NANCY KAY WEBB

WHERE THE WEST ENDS

A Story of Place and Community

Flying Turtle Press

Where the West Ends by Nancy Kay Webb

Powered by Flying Turtle Press—an imprint of Solano Press Books
Post Office Box 773
Point Arena, California 95468
tel (800) 931-9373
fax (707) 884-4109

Distributed by Alan Levine, 126 Steiner Ct., Santa Rosa, CA 95404
alevine@mcn.org, (707) 542-4408

Cover Photos (clockwise from top):
Marine National Monument/Stornetta Lands, Pt. Arena, Emerald Canary
Amaryillis, Nancy Kay Webb
Truck Garden, Nancy Kay Webb
1983 Storm taking down the Pt. Arena pier, Nicholas King
Rollerville and the flume (in background), Held-Poage Memorial House, Robert E. Lee Collection, Mendocino Historical Society

Title Page Photos (clockwise from top left):
Point Arena Hot Springs (Garcia River), Held-Poage Memorial House, Robert E. Lee Collection, Mendocino Historical Society
Marine National Monument/StornettaLands, Pt. Arena, Bureau of Land Management
Truck Garden, Nancy Kay Webb
Recent Pt. Arena, Alvis E. Hendley photographer, NoeHill.com

Map: Nancy Kay Webb

Editing contributions: Laura Schatsberg, Susan Webb Layne, Alan Levine

Graphic design, cover and interior: Emerald Canary

ISBN: 9 781938 166945 $26.95

ISBN for e-book: 9 781938 166952 $4.95

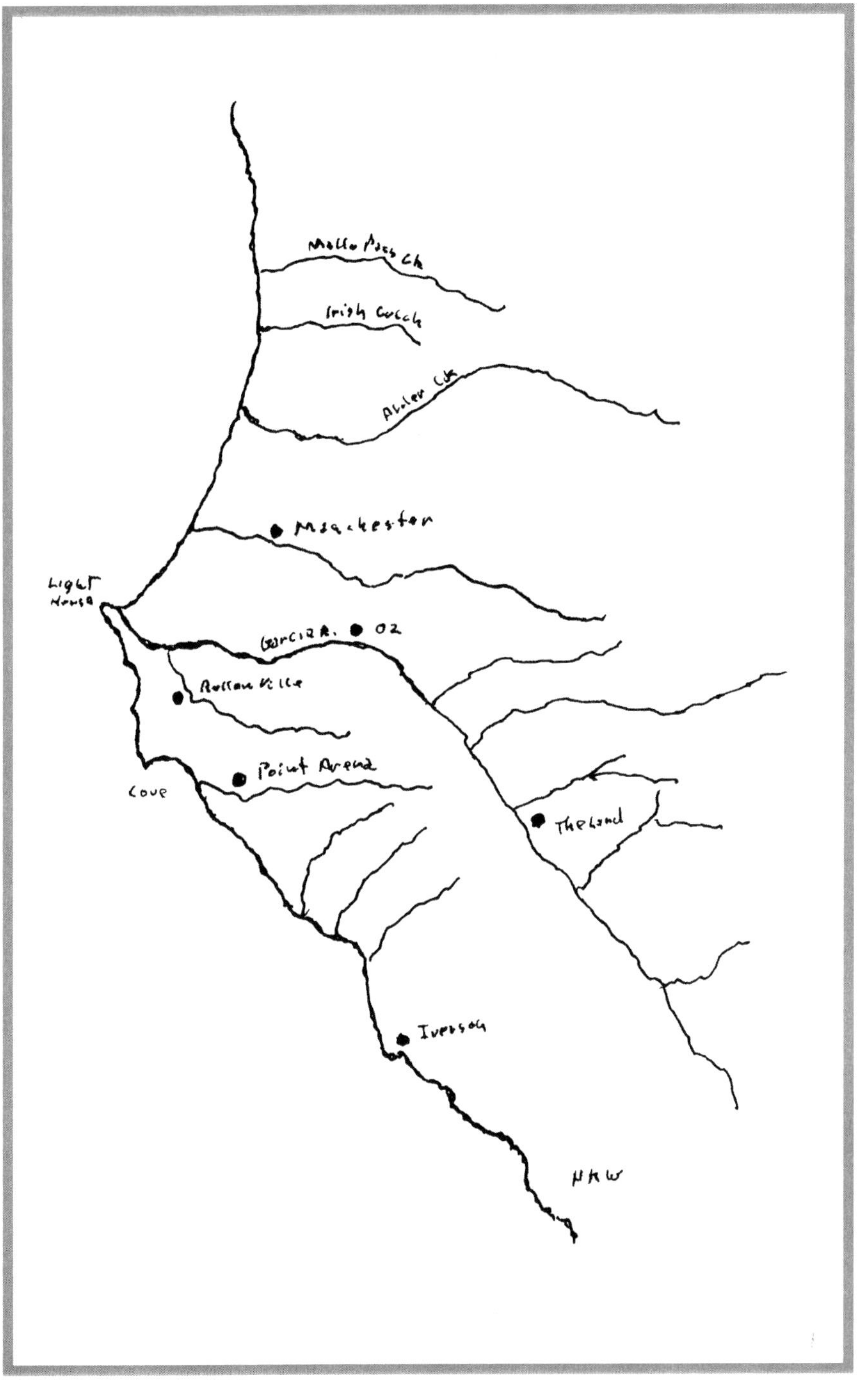
Mallo Pass Ck
Irish Gulch
Alder Ck
Manchester
Light House
Garcia R.
OZ
Rollerville
Point Arena
Cove
The Land
Iverson
HRW

Early cut.
California State Library, Georgia Pacific Collection

Felling Redwood. *California State Library, Georgia Pacific Collection*

Chute for loading ships after ties are transported from Rollerville. *California State Library*

Rollerville-at the bottom, ties delivered by flume on the way to the chute. *California State Library*

CONTENTS

Chapter One

WHAT KIND OF PLACE IS THIS ANYWAY?

The hazards are in the place, woven right into the place itself, so we learn to measure security like this: What a fine day! No storm ripped up my roof, no fox ate my hens, no temblor shattered my windows. The menace is in the place, elemental, but the menace doesn't reign alone. Its consort is raw beauty. A complicated duality of place. Unapproachable, the Redwood Coast beckons. Inhospitable, it invites. Attractive, it forbids. Exotic/provincial. Bounteous/closefisted. Binary compounds, matched pairs.

A splendid, eye-opening landscape, built of faults, folds, and fog, piles out of the ocean, straight up and out of the ocean floor to be scored, grooved, chiseled, trenched, and gouged by the dozens upon dozens of watercourses perpetually draining the high ground, freshets gushing past boulders and ferns and dark, wind-bent pines on their way to a white and green sea.

The Redwood Coast, shouldered between the wide Pacific Ocean and the low, rounded mountain peaks and ridges known collectively as the Coast Ranges, is raw, new land, land not altogether settled or ready for domestication. To the north, the Gorda Plate cleaves to the North American Plate in an implacable, rock-crushing embrace. In the south and west, the Pacific Plate grinds past the North American Plate. Two hundred miles in fifteen million years, pushing towards the northwest in sudden, violent lunges. During the famous 1906 lunge, all land west of the fault — that is land riding on the Pacific Plate — moved twenty-one feet in one exciting sidelong scoot which so staggered the surrounding land that almost everything to the west side of the fault line fell down, and much to the east was snarled and jumbled.

What happened to San Francisco is legendary, but Point Arena fared even worse. The little town was utterly devastated. Most of its buildings toppled over. The school burned to the ground. Trees, even giant redwoods, were bowled over. The lighthouse, tallest structure north of San Francisco, remained standing, but was so severely cracked it later had be pulled down brick by brick. The bridges over the Garcia River and Alder Creek collapsed.

Ponds suddenly drained. Fences pulled apart; afterwards the interrupted sections stood divided by fifteen to twenty-five feet. The Garcia, which ran straight down the fault line, changed its bed. One witness described it: "It just seemed to raise up out of itself and move hundreds of feet to the south. The fault continues heaving up the earth like a giant mole...."

The San Andreas Fault, as the rift between the Pacific and North American plates is now known, is in my backyard. It is an accepted part of life here. We in its neighborhood overbuild our houses, maintain generators for emergency power loss, store food and water — all this in everyday expectation of the Big One. A friend of mine from back east, a psychiatrist, says we are all "in denial." Otherwise, she insists, we wouldn't continue to live where we do. I say, "Balderdash. We know. We never forget."

Every Saturday's newspaper includes a "Seismo-watch," a colored map showing weekly activity along all faults in the vicinity — the San Andreas is a member of a considerable family. Each fault, large or small, is drawn as squiggly red lines; all quakes are represented by circles of different colors: red for magnitude of 4 or more, orange for 3 to 4, yellow for 2 to 3 and green for 1 to 2. Under 3 they are generally not felt, but every now and again a wee bump rattles the crockery, and trained eyes see, strewn about the landscape, elevated blocks, offset ridges, sag ponds, and drainage lines. We aren't likely to forget the fact that the Pacific Plate hasn't reached a final destination.

The peril is fundamental. Even when gratifyingly stationary, our ground includes a special, regional hazard: the Franciscan mélange. On the east side of the fault, the Coast Ranges consist of piles of rubbly, loosely-bedded rock — a young (nothing older than late Jurassic), unfinished geography. Until relatively recently, California didn't exist, at least not where it is now, nor all of a piece. It was scattered over the Pacific basin. Down through time the Pacific Plate, like a titanic bulldozer, shoveled far-flung and exotic rock formations from various marine locales and, heap by heap, packed them against the western edge of North America. Voila! California, with the Coast Ranges as the very latest addition. Geologists call this hodgepodge of oceanic rock and sediment from disparate continents all mixed together in a pervading mass of clay the Franciscan mélange. Initially sedimentary and volcanic, it was transformed over the ages by great pressures. It was folded, sheared, invaded. The geological story of the Coast Ranges is complicated — full of tales of uplift, subsidence, volcanism, and erosion — but underlying it all is the Franciscan mélange, a complex basement which can't be trusted entirely. Take a bite of rock from the wrong place and the whole face of the hill goes down. Rip out too much vegetation and your pond disappears, silted up in a season. Loose, chaotic ground easily eroded.

Geology holds the prerogative. It fixes the speed and direction of rivers and creeks. It limits how fast water sinks into the ground, and maintains its subterranean regulation as well, determining how much water there is and where. In league with weather, geology works on the vegetation. All things considered, geology arranges human affairs, regulating where populations can live, and in what numbers; supervising what they eat; fixing where they can build...safely. And woe, woe unto those who fail to heed geology's dictates. Their grazing sheep will get liver fluke, their fish will vanish from their waterways, their farms will dry up, their houses will slide down hills, and some of them, the heedless, will lose their lives.

Geology provides, it denies, it actuates, it halts. It bends history to its will. The same natural forces which made the coast redwoods possible are the forces responsible for the Redwood Coast's paucity of harbors. Mercantile pioneers discovered here a timber bonanza, a treasure simultaneously bestowed and withheld by local geology. The golden timber was worth nothing unless it could be gotten to market, so those early would-be tycoons were forced to vigorously exercise their wits devising new technologies for harvest and shipping.

Redwood Coast landscape thwarted more than the movement of giant trees. It thwarted simple, everyday travel. Until well into the twentieth century boats were the only practical means of coming and going. Overland transportation was the more expensive and time consuming. A land journey from San Francisco to Point Arena took two days at the very least. A ferry from San Francisco to Sausalito; a train to Duncan's Mills; a second train — narrow gauge — through the mountains to Cazadero; a horse-drawn, four-seat twelve-passenger shock-absorberless coach from Cazadero to Plantation and a night's sleep at the inn. Next morning, the coach again with its team of half-broken mustangs. It rattled and bumped through the Kruse Ranch, down to the coast, where, after a hard right turn, it rattled and bumped north to Point Arena. Two days if everything went right. If nothing broke; if the horses stayed sound; if the highwaymen were occupied elsewhere. Eventually a bus replaced the horse drawn coach, but the trip still took two full days.

The original road along the coast — now Highway 1 — was nothing more than a pair of wheel ruts. As a resident of Point Arena, here since 1906, put it, "Early travelers went the easiest way and the roads just followed."[1] Eventually the county graded the road and gave it a gravel surface, but it wasn't until 1935, when the state took charge, that it was paved.

Wherever the road crossed a property line, the property owner hung a gate travelers were obliged to open and close.

> Everyone who has had occasion to travel on the road between Gualala and Stewart's Point knows how very annoying it is to have to stop from 5 to 10 minutes at each of the dozen gates between these two points. These gates are a public nuisance, and it is high time the traveling public should have an open road along the entire Coast. *Point Arena News*, May 5, 1878

In the vicinity of Point Arena gate impediment gave way to the gulch impediment. A series of rivers and streams have molded the coastline to the shape of a stegosaurus's back. The Garcia, Gualala, Greenwood, Navarro, Salmon, Albion, Little, Big, Caspar, Noyo, and Ten-mile rivers, as well as a multitude of smaller streams too numerous to name — each watercourse carves a dramatic, wooded gully, a deep green cave, lush and beautiful, but a serious challenge to early transit. Down the chasm, across a wee scrap of a bridge, then steeply up the other side. Over and over again, through every dingle and dell.

Mal Paso and Irish Gulch north of the Garcia River were especially difficult. Mal Paso's sheer south wall and deep ravine were such a formidable obstruction that the pass apparently decided the important boundary between the two original Mexican land grants. The choices of later U.S. settlers too were shaped by Mal Paso. Most of those pioneers would do anything to avoid crossing it — toughing out an ill-favored homestead site or sticking with an offensive spouse — few things were as trying as that pass.

Before a bridge was built in 1870, Mal Paso hindered all communication between Point Arena and Greenwood. In the best of weather travel through that gulch was onerous; in winter it was just shy of impossible: "Part of the grade has caved in and Mal Paso is not passable for any vehicle except baby carts and wheelbarrows…."[2] The bridge made the ravine only slightly less dangerous. The road took a winding course down one side, ran a good half mile up the creek before crossing it, then drew itself by inches up the other side.

Today Highway 1 drivers are scarcely conscious of the numerous gullies and creeks. The bridges, eight or nine in forty miles, are merely part of the pavement, that seamless gray ribbon winding between trees, curving above a splashing, shining sheet of sea, twisting through mountains lumpish yet majestic in their rawness.

To reach Mendocino's coast from the south you drive west along the Russian River, then north up Highway 1. From the north you drive west along the Noyo or the Navarro river, then south on Highway 1. Either route is tortuous. Motorists tire. Passengers go bilious. After one visit, my brother-in-law swore he'd never come again unless by plane. My children's father believed — still believes, I suspect — there was an easy route somewhere, a route I was either too benighted to discover, or too mean-spirited to show him. Over the years every time he came to see the kids, he tried a different thin gray map line. He always arrived here wearing the same shade of gray on his face. These alternative routes are even narrower and more serpentine than Highway 1 and are only semi-paved to boot. There really is no fast and easy way to our secluded stretch of coast. Every artery is steep, or shaped like a corkscrew, or both.

The northern Coast Range runs north and south for 400 miles and is fifty-odd miles wide. Peaks average only 2,000 to 4,000 feet, although a few in the Range's northernmost reaches are taller (I got horribly lost once on a 7056-footer in Lake County). However, for the most part the mountains are modest. The highest point in the Garcia River watershed is a mere 2470 feet. Yet humble as it is, within Mendocino County the Coast Range effectively cuts the shoreline communities off from the inland valleys. Coast dwellers feel as though they live on an island.

Those of us who live near the mouth of the Garcia River do live on an island of sorts. The San Andreas Fault, skulking underwater, comes ashore just north of Point Arena, then travels south for a 43 miles before diving back into the briny deep at Bodega Bay. Everything on the east side of the Garcia River is happily situated on the more settled North American Plate, but those of us to the west of the river live on the Pacific Plate which is headed for Alaska, taking us (and Los Angeles) with it. The Pacific Plate travels an inch or two a year, but the dawdling pace doesn't dispose of the fact that my farm sits on the one plate while most of the rest of my fellow Americans live on the other. We may look connected but, deep down, we're not.

The northern Coast Range follows the shoreline, veering occasionally to the east to leave a stretch of good, flat farmland. The broadest expanse of such terrain anywhere on the Mendocino Coast lies between the town of Point

Arena and Alder Creek to the north. When everything else in the area went to timber, this bench land went to agriculture, bankrolling the local community when the timber boom went bust.

As soon as I set eyes on these sea-clipped pastures, I fell in love — impulsively, intemperately, impracticably. I bought eighty acres before I went back to Southern California for nine long months of lavish meditation and fancy before actually moving north.

Around 9 p.m. on June 16, 1981, an Audi Fox station wagon and a large green furniture-packed school bus crawled up the rutted, weed-choked driveway. Out staggered a grown woman (me), her two daughters, husband, his daughter, an over-excited Golden Labrador Retriever, and a car-sick cat. (Such stowaways as had begun the trip with us parted our company in the San Fernando Valley: Alan had made a sudden, unscheduled stop at a gas station on Ventura Boulevard. Following him, I wondered what was going on. Then the bus door flew open and out jumped six or eight mice. As we drove away we saw them running round and round the diesel pump.) We had arrived in Point Arena to stay.

Three days after the initial relocation to the realm of my golden dreams, I found myself sitting in front of a weather-chewed mobile home and watched the fog come toward me. It rolled in from three directions, north, south and west. Point Arena, I said to myself, with a little *frisson* of comprehension, is just that — *a point*. Beetling out into the ocean, it's bound to take all weathers full in the face. (During the coming months, locals were pleased to tell me Point Arena is closer to Hawaii than any other place in the continental U.S.A., a fact which does nothing to make the place a jot warmer.)

On that third day, sheltered from the wind, one of my daughters and I lolled in the old porch furniture I had been dragging around with me for years. Two white wicker chairs and white couch. They weren't going to last much longer, but for the moment were nested in the tall beige grass.

A quarter mile from the ocean, we could hear the surf. My bench land, stark and windswept, looked surpassingly picturesque to me. Rolling dun grasses. Tumbled down runs of weathered grape-stake fencing interspersed with stretches of serviceable wire and metal-stake fencing. Snatchy groves of dark Bishop pines — bull pines, they call them — relics of the Ice Age, a tree found, by fits and skips, along the California coast from Humboldt County to Lompoc, but only on the Mendocino flats, a bare hundred feet or so above sea level, does the tree reach the greatest height of forty to eighty feet. Bull pine was scorned by early lumber-lovers. The county's first historian, Lyman Palmer said of it: "Of the kinds of trees which are of no particular use the 'bull' pine stands first and foremost…it is scraggy and ill-favored and but little could possibly be expected of it."[3] The tree's pitchy wood, though heavy, is weak, coarse grained, and knotty. No commercial or practical value. But the tree's poor character reference wasn't going to put me off. I found these dark conifers, crowded into awkward groves of interlocking crowns, appealing. I liked the bull pines' tendency to huddle, but admired, too, the individual, the single tree which occasionally grew apart from its kind distorted by wind and weather. Today I had set my wicker chair near one of these stout, steadfast loners looking for all the world like a gargantuan broccoli.

In the background, to the east, ran the heavily wooded Ridge. Still east, but closer, was a turkey farm, so noisy Emily and I turned our backs to it. To our right, directly north, was the mobile home backed by the four-acre stand of bull pines from which the broccoli had escaped. Northwest, I could see one of our twenty-acre pastures, south and southwest, the other twenty-acre pasture, each bordered by single-file processions of bull pine and cedar. Between my seat and the south pasture, in a small straggling clump of bull pine, stood an empty rabbit hutch and chicken coop. Beyond them, another, smaller field. Southeast, our pond lay curled up in a little hollow. From this vantage point all I could see of the pond was its surrounding trees from their waists up.

Slowly, slowly the fog drifted closer while the distant Ridge held onto its canopy of blue sky. So far at our new home every day had been foggy or windy. Offhandedly I realized those three short days had transmuted trees from a source of shade to a source of shelter.

"Where you are alters the way you see things," I said to Emily, "If you stay in a place long enough, it's going to alter your personal cosmology." She, twenty-four days past her thirteenth birthday, looked up from her book and said, "Huh?" "I believe," I said, trying to clarify, "where you live squares things up in a certain way, shapes how you see things." She said, "Huh?" again, but by the way she smiled this time I saw she was making fun of me.

I took up my journal and I wrote: "The fog, like smoke, settles on the two flat pastures. There is no sky. Spiny black pines outline oat-colored fields. These trees are windbreak. The fog lifts only in front of the north wind."

When I first saw it, the Mendocino coastline put me in mind of the Suma coast where Genji spent his royal exile. Windswept shore, plovers at dawn, "unchastened longing for the deep-lying sea pine,"[4] and all that sort of thing.

Now I was here to stay, and the very images which had so charmed me now scared me. The land was too extreme. The weather was too passionate. Reading my old journal entries, eighteen years later, today revives precisely that past sensation of being thoroughly cowed by landscape and weather.

> 7/81 What I thought was smoke from a chimney I now know was a patch of cloud. A row of bull pine disappears. Then another row, and then the chicken and rabbit houses. Then the tether ball pole in the front yard. Finally the giant bull pine right outside the window, the enormous one holding the wind chime and the tire swing. Tufts of fog spill over the top of the trailer and down the sides. It swirls like a blues riff. There is something here that corresponds to a secret I have from myself.
>
> 7/26/81 Our old gray and white Venice cat sits outside the sliding glass door. She wants in. From her mouth hang four legs and a tail. She wants to eat it in here.... I am afraid of this piece of land. Maybe because I dreamed of it too often between now and last August. But I am afraid of it.
>
> 8/81 No tv. Scant radio. Where are you Spock? Captain Kirk? What kind of place is this anyway?

REFERENCE NOTES

1. Joe Scaramella, *Yesterday's News* interview, JS07.VIA.

2. *Mendocino Democrat*, January 29, 1968.

3. Lyman Palmer, *History of Mendocino County.*

4. Murasaki Shikibu, *The Tale of Genji*, translated by Edward G. Seidensticker, Alfred A. Knopf.

Chapter Two

THE WHARF AT ARENA COVE

Juan Rodriguez Cabrillo, sailing by in 1542, called the promontory *Punta Arenas*, and the name rode out the ages, shedding its Spanish duds along the way. Punta Arenas, Point Arenas, Point Arena. When, in 1859, U.S. settlers built a store and a saloon and called the place a town, they gave it the name of the point which was actually a few miles to the north, but the newcomers wanted to plant their town close to the cove, the best bight in miles and miles of a shoreline woefully deficient of adequate harbors. Ships sailing between Bodega and Humboldt bays were obliged to lay anchor wherever an awkward slab of headland protected some middling inlet. These treacherous anchorages came to be known as dog holes. Most accounts insist the term "dog hole" was coined by deep water sailors grousing about ports "not big enough for a dog to turn around in." But some students of the subject claim dog hole unfolded from reference to the "barking dog navigators," those Scandinavian seamen (as distinct from officers) who made up the majority of the Redwood Coast captains and were considered by most Europeans to lack the formal education to master mathematical navigation.

Whatever the word's etymology, dog holes were dog holes, and shipping from these narrow, rock-ribbed ports became practicable only after the Scandinavian sailors — capable if unscholarly — boarded the newest marine marvel: the schooner. Short, wide, with shallow-draft, the schooner was more maneuverable by far than other ships and it required a considerably smaller crew.

Each shipping point on the Redwood Coast spawned a shore community. Approximately sixty have been identified between Bodega and Humboldt bays, six of them — complete with chutes, stores and schools — between the towns of Point Arena and Gualala. Most of these erstwhile communities withered on the vine, but Point Arena endured because Point Arena was different. Her cove was roomier and it was well suited for a wharf, which an enterprising settler constructed in 1866. The wharf dispatched the yield of field and forest, granting Point Arena, a frontier town pitched beside a river hustling with nineteenth century timber traffic and flowing through the most extensive farming acreage on the coast, a permanent mark on the map.

Loading schooners was the early timber industry's biggest expense. Loading at the mill would have been the easiest way to do it, but the Garcia River wasn't deep enough, so loading was done in Arena Cove with lighters. The lighter, a shallow-draft boat or barge, was floated out on the tide to a moored vessel. Piece by piece, lumber was handed up from the lighter to the ship's deck, a lengthy, grueling task, and men clamored for a more efficient method. The prodigious Yankee ingenuity, which powered the redwood enterprise over its many hurdles, introduced a contrivance called a chute.

The first chute was the slide or apron chute. By 1860 it was on the job all along the coast; nearly every shipping point had an apron chute at one time or another. Nickerson & Baker, owners of the Garcia Mill, erected one above the wharf. A chute system was composed of two parts: the chute proper, and its supporting structure. The chute, an apron-shaped wooden trough or slide, extended from land to the deck of a ship. To compensate for tidal changes, the slide was raised or lowered with block and tackle. The slide was attached by ropes or wire cables to a wooden frame built on a bluff. Slides could be very long — some as long as two-hundred feet — and often needed further support. Tall pyramid-shaped props of two, three, or four converging poles were fastened to rocks onshore or off. From the high bluff, gravity brought the load to the boat. Tracking down the slide along with the load was an iron-footed hinged gate designed to slow the lumber traveling beneath it. At the deck end of the slide was another brake, the clapper, a long, flat board fastened at one end, then levered up and down by the clapper man charged with slowing the descending materials enough to allow deck hands to grab them.

> A bull belonging to Mr. Abbot was found one morning recently standing in Nickerson and Company's chute at the first brake contentedly chewing his cud. He had slid down there during the night, and lodged at the brake about 100 feet from the top. Before help arrived to rescue the animal he had jumped from the suspension and was killed on the rocks about 50 feet below. *Point Arena News*, August 25, 1878

Chute loading, though easier than the lighter method, was nevertheless a shaky, vexatious affair. Dangerous work it was which took a long time. Also, the wooden slides were vulnerable to rough weather and seas; winter storms damaged many of them and some were washed entirely away. Then when steam schooners began to replace vessels with sails, the apron chutes presented an even greater drawback: steam powered boats could not raise their centerboards as the sailing schooners had been able to do, thus they often couldn't get close enough to shore to use the chutes at all. A new type of chute was needed, and right on cue came the wire chute, invented in Gualala by Will St. Ores and his brother. The wire chute was sturdier, safer, faster to use, and could deliver loads farther out into the water than the apron chute. The "wire" was a heavy cable stretching from a framework erected over a platform on shore to a heavily anchored buoy beyond the mooring site. A later refinement called for two separate cables, one brought from the land to the boat's deck where it was coupled, by means of a slip hook, to the other cable running from the buoy. The wire, made taut from the shore end, was hung on a boom so it could be raised and lowered.

The ship to be loaded positioned itself beneath the wire, and loads were transported to it in slings by means of sling ropes attached to a pulley-fitted framework called a traveler. The load was lashed to the underside of the traveler with sling chains, and gravity carried it, under the control of a brake at the shore end, down to the ship. After the load was released onto the deck, the traveler returned to the land either by counterbalance or steam power. In some ports the passengers rode to the ship on the wire instead of being ferried out on a small boat. "To get on the schooner you had to get into a little chair that went out on a, what they call the bosons chair now, probably then, too. But it went right out like the lumber did and sat you down on the deck."[1]

After a new owner, L.E. White, bought the Garcia Mill properties in 1891, he built a second apron chute at the wharf. Soon, though, he decided he needed a wire chute and had the cove surveyed for proper buoy and anchor sites. Standing a thousand or so feet northwest of the old chute, the brand-new state-of-the-art wire chute was ready, and half the town of Point Arena traipsed down to the wharf to watch the loading of the first schooner. The vessel sailed into port, and was anchored in place. As was customary, a cannon on shore fired a slug to carry a cord to the deck. When it landed, the crew was supposed to attach it to the ship's steam winch. But, while the eager crowd watched, the shot dropped considerably shy of its mark. Shot number two landed in the water as well. And three, and four. Over and over the slug fell short until the Eddie White gave up and sent the schooner north to load at another company landing at Greenwood. The engineers scratched their heads and took up their pencils.

An eighty foot chute plus a two hundred foot high bluff equaled a distance too far for the cannon delivery. Solution: an eyebolt in a big offshore rock. The rock was exposed only at minus tides so it took a series of minus tides for three men to drill the rock and set the eyebolt to which they attached one end of a five-eighths inch cable. The other end of the cable was made taut to a post on the bluff, and a pulley carrying a heavy weight fastened with a manila rope was hung on the cable. When the next schooner arrived, it was fixed securely in its designated place, and the manila rope for hauling out the loading cable was let down from shore — from loading point to loading point, its exact position would vary with the tide. Sailors in the ship's work boat secured the end of their rope to the line from the bluff, and the combined lengths got the loading cable to the schooner.

Some years after the eyebolt was installed, the L.E. White Company superintendent, ambling along the headlands, noticed the taut line had somehow become detached from the submerged rock. Point Arena now included a local Coast Guard station, so the superintendent asked the Coast Guard captain to send some of his men to install a new wire. The captain agreed, but on the day he was to effect the repair, the captain did an about-face. He telephoned the superintendent to say his rule manual forbade him to jeopardize a Guardsman's safety for any commercial enterprise. "The duty of the Coast Guard," he pronounced, magisterially, "is to save lives, not endanger them," and he hung up.[2]

The steamer *Alcatraz* was due next morning. It was late in the day now and the ship's office would be closed so that the superintendent wouldn't be able to warn the ship away by phone. How was he to make contact? He fumed and fretted until he finally hit on the idea of getting someone from the Coast Guard to talk to the *Alcatraz* with semaphore signals. He told his chute foreman, Tom Moungovan, "They brewed this fine kettle of fish, by god, they'll just have to help dish it up." He left Tom with instructions to have somebody from the Coast Guard down to the wharf first thing in the morning.

Tom hated to turn the steamer away. Surely there was an alternative. After ruminating on the problem, he called Rollerville, where the White Company fished its timber from the river to move it on by rail the short distance to the cove. He coaxed the engineer to drive his locomotive to the chute that night. "And bring three hundred feet of half inch manila rope, two half inch wire clamps and a ten inch crescent wrench." When the engineer arrived, Tom told him exactly what he wanted him to do, then lowered the cable over the bluff. Using the rope to help himself down, Tom descended the steep face of the cliff. At the bottom he attached the rope to the cable with binding wire. Now in the dark cold water, Tom set off swimming with the wrench, two clamps — he carried the load around his neck — and the end of the rope. When he got to the rock, he discovered his line was short by a few feet. The engineer was supposed to be controlling the line's tautness, but the northwest wind prevented him hearing Tom's call for more slack. Tom hollered himself hoarse until, finally, the engineer got the message and Tom was able to complete his task. Then he swam back, and, by moonlight, managed to scale the treacherous rock wall.

Next morning the superintendent nearly had a heart attack when he heard the steamer's coming-in whistle. On a panting horse he galloped to the chute where Tom calmly assured him the ship would have no trouble tying up. The engineer, not so calmly, tattled. "If you want to know," he said, "here it is: That long fool there swam out and fastened the line to the eyebolt! I know — I helped him!"

The superintendent had the story repeated several times before he was willing to credit it. In silence he watched the ship tie up and get loaded, then he turned to his chute foreman. "Tom," he said, "if you took the most brainless of all of the inmates of all the asylums in California, he would still have sense enough not to do such a damn fool stunt."

Over the years Arena Cove employed an assortment of loading methods: lighters, two chutes — actually three, but never more than two in operation at once — and a wharf. All other wharves along the Redwood Coast were owned by various lumber companies, and thus were available only to parties doing business with the company. But Arena Cove's wharf was a free wharf; anyone willing to pay the "wharfage" was permitted to load and unload there. The cove was a busy place. In the year 1879 alone 2,300 tons of merchandise, 70,000 fence posts, 223 cords of bark, 13,500,000 shingles, 228 rolls of leather, 1,042 bags of potatoes, 940 boxes of butter, 274 cases of eggs, 130 sacks of wool, and 4,000 reams of paper left the port.[3]

Then the schooners traded their sails for steam engines. At first the engines were merely tacked onto the existing craft. A cabin was installed on the afterdeck with boilers and machinery below and a smokestack forward of the main mast. The masts and rigging stayed put; they might come in handy if the newfangled engine broke down. But these clumsy hybrid crafts were soon replaced by boats designed for engine power. Fifty feet longer than their predecessors, they nevertheless were more maneuverable than their sailing counterparts. Better still, in the face of big storms, they could more easily cut and run.

Until the early 1930s more than a dozen schooners shuttled passengers and freight up and down the coast. Drummers, sales people, came through on a monthly basis to take orders. The orders were filled and shipped to be picked up at the wharf.[4] A schooner called at Point Arena twice a week — if it wasn't too rough — Tuesdays and Thursdays. Supplies for the residents, all the merchandise for the stores. And the passengers. The local newspaper *Point Arena Record* (at first called the *Point Arena News*) kept readers informed as to who had come in and who had gone out with each sailing.[5]

But after the internal combustion engine came along, and roads were improved, wheel transportation became more convenient than the trip by sea. All over the U.S.A. travelers took to automobiles. At about the same time the lumber industry languished. Both changes sapped life from the Point Arena Wharf. Above it on the hill, the grand old Coast Guard house, once the center of rescue station operations, stood empty, its empty windows confronting a discarded sea crisscrossed only by an informal and ragtag fleet of fishing boats.

During the 1940s a new owner transformed the empty wharf warehouse, once jammed full of sorted and stacked merchandise, into a cafe and bar. A great place for beer. The hamburgers and fish and chips weren't half bad either. The bar was still a popular hangout when I arrived. The building was tiny and when the joint was jumping, it was mighty crowded. A big noisy fan above an unused side door sucked out heavy, greasy, smoky air.

Roy Fox went partners with the owner, and ran the place for over forty years. Roy welcomed everybody. Louie Frasier, who arrived in Point Arena with the counterculture influx of the '70s, said of Roy, "You're a fisherman or a timber guy or you're a hippie or you're a back-to-the-lander, he didn't care. That's where it all came together down at the wharf. The Indians and the cowboys were all there."[6] Strong, lean and tall, snow white hair, affable, Roy was a popular person. So was his cook, Sophie Harper, a Greek woman who had married a G.I. and had come to Point Arena after WW II. Sophie was as short as Roy was tall, as homely as Roy was handsome. Under five feet, she nevertheless had a huge personality, and had no trouble holding sway in the cafe kitchen — holding sway throughout the entire establishment, some would say. Sophie had unique ideas and told some pretty wild stories, though, I have to admit, I couldn't always understand, through her accent, exactly what she was saying.

Alan and I used to take the kids there once a week to eat and watch the surfers. After dinner, attentive to bandy planks and gaps from missing planks, we took our ritual strolls to the end of the wharf. A year after we moved here, an enterprising soul restored the fish house and during the '82 fishing season I sent Alan several times a week to buy fresh fish and crabs. Very nice, but it didn't last.

The next winter brought spectacular storms, passionate affairs which shook our house and knocked down our trees. The ocean went wild. Even after rain and wind eased up, the sea continued to run savage. On the morning of January 26, 1983, the stormy, rampaging sea was also in the throes of a +7 foot tide. The Arena Cove parking lot was flooded when our friend Nick King arrived. In yesteryears, Nick had been a professional photographer and now, whenever the sea promised a show, he came to the cove with his cameras. He and his son were sitting in the cafe eating breakfast when a monumental wave broke down the cafe door. Saltwater swamped the floor. Everybody jumped onto a table, or headed for the back door. Without breathing space between, three more monster waves exploded. They seriously damaged the cafe and the boathouse, and utterly destroyed the fish house and the wharf, ripping both apart and dragging them to Davy Jones's locker. Nick got pictures of the whole frenzied sequence.

The wharf was gone. Everybody wanted it back, but democracy makes the winnowing of problems and possibilities a complicated affair. And then there's the perennial snag: money. Three and a half years were needed to accomplish the twin feats of accord and funding. With the City of Point Arena as the lead agency for the project, a new pier was built, 15 feet higher than the old wharf, and standing on steel-jacketed concrete rather than wooden pilings.

Construction crews witnessed the two or three local divers who first began to experiment with harvesting sea urchins, *Strongylocentrotus franciscanus* and *S. purpuratus*. Something new for this neck of the woods. The divers had no pier to work from, nor were they certain of a market, but because the otters were gone, the urchins abounded, so a few of the hopeful went down and picked them.

They were fortunate. A market did, indeed, exist, a market with its tongue hanging out. When market and supplier made contact, lights flashed and bells rang for everybody. By the time the new pier was operating, the cove was filled with boats queuing up to unload. Every evening, toward sundown, Alan and I went to watch. Summer, and the green Pacific surged and sparkled. Spread out over the water, thirty or forty boats headed for the pier where other boats, already moored, bobbed up and down.

When a vessel came alongside the pier, its diver stayed on board while his tender climbed the long ladder. As soon as a boat was ready to unload, the *Ocean Fresh* truck backed down to it. At first eight different companies competed for prices right there on the new pier, but four of them quickly competed themselves out of business, leaving *Ocean Fresh* as the biggest buyer, so more often than not it was the *Ocean Fresh* boy who jumped down from the flatbed, swung the huge crane around, and lowered the hook toward the boat thirty feet below. The diver fastened the hook to one of the several full nets waiting on his deck. Above, the boy leaned against the hydraulic lever and the crane lugged the bulging net upward. At a certain level the boy paused to let the tender record weights from the electronic scale on the hook. About that time a woman, the weighmaster, would come jogging down the pier with a clipboard under her arm.

With a hydraulic whine, the crane finished the lift, then swung its load toward the half dozen four-foot-square boxes on the truck. There the sea urchins hung, clumped together in the net, one spiny cluster of hundreds of spiny balls — wine-colored, magenta, plum, sienna, cinnamon, liver-colored, chocolate-brown, salmon-brown. Climbing onto the back of the truck, the boy would reach up with a bent pitchfork to release the bottom of the net. A number of urchins spilled out before a tangle of spines inevitably stopped the flow. The suspended net now was no longer a ball but a gorilla — arms, head, torso. A large, prickly King Kong. The boy raked at the bottom urchins until the mass broke loose, thundering into two of the white boxes.

The wharf's renaissance was the setting for Roy Fox's physical decline. The man who was everybody's hero developed cancer, and sank as quickly as the urchin business rose. It was painful to see him — once the epitome of strength and energy — bedridden and struggling for breath. My daughters' high school French teacher, Anita, helped Roy during his last weeks. Miserable, shut up in his house, he wanted more than anything to be back down at the wharf even for just a while, so one day Anita decided to take him. The Foxes lived within five hundred yards of the cove, so it was only a matter of bringing a wheelchair, contriving to load him into it, and steering him down the rutted road.

By the time Anita got Roy to the water's edge the sun was low, but the wind off the sea was gentle, and they decided to venture all the way to the pier. Roy tried to talk but it brought on a coughing fit so violent that Anita held her breath and helplessly patted her own throat. She was worried the outing was going to kill him. They watched a gray urchin vessel hove into sight. It chugged up alongside the pier. After he unloaded, the diver climbed up the ladder to read the last weight.

"Pretty damn good. Where the hell's the weighmaster?"

A few urchins had tumbled onto the pier, and the boy jumped from the truck to get them. Very carefully, one at a time, he chucked them into the boxes. The diver picked one up — a large dark urchin — and, holding it on his outstretched palm like a small hedgehog on a platter, asked Roy if he wanted some. Roy, who hadn't been able to eat anything for several days, nodded yes.

"This stuff 'll put lead in your pencil," the diver said breaking the urchin open with the heel of his rubber boot. Then he scooped out the mustard-colored mass of roe and fed it Roy to with his fingers. Roy ate slowly, sucking his tongue and licking his lips after each small bite. When he said thank you, his voice gasped up from the miasma, the unwholesome thicket flourishing in the cage of his ribs. After that, he closed his eyes and either slept or pretended to sleep, while Anita sat on a bench and watched the corrugated sea until it was time to take the sick man home. The urchin roe was his last meal.

Ninety-five percent of the urchins harvested here go to Japan where the fresh roe — urchin roe is not eggs, but ovaries and testes — is popular in sushi bars. Freshness is of supreme importance, so, boat to dock, dock to forklift, forklift to truck, the white boxes are hurried to air freight depots.

The Japanese love sea urchin roe and don't mind paying for it. An urchin boat with one diver can count on bringing in over a thousand dollars a day. At the height of the urchin business, the City of Point Arena collected around $80,000 a year in revenues.

Divers, tired and hungry and flush, left their boats at night and spent money in town. My stepdaughter, Carey, when she was a senior in high school, waited tables. She came home talking about one diver who ordered a pitcher of beer, two complete pork chop dinners, soup, salad, and a hamburger. "His buddy had said, 'The same but double,'" she told us, "and after that, they started in on pie!"

The supply of urchins was great but not infinite. With each new season the divers had to go farther and farther away to find the same quantity of urchins they used to find right here in the cove. Moreover, the Department of Fish and Game regulations got persistently stricter. Urchin diving is no longer the bonanza it once was.

The commercial fishery, too, has fallen on hard times. Salmon fishermen must supplement their catch these days with rock fish and crabs. But the wharf finds other attractions. A city council member renovated the old Coast Guard House, transforming it into a chic bed and breakfast inn. An out-of-town entrepreneur tore down the cafe, and replaced it with a grand two-story building with shops below, a restaurant above, then built an upscale motel on the hill beside the Coast Guard House. He cleared away the shabby trailer park — to the great ill will of those who lived there — and tried to put in a high density RV park. This is where the community drew the line. The entrepreneur blew town, selling, on his way out, the restaurant business, but not the building, to a local boy who continues to serve a large clientele. The old, once seedy cove, decked out now in a new bib and tucker, continues to feed the kitty — some revenue from urchins, launching fees for sport crafts, per pound fees for commercial fish catches, as well as bed and sales taxes. And, beneath an everlasting diadem of gulls, the waves keep pounding, and the surfers keep surfing.

REFERENCE NOTES

1. *Yesterday's News* interview, wa05via.sea.
2. "Incident at Arena Cove," *Where There's A Will, There's A Way*, Mendocino County Historical Society monograph.
3. Lyman Palmer, *History of Mendocino County*, p.373.
4. *Yesterday's News* interview, tg04.sea.
5. *Yesterday's News* interview, rb04.sea.
6. Louie Frasier, *Yesterday's News* interview.

Chapter Three

POINT ARENA, THE TOWN

The first business established in Point Arena was a general store, giving the few settlers here in 1859 a locus, a campfire to gather round. Even though the area had not yet been surveyed and officially opened to settlement, the population expanded. When federal townsite requirements were liberalized in 1865, '67, and '68, Point Arena, with businesses strung all up and down its main street, joined the throng of California towns taking advantage of the new legislation by registering a patent on the land it occupied. The process by which towns acquired public lands was based on preemption rights similar to the ones by which individual settlers acquired homesteads. After the town's patent was registered, it took still another five years for the survey to catch up. The federal surveyor finally made it to the coast in 1873, surveyed the land, and filed it with the county. The City of Point Arena followed up by complying with the newly devised state procedure for procurement of title to become a bona fide town.

MAIN STREET - 1880:

1 brewery
2 blacksmith/carriage shops
2 hotels
1 barbershop
1 meat market
2 shoe shops
1 drug store
1 harness shop
2 livery stables
4 saloons
5 general merchandise stores
1 tin store
1 jeweler
1 tailor
1 milliner
1 Templars Lodge
1 Methodist/Episcopal Church.

Point Arena arrived on the scene loaded with cultural baggage. From the beginning, or very soon thereafter, the town was fully outfitted with a newspaper, a coronet band, secret societies such as the N.S.G.W. Broderick Parlor, No. 117, which met every Thursday evening in the Good Templars Hall. Point Arena even had a theater, Scott's Opera House, where, in the fall of 1893, a cast of seven performed *Ici On Parle Francais.*

Point Arena was a rawboned little town with a fat cigar in its pocket, waiting, always waiting, for the big time prosperity just round the next corner, the pot of gold beyond the next hill. "Prosperity would be ours if only...." The railroad was always just about to link Point Arena to the rest of the world. Or the neighborhood was just about to strike it rich in oil. Eighteen fifty-nine was the year petroleum turned to gold. The nation's first oil well, drilled that year in Pennsylvania, sparked a new profit mania. Point Arena organized the Garcia Petroleum District in early 1865. The venture was a total loss, but over and over, continuing on into this century, the unrequited lust for oil reappeared again and again. Wealth was on its way. Always something: Hey, they found copper in Cloverdale! Gold in Hopland! Or coal, even coal would do.

> There is some talk of working the bituminous rock mines. If every citizen would do his duty in encouraging enterprise — great and small — Point Arena and vicinity would experience a substantial boom. This is the most favored spot in the county. Nature has smiled with favor upon the lands, and placed resources within easy access. It now only remains for man to exert his energy and use his means in developing them, and in doing so his wealth would increase and the southern part of the Mendocino coast would flourish as never before. *Point Arena Record*, March 5, 1895.

The bit of coal unearthed here proved too young to be of commercial value. The same was true for the value of local deposits of mercury and of mica. Soon the newspaper was off on another track, ballyhooing the asphalt which exuded from a bluff, but in the end no one got rich from it.[1] As far as minerals were concerned, the best this community did was a ledge of graphite mined during WW II between the Garcia main stem and the Garcia North Fork.

Half-baked grand schemes make up the chronicle of our hapless little town. In 1867 a wiry Irishman named Thomas Nugent built a paper mill on Brush Creek. The earliest days of the nation had been plagued with a serious paper scarcity. The thirteen original states published newspapers irregularly because of the shortage. People wrote letters on pages torn from books. Even

General George Washington, during the Revolution, obliged to send his dispatches on the backs of odd scraps of this and that. Envelopes were out of the question. It, therefore, made historical sense for a new settlement to aspire to produce its own paper.

At first the Brush Creek Paper Company prospered, manufacturing the highest grades of paper from cotton and linen rags, burlap, rope, and scraps of used paper. But Northern California's coast was only sparsely populated. Nor had the few people living here had time to accumulate excess bits of rope or chests of rag they wanted to sell for a pittance. When Nugent saw his supply of raw material begin to dwindle, he resolved to unload the business while it was still profitable. In order to be able to guarantee a potential buyer a steady supply of water, he bought forty additional acres on Brush Creek from an adjacent property owner, Joseph Sheppard. The extra water in league with his account books were a strong inducement for the investors Nugent lassoed: "Captain Neils Iversen, William Shoemake, Jess Dodson, Joseph Sheppard, A.B. Kendall, Henry Fairbanks, Henry Vinegarholtz, H.N. Stevens, G.G. Stevens, William McKinner, Peters and Weinberg and Louis Gerlock." The deed catalogues a flock of hardheaded local businessmen whose new enterprise, The Eagle Paper Company, immediately began to drink money.

Situated in the timber capital of the universe, the company might have looked to the woods for raw materials. Instead the mill was set up to manufacture paper from items which turned out to be in short supply. Without rags and rope, the mill tried processing straw, a material commonly used for making paper elsewhere, but the damp sea air and fog made stale and moldy straw. Then, as if the quality of the straw were not problem enough, the farmers got greedy and decided to raise the price of their straw from $2.50 per ton to $7.50. The paper mill owners hung on, bleeding themselves and their friends dry, until, finally facing fiscal facts, they closed shop. The Eagle Paper Company "has been 'put upon its feet' three several times, and several thousand dollars have been invested, and yet to-day it stands a monument of miscalculation and misdirected energy and capitol, the hum of its machinery being dead, presumably beyond the power of human agency to resurrect," county historian Lyman Palmer wrote in 1880, just before the mill was sold and carted off piecemeal to Santa Cruz.[2]

Palmer went on to say, "It is evident however that the old residents of [Point Arena] hope to better things in the near future and are investing money in property with as much avidity as in the 'flush' days of years agone."

At the time he was writing, "years agone" amounted to barely a score and nine or ten. Already Point Arena, not yet thirty years old, was a town fallen from grace. "We bespeak better times.... It is to be hoped that the day is not far distant when the arteries of industry and trade will be again opened by a strong and healthy flow of money into the coffers of the citizens of this lovely little village by the sea-shore."

Hopeful bespeaking and rampant boostering never ceased. A couple of years before I moved here, Point Arena was licking its chops for the prosperity soon to arrive in the form of a nuclear reactor. PG&E had purchased the land (land semi-surrounding the eighty acres I eventually bought), and the citizens of the lovely little village by the sea-shore dreamed at night of some strong and healthy flow of money headed their way. Alas, the proposed nuclear reactor site was situated smartly between the San Andreas Fault and an impressive string of major faults offshore. Back to the drawing board…

"West" is a direction. "West" is a set of images. "West" is a state of mind. Point Arena unarguably meets the criterion of West-as-direction: It is about as far west as the continental U.S.A. goes — only Cape Mendocino reaches farther out into the Pacific Ocean.

As a set of images Point Arena seems at first not to fit the bill: West is supposed to be arid. The coast of California appears an exception, but, in fact, it is not. From San Francisco north, the winter season is rainy, yet the rest of the year rarely sees a drop of precipitation. Summer crops want irrigating. Wells go dry in September. Seasons of diminished rainfall are sorely trying. The green Redwood Coast, though apparently juicy, has to scramble for its water just like the burnt sienna and terra umbra portions of the West.

> As a state of mind the West reflects a nineteenth-century frontier ethic: Rugged Individualism, Manifest Destiny, Unfettered Capitalism, Absolute Property Rights. Traditionally the West has meant opportunity without the restrictions associated with the not-West. An honest-to-god Westerner doesn't like anything to get in his or her way. The honest-to-god-Point Arena Westerners from the beginning and up until today insist their hometown would blossom into prosperity if only certain people weren't so perversely obstructionist. Things would be different "if only" wrongheaded thinking would not make trouble. "If only" the populace would make more effort. What a shame the town doesn't embrace the chance to stay alive

with a business such as the concrete plant that is being offered... *INDEPENDENT COAST OBSERVER* 5/22/1992

Point Arena's isolation keeps it, for better or worse, small, relatively homogeneous and developmentally retarded, leaving it one of the last bastions of the nineteenth-century frontier ethic. Here experience hasn't thwarted, choked, obstructed, or arrested the naive and muleheaded expectations of the Western booster.

The concept of prosperity hasn't altered over the hundred-odd years of Point Arena's life, even though economic reality has. However, it won't be grand schemes, or strike-it-rich resource extraction, or even tried-and-true agriculture buttering the community's bread. From here on, the city is going to be maintained by sales taxes and bed taxes. It is going to rely, more and more, on tourism, and such enterprises as Peter Reimuller's mail-order nursery, Warren Jones's publishing company, Solano Press, and Steve Oliff's comic book coloring and computer animation business, Olyoptics. Enterprises of this sort can be situated anywhere and conducted through the expanding array of communication methods: FAX, FedEx, e-mail, U.P.S., overnight postal service, and so forth.

When I arrived in ungentrified Point Arena, the town had two or three commercial enterprises which set it apart from other backwater agricultural communities in the area. It had a tiny bookstore with a strange assortment of esoteric books on its shelves. It had a thriving natural food store, the Natch. And it had two venues for movies. One night a week, above the Natch, in the big room adjoining the Upstairs Cafe, you could watch a 16 mm film — always a good one, the kind I had enjoyed at the big-city retrospective theaters. The Wednesday Night Movie was the hub of our social life. The whole family ate dinner at the Upstairs first, then we went through the double doors to help set up folding chairs. Half the audience brought kids who sacked out on the floor in their sleeping bags when they got bored with subtitles.

Point Arena's "real" movie theater, popular for decades, had degenerated by 1981. It had developed a reputation for screening such films as *Friday The Thirteenth* and *Porkies*, and very little else. The audiences consisted primarily of teenagers who went to throw things at each other more than to watch the show. In 1983 Raven Earlygrow, organizer and perpetuator of the Wednesday Night Movies, got a chance to lease the theater, the only one between Monte

Rio and Fort Bragg. The building had been built in 1927 to replace Scott's Opera House, the old opera house (i.e. vaudeville theater) destroyed in one of the numerous fires which periodically laid waste to Point Arena in its early days. Raven formed Fly-By-Night, Inc. Fly-By-Night bought the movie business then rallied local movie lovers to the cause of refurbishing the interior. The theater equipment was archaic. The old carbon arc-lamp projectors turned all sorts of movies into a horror flicks when the film jammed and a spreading center of melting celluloid slowly devoured each image on the screen. Raven went shopping to replace the wonky sound system and found a great bargain in Texas, a complete Dolby sound system newly installed in a Texas prison. When a riot broke out, prison officials decided the inmates didn't deserve movies and put all the equipment up for sale. Fly-By-Night bought the Dolby.

The Wednesday Night Movie disappeared, but the new theater gave us two films a week, and Arena Renaissance Company gave us plays, dance performances and music concerts, local performers alternating with whatever world-class performers could be lured here. ARC also organized two annual fund-raisers: the Black & White Ball, where "formal attire is required but not expected," and the notorious Talent Show.

After the theater opened, the bookstore, the Upstairs Cafe and the Natch closed. A sad loss, but in time a new bookstore opened in the old pharmacy. To fill the niche left by the passing of the Upstairs, the new bookstore, Bookends, began to serve food along with books. Soon the store/cafe had grown so much it moved into the newly renovated office of the *Point Arena Record*. During the same time, the town's heavy readers, lusting for more ink than a medium-sized bookstore and a once-a-week bookmobile could deliver, founded a library. Magnanimous newcomer, Warren Jones, provided the library a free building for eight years.

Next a local chef opened a four star restaurant, Pangaea, which drew diners from all around Northern California. A new doctor moved to town; a new pharmacy opened. Adding all this to the developments at the wharf, we figured our wee outpost had acquired most of the trappings of a real city, a full complement.... Then I'll be damned if they didn't come in here and red tag our movie theater!

Although the community rallied its resources once again and restored the theater to a glory greater than it had ever known, the lesson was clear: I was never going to be able to pin down the place. I was never going to be able to say: this is it, my town. This is how it looks. This is what it has to offer. No,

Point Arena was too mutable, not from instability, but from an odd process of perpetual metamorphosis. At one early point in time Point Arena had two general merchandise stores, a string of bars and brothels, a hotel and two livery stables. Now the hotel is a liquor store, one of the livery stables is a gas station and the other has long been displaced by a motel. One of the general stores became a second gas station which was slowly balkanized into feed store, laundromat, and beauty shop. Flux-without-end. A meat market becomes a pharmacy. A newspaper office becomes restaurant, then a bookstore. A home becomes video rental shop then a library. And so on. Form remains (relatively) fixed, but makeup varies. Probably this is the case with all towns, but in the big ones it is not so noticeable.

Raven was mastermind of much of Point Arena's current municipal activity. His detractors call him a hippie and a dope grower, but in point of fact he is a thoroughgoing capitalist and entrepreneur. He has instituted any number of businesses, including the movie theater, the bookstore, the natural food store, and a prosperous travel agency booking river trips all over the world. His proudest achievements are his organizing of the annual Fourth of July fireworks at the Cove, and his founding of the Farmer's Market.

Raven is an imposing figure in demeanor if not in physical size. Not slight but a short, compact man, he carries himself with great assurance. He was born in New York City in 1946. Like the rest of us, he is not getting any younger; over the years I've watched his dark hair get sparser and grayer and his swarthy complexion take on more and more wrinkles. But despite his age, he has a perpetually boyish countenance, especially when he smiles.

After Raven graduated from City College with a degree in American history, he worked at city planning and as a social worker. In 1971 he decided he was heartily sick of the urban scene so he hitchhiked to California and made straight for the Mendocino Coast. Within two years he owned land on the Ridge above Point Arena and had built himself a house.

Before he achieved the status of Point Arena's number-one employer, he was gainfully employed by marijuana. His success in the dope business came to a spectacular halt when, while taking off in his private plane full of marijuana, he ran head on into another plane taxing the wrong way down the runway. The game warden, long itching to nail Raven, was too hasty about searching Raven's plane, so the case was thrown out of court, but the close call put Raven on a straighter path, and has profited more as an honest businessman than he did as an outlaw.

Raven has even risen to the respectable office of mayor now, much to the consternation of his enemies who registered a passel of bogus voters in an attempt to vote him out of office. In a town with a population of only slightly more than four hundred, the fraud was easy to spot, especially as the bogus voters mailed in their registrations all at the same time. The County Clerk phoned the City Clerk, and the fat was in the fire.

Though the Voter Fraud was a big local scandal, Mendocino's District Attorney never pressed charges. Perhaps she was still galled at how Raven cunningly eluded her grasp in the dope/plane fiasco. Yet it was a big scandal. Bona fide voters were indignant: "This is an unprecedented outrage!"

Outrage, yes; unprecedented, no. Point Arena has ever been the scene of sharp practice and contentious electioneering. One of the hottest conflicts galvanized around the ardently contested local option liquor laws. On May 17, 1915, the hotels in Point Arena filled with pro tempore "residents" whose votes would be tallied along with those of the qualified voters. Everyone was urged to the polls. Local citizens who were bedridden were carried to the polls. However, women were not yet allowed to vote, so in the final count "wet" won by nine votes.

Then there was the earlier pocket-sized civil war. It attended the special 1908 election to incorporate the town. For eight years the Point Arena Record editor, William Hanen, had been waging a campaign for incorporation. Finally Point Arena petitioned the County Board of Supervisors requesting a special election allowing the town's citizens to decide the matter.

If incorporated, Point Arena would retain two-thirds of the tax money it currently sent to Ukiah, the county seat. Advocates of incorporation wanted to keep the extra funds in the city, arguing that the money could be used to fix the woeful roads, keep the sidewalks clean, and generally provide more for the local infrastructure than the county provided. On the other side, the citizens opposed to incorporation feared that, if autonomous, the city would raise the tax rates.

Required for incorporation was a minimum population five-hundred residents. To take in the requisite number of bodies, the city had to extend its boundaries. Newly included ranchers did not want their property to be located within the city limits, so they lobbied strongly against incorporation.

Everyone was in a tizzy. The town at the time had thirteen saloons and the saloon keepers decided incorporation was a church deal — if incorporated, the city was going to raise their license fees high enough to force them out of business and thereby rid the town of alcoholic beverages. For their part, the churches believed the city, if incorporated, would be completely controlled by the saloons, and would reduce license fees to a merely nominal sum.

Watching the fracas, editor Hanen wrung his hands and tried to explain. "The only object of incorporation," he insisted, "is better control of the town.... We can only secure our rights by becoming a self-governing community."

When first the petition was presented to the Board of Supervisors, a minor omission in the document gave the Supes an excuse to postpone the matter. County government did not relish the idea of relinquishing Point Arena's revenue. But the postponement proved an advantage to incorporationists. During the delay, they recalculated the town's population and discovered that the extended boundaries had corralled well over 600 residents, more than was strictly necessary. Able now to re-compress the town limits enough to leave the protesting ranchers outside, they eliminated the ranchers' "no" votes, as well as their grounds for opposing incorporation.

The week the petition was put on the Board of Supervisors agenda for a second time, the weekly issue of the *Point Arena Record* by chance, included midst all the incorporation news, a letter from Lewis Morse and J.C. Halliday. The previous spring J.C. turned over the blacksmithing half of his business to his partner, and his son was pretty much running the other half, the hardware and implements store. This change in affairs left J.C. a good deal of spare time. Despite his age, J.C. was not a man to sit around in idleness, so one day he pried his friend Dr. Morse out of his rocking chair — for the good doctor had no problem at all with the contemplative life — and the two old geezers paid a visit to the County Farm. I don't know what they expected but they came away appalled by conditions and immediately drafted a letter of complaint to the newspaper. The farm's inmates, they said, were ill-clad and underfed. Was the county trying to starve its indigent population into extinction?

The letter, authored by two pillars of Point Arena society, infuriated the Board of Supervisors who were irked already by the town's proposed fiscal defection. Though they would have dearly loved to deny Point Arena the special election, the supervisors couldn't legally take such a position, so they scheduled the ballot for the last day in June. But in their rancor they stipulated: 1) the town was not allowed to shrink back to its originally proposed boundaries, and 2) if the proposal passed, the town must not raise its municipal tax to a rate any higher than county's. Furthermore, obliged to publish a Notice of

Election, the Supes, in an impotent gesture of displeasure with Hanen, refused to pay *Point Arena Record* to print the notice, choosing instead another town's paper. Unabashed, and hooting with his victory, editor Hanen published the Notice of Election free of charge.

The Board of Supervisors' frail attempts to undermine the election actually promoted the cause of incorporation. Realizing Point Arena was in the Board of Supervisors' "black book," and afraid of reprisals if their town remained in the county's yoke, some of those citizens opposed to incorporation began to campaign in favor of it. Others, previously opposed, were reassured now by the county limit on tax rates and so were willing to vote for incorporation. Saloon keepers signed a statement promising not to ask for a reduction in the cost of their licenses, and on June 30, 1908, the vote to incorporate passed, and the city elected its first board of trustees, later to become the Point Arena City Council. The trustees' first meeting took place in July. In October — licensing was done quarterly — the city issues twelve liquor licenses, which became Point Arena's greatest source of revenue until the Volstead Act closed the saloons in 1919.

Point Arena was born fully matured and, in its essentials, has grown little since its birth. The population of the overall area has increased drastically, but the city itself is roughly the same size it was at its inception, and it grapples with many of the same problems. Fire protection, waste disposal, roads — throughout the years the minutes of City Council meeting show astounding continuity.

The governing of Point Arena has never been serene. All interests make a stand then duke it out. That's the way of a vigorous democracy, but the process takes its toll on City Council members. Whatever choice they make, they are bound to vex somebody who proceeds to rake them — either one by one or as a body — over the coals. Occasionally, a city council member has been heard to cry in despair: "We ought to disincorporate!"

"Point Arena had no business being incorporated, but in my judgment it was a good thing," said ninety-seven-year-old Joe Scaramella, former City Council member, mayor, County Supervisor, and State Coastal Commissioner, "because it gave us local control we wouldn't have had otherwise. With all its faults and weaknesses, in my notion, it was a good thing. We could do things here ourselves without going to Ukiah for everything we wanted. I went through the records and at one time the town had an actual cash balance of $1.15. When they would put gravel on the street they would tell the guys who did it, 'You'll get your money when the tax money comes in.' Now I hear them talk and they want to disincorporate because of some political action on the part of the council or something that they don't like. When they talk to me about it I tend to discourage it. It's not in the best interest of the people of the town. If you have home rule, then keep it. That's the way it's been all the time since 1908."[3]

REFERENCE NOTES

1. Aurelius Carpenter, *History of Mendocino and Lake Counties*, 1914.

2. Lyman Palmer, *History of Mendocino County.*

3. *Yesterday's News* interview, JS04.PA.

Chapter Four

BEST LAID PLANS

My husband never intended to become a patrol boy of natural resources, but things had a way of happening, things he simply could not shut his eyes to. The R.V. park was the first of them. Alan has been a surfer since he was old enough to figure out how to cut school and take a bus from the San Fernando Valley to the beach. Point Arena is a surfing (albeit a chilly one) Mecca, so Alan spends his lunch time at the Cove watching the waves. He likes his walk on the Wharf of an evening. In short, he loves Arena Cove, and judged that a sixty-nine space R.V. park would destroy it utterly. The setting might survive forty spaces, but the proposal was for sixty-nine. *Sixty-nine!* No sireee bob. No way. Alan went into action.

Next came the Bed Rock sortie. In the middle of the night our bedroom window was suddenly open to a functioning rock crusher and asphalt plant a mere quarter mile upwind of us. This battle was followed by another, then another. Alan's forces won more often than they lost. Armed with his native doggedness, he gradually gleaned enough about environmental law and developed enough sense about how use it — how to tread the intertwist of government bureaucracy, how to talk agency argot — to become a genuine barb in the butt of his adversaries. Considering his reputation, Alan was the last person on earth AT&T would have wanted to find, that fateful July day, poking around back in the woods on that unnamed tributary of the Garcia.

It was hay season, and Alan had hired a strapping lad to help him bring in our hay crop from the Hallidays' big north field. As the two of them loaded bales onto the flatbed truck, they caught glimpses of people, strangers, behind the trees on the other side of the field fence. Odd. Who could they be? What could they be doing? And those trucks? They looked for all the world like water trucks. First one lumbered by, then another. Not-knowing drives Alan crazy so after some time he went over to find out what was going on. At his appearance, a gaggle of bright young women broke from their huddle in surprise.

The hired lad probably thought his employer was flexing his elegant biceps and winking at the pretty young women, but it was overweening curiosity, rather than a slavering lubricity, which kept Alan hanging over the fence, while behind him the strapping lad bucked the bales all alone.

The women told Alan they were consultants on the AT&T job, but would surrender no more information than that despite the persistence of Alan's probing.

AT&T's big project was no secret: a five-hundred-million-dollar fiberoptics cable. It had been inching its way across our neighborhood for, lo, these many months. Lined across the United States in a cement encased trench, the cable was to make a sharp right hand turn at San Francisco, then run north to Manchester Beach where it would join the undersea line from Japan.

No secret at all. Big news, in fact. For several weeks Windy Hollow, a primitive little farm road, had been bustling with men and equipment. The south-bound lane was trenched right down the middle for the whole length of the road. After the pipe to house the cable was laid in the trench, the scar was filled and repaved.

A five-hundred-million-dollar project. And AT&T, by god, was going to do it right. The company was determined to leave nothing for local residents to complain about. Many studies, much negotiating. The AT&T plan of action included a close survey of sensitive species along the cable's entire right-of-way. The scene was set for AT&T, currently the nation's third largest public corporation, to make the acquaintance of *Aplodontia rufa*, a small, elusive Point Arena resident of little celebrity.

Aplodontia rufa, the Mountain Beaver, isn't actually a beaver at all but a rodent more closely akin to squirrels and muskrats than beavers. For at least thirty-five million years *Aplodontia rufa* has been living along the Pacific Coast from British Columbia to Point Reyes, California, in labyrinthine burrows of rambling, haphazard tunnels. Mountain beavers spend three quarters of their lives underground, and when they do emerge, it is usually in the dark — apparently sunshine makes the little beasts drowsy causing them to fall sound asleep in the middle of eating or even fleeing danger. But mountain beavers do occasionally make daytime appearances and I once saw one walking up our driveway. A dark shade of brown, it was about a foot long, or oblong, I should say, with a little blunt face as round as its round, tailless little rump. The mountain beaver has long whiskers and tiny feet with five toes on each foot — nice long toes on its forefeet for digging and grasping. The whiskers and toes were details I couldn't see, but read about later when I finally was able to identify the unfamiliar animal.

The mountain beaver has never been popular with humans. Because it burrows, farmers class it with their archenemy, the gopher. And the timber industry's attitude toward the mountain beaver — "boomer" is what the foresters call him — makes agriculture's dim view look like fondness. Mountain beavers are voracious herbivores with an appetite for shrubs and small trees. They gnaw the limbs off of full-grown Douglas firs, and chow down whole seedlings. In Oregon, mountain beavers reduced several sites planted with six hundred trees per acre to one hundred trees per acre in very brief span of time.

Aplodontia rufa has seven subspecies, three of which inhabit the Redwood Coast. The Point Arena's *Aplodontia rufa* is of the subspecies *nigra*, named for its dark-tipped hairs. (Other mountain beavers are somewhat lighter.) The Point Arena Mountain Beavers aren't tree eaters, but feed instead on roots and ferns. A fair quantity of their favorite foods — bracken fern, sword fern, foxglove, stinging nettle, thistle, salal — are plants distasteful, even toxic, to other animals, so *Aplodontia rufa nigra* has little competition in its food niche.

Aplodontia, the oldest living rodent, has some odd and primitive physiological characteristics. It lacks the ability to reduce heat stress by panting, salivating, or sweating. It also lacks the anatomical features needed for effectively concentrating urine, and so must take in large quantities of water to replace what it loses through excretion. The animal's limited ability to thermoregulate and its inefficient excretory system confine it to a narrow domain of moist, mild, stable climates. It likes the well-drained soils and lush vegetation of cool ravines, evergreen forests, and coastal strands.

Mountain beavers are solitary, irascible little beasts, hardly more sociable with their own kind (except in mating season) than with the human species, whom they would as soon bite as look at. Held in low esteem already, Point Arena's particular mountain beaver subspecies had the effrontery to become an official Endangered Species. Thus when AT&T began mapping the fiber-optics cable route, it had to avoid disturbing the mountain beavers. The AT&T monitors were so conscientious they located previously undiscovered populations, revealing *Aplodontia rufa nigra* to be far more common than anyone had thought. Wholeheartedly committed to protecting the animal, AT&T decided to bury the cable beneath local watercourses rather than risk going through them. To this end the company hired an oil drilling crew from Texas to drill horizontally under all streams needing to be traversed. The irony is that if the drilling, devised solely to protect the mountain beaver, had not been done, the poor creature would have fared a lot better.

In the course of drilling near a small stream, which came to fame as The Unnamed Tributary, the crew, using bentonite clay as a lubricant, unexpectedly hit a strata of very hard rock, promptly breaking their drill bit, but they kept right on drilling, all the while injecting bentonite into the fissure. At one o'clock — shortly before Alan began to pester the biologists from his side of the field fence — the site superintendent informed the women that he had "lost circulation." The biologists were alarmed, but the oil drilling boys from Texas, without the vaguest misgiving, neither paused nor slowed their pace. Bentonite flooded approximately six acres of hillside then bled down into the Unnamed Tributary, eleven thousand gallons of it.

Bentonite is inert and non-toxic, but its thickness and viscosity suffocate. Not only were the mountain beavers, burrowed directly below the spill, affected, but the amphibians, including red-legged frogs, yellow-legged frogs, Pacific giant salamanders, fish, and a host of invertebrates were blanketed in clay. Even creatures on the banks who survived — cray fish, the western toad, sculpin, garter snake, etc. — were now scheduled to die from lack of food if the spill managed to kill enough aquatic invertebrates.

Late that afternoon Alan came home from the hay field with no inkling of what he had witnessed, so he was unprepared for the call. Telephone receiver to his ear, blinking like a frog, he listened to the biologist's tale. For once in his life he was speechless. A *pro hac vice* loss of words. It wasn't until he hung up that words came, and then all he could do was rave since the biologists had already notified the Department of Fish and Game as well as their employer, AT&T.

Thursday saw the local game warden tromping up and down the river. Finding mountain beaver burrows buried in clay, in league with a Fish and Game biologist, they tried to formulate a cleanup strategy. The first plan was to vacuum the riverbed, a plan they dumped when they realized vacuuming might finish off whatever had survived the initial spill. By Monday they had settled on a scheme to divert the Garcia around the two most affected areas, then go into the mess with a crew and manually remove the bentonite, which had seeped so deeply into the riverbed that it might be necessary to excavate to a depth of three, maybe even six inches.

The bypass channel was completed on Tuesday, and a group — which, by order of AT&T, included the drilling Texans — was assembled to move frogs, fish, salamanders, et al., to the newflow. The channel was begun, but the sandy soil wouldn't hold back the water. The bypass was doomed to failure, and everybody began to fear they might have to vacuum after all.

A first-class disaster. Over the past year the community had poured immense amounts of work, countless hours, much energy, and all available funds into improving the condition of the Garcia River. Now it all seemed to be wasted. And worse still, a community's optimism, its hope for the river's health, was sadly undermined. The good folks who had been working hard to restore the river, to salvage what was left of its fishery, were exasperated: Why had AT&T's boys kept on pumping when they knew they had a rupture?

Friday we were slapped with a further development: after fouling the Garcia, the drillers had trundled down to Moat Creek and to Point Arena Creek, two smaller watercourses south of the city, and done precisely the same thing on both of them!

"They were rushing," Alan said. "They were in too big a hurry." He was bitter, and he began to spend ninety-nine percent of his waking hours on the telephone, calling everybody he could think of — managing agencies, elected officials, newspapers.

That August 4 was my birthday, and I was determined to celebrate with an outing calculated to temporarily extricate my husband from the bentonite. Lake Sonoma should do it, I thought, a drive along an obscure road, a hot walk, a swim. For at least one day we would escape the wearisome AT&T business. But, alas, the demands of irony were more powerful than birthday-girl prerogatives. We left the main road, passed through an open gate, and following a squiggly, broken red line on our minutely detailed road map, we headed straight into the arms of the very enterprise I had so cunningly contrived to evade.

My car bounced slowly through the dust. The day was hot, but the road was shady and the scenery was fine, and we drove on in wordless contentment until, gradually, a distant noise began to trespass on our woodsy silence. It couldn't be bulldozers; up to the time we actually saw them, I argued vigorously against the presence of bulldozers. As it turned out, AT&T was running the fiberoptics cable down the side of the squiggly red line road, and before we had reached the lake, Alan had spotted at least two blatant violations of rules he now knew were supposed to be governing AT&T's actions. The next day — no phones at the lake, thank heaven — he contacted the State Regional Water Quality Control Board and the Sonoma D.A.

Over a barrel now, AT&T was wildly anxious to set things straight, and its representatives arrived in town en masse. Not only was the telecommunications giant determined to be "a good corporate citizen," but also, with almost half of the fiberoptics cable's forty-thousand circuits already leased to the federal government, the company was faced with contract deadlines, and its multimillion dollar project was now at a complete halt!

The state agencies documented, analyzed, and evaluated. Finally, after three months of scrutiny, California advised Mendocino County to take legal action, civil, criminal or both, against AT&T for "obvious violations of the state's pollution and water quality laws."

Local entities affected by the spill — the County of Mendocino, the City of Point Arena, the ranchería (which gets its water directly from the river right beside the spill), the Resource Conservation District, the Watershed Advisory Group, the Friends of the Garcia, and the Surfrider Foundation, all (with the possible exception of Surfrider) — were chronic paupers. AT&T was the third largest corporation in the nation, had the second highest market value, was ranked fourth in sales and fourth in profits. And, by the sheerest chance, these impoverished local entities now had this incredibly wealthy corporation in their collective clutches.

At the point the advisement had come down from Sacramento, AT&T was in the process of negotiating a new route for the cable. Toward the end of November the cable link from Sacramento would be completed, allowing the cable to go "on line," thus fulfilling AT&T's most pressing obligations, but pressure to complete the San Francisco/Manchester Beach link persisted. Because the Department of Fish and Game forbade the original route, AT&T needed to wangle new permits from Mendocino County and the City of Point Arena. Confronted with a multiplicity of lawsuits, the corporate giant hustled to settle with local interests.

Point Arena wasn't greedy, but it was determined to come away with its share of the poke. Steve Oliff was mayor during this episode of Point Arena history, and a cadre of local environmentalists counseled him to bide his time, and cautioned the City Council to hold out for more. Both mayor and council were peeved, and labeled the holdout camp "nay-sayers" stubbornly impeding the goose which was trying its best to deliver a golden egg.

Similar discord reigned in the Watershed Advisory Group and, to a lesser extent, in Friends Of The Garcia. Should they accept what was being proffered, or risk getting less, getting perhaps nothing at all, by holding out for a fatter, and, as they saw it, more equitable sum? The river, after all, was to be the beneficiary; whatever they came away with would go into the much needed restoration.

Local interests rallied themselves into a roundup of skittish mistrust. Whenever anyone met with an AT&T envoy, either formally or informally, everyone absent from the encounter snorted and pawed the dirt.

The rodeo went on and on with accusations and counter-accusations, standoffs and recapitulations. AT&T representatives pirouetted wildly around the arena, dodging the mad steers and the bucking broncos. Towards the end, one tired spokesman said, "We got in there with all fours, and rolled up our sleeves and did everything we could...we're trying to act responsibly. I'm not sure you people know that." The guy was close to tears.

Eventually AT&T managed to settle out of court with each separate party. Bill Hay's Point Arena Water Works was reimbursed for a new well — the bentonite thoroughly plugged the original one. And the County D.A.'s office received $132,770.20 to be dispersed among several agencies, including the State Regional Water Quality Control Board, the Mendocino Resource Conservation District, and the Department of Fish and Game.

The array of environmental groups got their portions through the Resource Conservation District. From the total of $203,500, the RCD kept $18,000 in administration fees. Then $9,250 was allocated for Native American education, Friends Of The Garcia got $26,600 for monitoring and mapping, the Watershed Advisory Group got $34,150 for immediate watershed activities with a $65,000 for future projects, and Surfrider Foundation got $50,000 for Moat Creek. (When Florence Silva, ranchería representative, asked, "Why so much to Surfrider?" a local surfer told her, "Man, was our attorney ever a go-getter.") Also, the DA's office allotted $82,450.78 of its AT&T settlement money to the Garcia and Moat Creek. A portion of the money was set aside to cover the costs of the investigation.

Later AT&T, not content to pay only what was exacted, expanded its largess by contributing to the community library generous amounts for new environmental education materials and computer equipment.

And then it was over. Back to business as usual. At intervals, a memento, a souvenir trophy. At the library, I'll find a new book with a note: Needs plaque. And I'll affix "This Book Donated With Funds From AT&T" onto the frontispiece of something previously backordered. Or someone from Point Arena will go to the Water Quality office in Santa Rosa and be surprised to see an entire room full of brand new computers. Or those snatches of fretful dialogue still heard now and then: "Damn. I just read that Rosenfield and those guys got fourteen million from Chevron. We shoulda held out."

"It doesn't do to be too grabby. It isn't honorable."

"Where's the dishonor in getting money for the river? Maybe the dishonor was in not pushing for a better settlement."

And the beavers? The beavers remain elusive as ever.

Chapter Five

LOCATION, LITIGATION, FRUSTRATION

The VFW Hall is packed. The members of Point Arena's City Council sit on a dais, only their name plaques stand between them and their constituents. The hearing has been in progress for an hour, and things have gone smoothly. Surprisingly smoothly. Each speaker, formally recognized by the mayor, walks politely up to the microphone to speak.

"For the plan to work, and for Point Arena to survive, the Council must adopt strict project review procedures. I'd like to reintroduce the idea of a separate planning commission...."

Is it possible the wild, wild west is at last coming to terms with civic responsibility? Is Point Arena, ever the model of small government wielded by private interests, really capable of conducting business in a seemly, courteous, proper fashion?

"Mr. Mayor, I'd like to say that the analysis in this plan is the best I've ever seen. It's just what Point Arena needs...."

Each speaker is allotted three minutes, not a second more. The City Council has vowed to strictly enforce the time limit. Otherwise we could be here until tomorrow's sun comes up. The public listens, uncharacteristically quiet. The Council listens, silent as stones. Everyone has promised: No interruptions, no matter what the speaker says.

"The rules and guidelines in the General Plan will stifle development and make building costs too high. I don't think this draft proposal reflects the work done by the citizens advisory committees."

When the meeting closes I expect half the audience to hurry to the medical center to have their tongues sutured.

"Even though I worked on both the Land Use Committee and the Open Space Committee, I'm afraid that parts of the General Plan impinge on the rights of individuals..."

"Time was there wasn't much need for us to have rules, or General Plans, or anything else, but times are changing. More people, more rules..."

We are in the process of making history. Right now. Right at this very minute. Point Arena — smallest city in California to do so voluntarily and by means of its own resources — is drafting a general plan, a state mandated outline of development policy. The task is not easy, but since we are under injunction, we have no time to waste, and thus must dispense with our characteristic brawling. Tonight nary a peep of argument will be allowed.

"This thing represents a good program for bringing more jobs and more business to the community without jeopardizing the town's quality of life."

"Amen!"

"I said before," Mayor Earlygrow looks stern, no sign tonight of his winsome smile. "I don't want to see anyone calling out from the audience! I said so right at the onset…"

The promise of a rebuttal hearing, booked for two weeks hence, helps maintain this contentious community's good behavior.

"You have fifty percent open space in this draft. That was not our recommendation. If you go with your fifty percent open space, you're not going to have very much land to build on."

"What Mr. Hay just said is misleading. It is only multi-unit residential developments that are required to allocate half their land to open space. And they still can build as many units as their permit allows, but they'll need to cluster them."

"Balancing development with open space is really the heart of the issue. That's what planning is all about — make a place you can actually live with. I don't want to have to 'escape' from Point Arena someday."

Good behavior. Voices tend to rise an octave or two, but everything remains under control. Standing at the back of the room I listen, quietly jouncing a friend's newborn infant on my shoulder. Periodically, with a gentle hiccup, he deposits runnels of warm cottage cheese down my back.

A general plan is a projected design for local development, a "constitution for all future developments." Before 1971, general plans were merely advisory guidelines, but California decided local zoning and subdivision approvals must be consistent with an adopted general plan. The state Legislature acted in 1972, but it wasn't until 1990 the state Supreme Court gave the doctrine the judicial go-ahead. It took a while for Point Arena's City Council to figure out that in order to be consistent with a general plan, it must actually *have* a general plan.

Belatedly but gamely grasping this plain fact, our august municipal body was soon adrift in a wide sea of confusion. A succession of mayors and city attorneys tried to disentangle the mesh of inexperience and indifference from the city's disabled motor, but the municipal bark was about to sink when providence intervened, placing upon the sacrificial alter the person of Warren Jones.

Warren is a sophisticated man — cosmopolitan, well-bred, suave, urbane — but if this description told the whole of the story, Warren today might be less gray of head, less furrowed of brow. As it turns out, for all his learning and worldly wisdom, Warren Jones is most wonderfully naive.

For many years he lived in Berkeley, teaching urban planning and publishing planning law books. When the time came to retire, he contrived to get away from the stress of the big city. Leaving his position at U.C. Berkeley, he bought a simple, tasteful home in a bucolic setting, and relocated his publishing enterprise to the simpler, quieter life of Point Arena.

Lovely place, Point Arena. A town of honest folk, colorful characters, all going about their business in a nineteenth-century frontier setting. Warren, a great lover of good food, discovered a quaint cafe above the natural food store. The Upstairs Cafe. It served hearty, tasty food on Wednesday nights, so, come Wednesday night Warren — trusting as a babe in the woods — ascended the stairs for a leisurely dinner. All the tables were occupied, but as he stood looking around and salivating, an attractive, redheaded couple beckoned him to join them. In good natured and trusting innocence, Warren sat down to a fateful dinner with Jeff and Lena.

Salad went down with offhand chat, getting acquainted chat, but the pesto lasagna, was transformed by a sudden, unseemly whoop from Jeff: "Eureka!" The angel assigned to guard muddled municipalities had placed Warren Jones, unwary city planner, at table with a desperate city council member.

Point Arena tapped Warren like a Vermont maple in February. When I asked him if he had understood what he was getting into when he agreed to help, he said, smiling his seraphic smile, "Yes and no." Yes, he knew that offering his time and expertise would mean meetings, phone calls, pullings, tuggings, grindings, plungings, scuffles and tussles, followed by more meetings and phone calls, but, no, he hadn't realized how much he would be going it alone. He had expected more help. A good deal more help.

The City never could have afforded to pay Warren, or anyone like him, so without Warren's pure benevolence, the city would have had to endure the State of California circling it like a shark. Already the State had imposed on the city a building moratorium, a most inconvenient moratorium which remained in effect for two years. Time was running out. Point Arena had to create and adopt a comprehensive, long-term general plan containing seven mandatory elements: Land Use; Circulation (traffic); Housing; Conservation (flood control, pollution, conversion of farmland, endangered species, etc.); Open Space; Noise; and Safety. These elements had to meet state requirements, or the plan would be "deemed legally inadequate." A tall order for a bunch of sheep farmers and hippies.

Warren set things in motion. First, the City Council needed to muster committees, one for each element. Everybody in town was pressed to join one. For the next five years, plan drafters worked and fought and held public hearings and fought and wrote and telephoned Warren. Warren introduced his troops to appropriate written resources, then stepped back to let them duke it out for themselves. But they needed him, all of them, all the time, so he ended up a de facto member of every committee.

Though his emphatic step backward never removed him from the fray, he tried to remain politically neutral. His neutrality — or at least his reassuring semblance of neutrality — though essential, was hard on his social sensibility. Warren, though, was too amicable, too charming, too much of a bon vivant to give up all camaraderie.

One morning he invited a gaggle of hard-core environmentalists over for brunch, a clandestine gathering since it wouldn't do for him to be seen consorting with one of the factions. While Warren cooked, the rest of us, nursing stoically-awaited cups of coffee, watched a young doe nibble the salal outside the kitchen window. Warren, busy with a huge cast iron skillet full of eggs, mushrooms, onions, peppers, cheese, suggested one of us "shoo her away." But the rest of us were too lustful for a second cup of coffee to leave the kitchen. More efficient at city planning than breakfast planning, Warren was trying to exact from a single, one-cup coffee filter a morning's fix for six serious coffee addicts. Whoever went outside to confront the deer risked missing a turn in the go-round. So we equivocated and stalled.

"He used to feed them," Anna Dobbins said. "The deer. Can you believe it? Now he begs, 'Go shoo her away,' but when he first moved here, he fed them. I think he deserves defoliation."

In the middle of the table, between the bouquet of columbine and a pitcher of fresh orange juice, sat a huge platter of the scones and muffins Warren's friend Sylvia brought from Berkeley.

"We need a bakery around here. I thought of opening one," Anna said, "but I don't know…I doubt I could make a living."

"The new bakery in Gualala, what's it like?"

"Awful," Alan answered.

And I told the group, "That's a sober indictment coming from a man who considers Winchell's Donuts a good bakery."

"We need somebody to bring bread to us from the Bay Area on a regular basis. Peet's coffee, too."

"Maybe Sylvia should get a helicopter."

"I can see us lying here on Warren's floor, gasping, waiting for her. Like a crack house."

We sat down to an impressive meal, and I began to count the beats. With my husband, the Dobbins, and Warren it was only a matter of time before the topic perpetually waiting in the wings took the stage.

"Did you know Billy's asking for two more permits to mine 10,000 yards of gravel besides the 10,000 he already takes." Peter Dobbins, right on cue.

"The 10,000 yards he's supposed to take. He takes a lot more than that."

"The Planning Commission's going to let him have them, too. The permits."

"Not without an EIR..."

"Yes. Without an EIR. We can sue, but even if we win, Billy'll take however much he wants. He just takes it anyway. Stashes it somewhere."

"Human beings are so damned greedy. So shortsighted. Sometimes I see us as a hoard of army ants, scraping the face off the globe bare."

"People are the exact opposite of bees," said Peter. "Bees are very stupid as individuals, but smart as a group."

We sat in downhearted silence for a minute or two. Then Warren in his let's-jolly-up tone said, "Raven tells me that Billy has a life-sized statue of John Wayne in his living room."

Incredulous laughter.

"Is it anatomically correct?"

"Undress it and see."

"I wonder if Billy dresses and undresses it. Has all sorts of little outfits." General hilarity.

That power breakfast was in May. By January Point Arena had a new general plan…Well, almost.

> HEARINGS CONTINUE
>
> The Point Arena City Council heard public comment on the Housing and Land Use elements of the proposed General Plan Tuesday night.
>
> Despite the heavy rains, the meeting drew a large crowd of concerned citizens eager to add their voices to the planning process. While there was much debate and argument over a few specific points, the overall tone of the hearing was one of compromise and cooperation...Though there was some contentious debate about the zoning of a few specific parcels, the expected clashes were for the most part avoided… *Independent Coast Observer*, January 22, 1993

Mendocino County was the last county in the state to adopt its required General Plan. Point Arena was the last city in the county to adopt its required General Plan. On January 24, 1995, the Point Arena City Council voted four to one to accept the final draft, complete with an Environmental Impact Report. Some people were upset, but Jeff spoke up, "All changes in the final Plan were made as a result of review of all the public input, which went on officially for almost two years and had to be brought to an end eventually. You can get bogged down out of control. We've actually had years of public input since 1985 when we first started talking about it. I've read the Plan word for word and I think we have a good document and a good process and I just can't stand naysayers."

Mayor Earlygrow said, "It's been a long time coming, and it has been an outstanding effort by everybody in this community. I'm proud to vote Yes."

Bill Hay said, "We can get along without a General Plan and EIR if we do it correctly." Ah, for the good old days. The good old boys and the good old days when, "…the white man does as he pleases."

At one point while the General Plan was being hashed and rehashed, Bill Hay decided to build a batch plant and concrete recycler directly adjacent to town. Everybody downwind of the proposed site was disturbed. They had already had a sampling of three a.m. rock crushing while Bill was rushing gravel to AT&T's hurry-up job. The townsfolk had not enjoyed the noise, the dust, or the truck traffic, so now they banded together to launch a lawsuit to nip the new plant in the bud, or at least force Billy to locate it in a more suitable spot. Billy, though, had his supporters who deluged the local newspaper with indignant letters:

> EDITOR: I am shocked and outraged by the lawsuits being filed against the City of Point Arena… Anyone who cannot accept this [batch plant] might be well advised to find another town to live in Marlene Soldani, ICO, May 22, 1992.
>
> EDITOR: What is happening in Point Arena? Being a lifetime resident (79 years) I like the old time residents and the new, but do not agree with people who sue…We get along without this type of ill love, [we] respected people's property rights. Victor Soldani, ICO, May 22, 1992.
>
> EDITOR: What has me worried is a change in attitude. It seems like some of our urbanite refugees are so afraid of spoiling our area that they are doing just that. Perhaps they should relax and learn to get along with other people. If you want litigation and frustration, try another location. Jim Soldani, ICO, May 22, 1992.

It would have been useless to debate Jim Soldani on the merits of setting up a batch plant and cement recycler in a quiet, rural community, but I could have set him straight about the other part, about the newfangledness of litigation. Litigation here is old hat. In fact, Point Arena entered American history sporting a dandy and protracted lawsuit.

When the United States, by capture and purchase, laid hold of California, Mexican citizen Rafael Garcia did his best to keep title to his forty thousand acre land grant in Mendocino County. Articles VIII and IX of the Treaty of Guadalupe Hidalgo guaranteed the security of all Spanish and Mexican grants, and, as final and perfect evidence of title, the U.S. issued patents to all claimants with Mexican titles valid before August 7, 1846. Titles issued after this date, arbitrarily assigned as the end of Mexican rule, were thrown out. The Mexican government, sorely pressed to hold body and soul together during the years sandwiched between Spain and the United States, had been inattentive to the recording of their grants, many of which, especially during the final hectic months of Mexican rule, were scooted through with not so much as a nod in the direction of proper procedure. The United States, in its turn, did not make haste to tackle the problem so that by the time the California Land Act of 1851 created a Board of Land Commissioners to decide the pending claims, the situation was a vast muddle of honest confusion and deliberate hanky panky.

On March 23, 1852, Garcia filed his U.S. claim for Rancho del Norte. Along with written evidence, he produced witnesses to testify that he had occupied the land since 1845. The three Land Commissioners accepted as evidence the Mexican "passport" allowing Garcia to come north to look for land, but they decided his application for the land, made three years later to Mexican Governor Pio Pico, was not a valid title. "…there is nothing in all this from which a grant of land can be inferred or from which an obligation to make a grant could justly proceed under colonization laws then in force."[1]

After the Board rejected Garcia's claim, he petitioned the District Court for a review of the Commission's decision. If the District Court went against him, he could go to the Supreme Court. In 1857, three years after Garcia appealed his case, the District Court reversed the Board's decision. To the judge it appeared as though Governor Pico was on the brink of issuing Garcia a title when the U.S. takeover stopped him. A victory for Rafael Garcia, but, alas, a short-lived one. In 1860 the U.S. Supreme Court overturned the District Court decision. Nine long years of legal wrangling had exhausted all possible avenues of redress. The last leg of the struggle had been waged by Jose Leandro Luco, a Mexican citizen who purchased the property from Garcia. Now the Rancho del Norte land grant was finally and permanently invalidated, and his forty-thousand acres was declared public land.

Although the United States assured Mexico that both Mexican and Spanish land grants would be honored, the burden of proof lay with the claimant, and, in the long run, eighty percent of the contested land went to U.S. settlers — or to their lawyers, who generously offered to take their fees in land. Garcia lost. I suppose it matters little if the decision was fair, or if his claim was honest, but my overweening curiosity yearns for satisfaction. The good old U.S.A., like most nations, favored its own. And with Manifest Destiny riding shotgun, Uncle Sam was managing to get what he wanted by fair means or foul. A good deal of western land was violently wrenched from

Spanish and Mexican holders, but a "shotgun title" wasn't what defeated Garcia. Rancho del Norte was acquired by U.S. settlers playing by the judiciary rules.

But, within the putative bounds of legality, was the rip-roaring U.S.A. brash in this instance? Or did Garcia lose fair and square? His story includes uncertainties. As its plot thickens, its motif becomes more and more obscure. The Garcia grant lay beside another Mexican land grant, one claimed by William Richardson only one day before Garcia wrote to Pico asking for "... nine leagues on the northern Coast of the Russian Presidio, as shown in the respective map, bounded on the North by the land of Don Guillermo Richardson and following the Coast sotherly until the nine leagues are completed."[2]

Richardson was a native of Kent, England, who moved to San Francisco in 1822. He taught art, navigation and carpentry to Mexican citizens until he got himself baptized Guillermo Antonio Richardson and married the Comandante's daughter. Soon he was a full-fledged Mexican citizen. By 1836 he owned several launches and was collecting produce from various points around San Francisco Bay to make up the cargoes of trading vessels. The next year he became Captain of the Port of San Francisco. He lived on his *Saucelito Rancho* on the bay's north shore. He claimed that when his job as captain of the port ended in 1844, and he asked for his back pay, he was told the treasury hadn't enough money. Would he take a northern land grant instead? Yes, he would indeed. Richardson signed a waiver on November 12, 1844, and lit out for the north. On March 3, 1846, he wrote Governor Pio Pico to say he had picked a tract of land that began at 39° 18' North, followed the coast to 38° 48' and went inland for two leagues. He sent the required hand-drawn map, the *diseño*, showing his southerly boundary to be Mal Paso, the precise boundary of Rafael Garcia's northern limit.

Were Garcia and Richardson in collusion? If so, for what purpose? That Richardson recognized the value of northern timber is clear from the fact that, straight away, he built sawmills, first on the Albion River then on the Noyo River. Richardson may have grabbed the land for the trees. But if Garcia was grabbing land for timber, he showed excessive restraint in garnering his prize. No evidence whatsoever exists to indicate he ever sold one board foot. It appears as though he built a mill on the Garcia River at Allen Gulch, but it was a very small mill used only for his own ranch needs.

If Garcia and Richardson were in cahoots, were they merely opportunists taking advantage of Mexico's general discombobulation? Or, premeditating, did they anticipate the U.S. takeover with all its attendant confusion.

Of course, it's possible the two did not know each other before claiming land on the northern frontier, that Richardson, already established there when Garcia arrived, merely offered a neighborly hand. Such things happen, even today: a developer blows into town where the like-minded offer their support. Richardson's written description (as opposed to the depiction) claimed property south to 38° 48', a latitude south of Mal Paso, but his diseño shows his land ending at Mal Paso, the north boundary of Garcia's grant.

The hand-drawn maps are unquestionably the work of one person. Maybe Richardson met Garcia, and in a spirit of neighborliness, surrendered a few degrees of latitude, then kindly drew up two *diseños*, one for each of them.

Initially both men appear to have acted in good faith. Each got a passport, each "proved up" on his land, each petitioned the governor for title. At the Board of Land Commissioners hearing, Richardson acted as one of Garcia's witnesses, testifying to the house Garcia built and to the "agricultural and grazing" use to which Garcia had put the land. But the petitions to Pico look suspicious. Richardson's was made on March 3, 1846; Garcia's was made the very next day. That, along with the two-of-a-kind *diseños*, suggest these guys were in league. But were they? And if so, does it have any bearing on the validity of their respective claims?

The Board decided Richardson's title was valid. Even so, the Richardson litigation lasted fourteen years. He didn't live to see the end of it. Was William Guillermo Richardson yet again another Mexican citizen flimflammed out of his property? If the Land Commissioners readily admitted the Mexican governor intended Richardson to have title, what prolonged the legal process? The signature was the problem; the commissioners decided the Mexican governor's signature looked funny. When I first read about the signature, I thought the Board was obviously determined to get the man's land by hook or by crook. But as I kept reading, the plot thickened once again.

Enter Jose Limantour. Señor Limantour claimed a four-league hunk of land which included most of the city of San Francisco. When his case came before the Board, his documents were all in order, his witnesses were squeaky clean, so Commissioners approved his claim without to-do. Two years later a judge discovered Limantour's papers had all been antedated, the signatures had been forged, and many of the witnesses had lied. And the most damning evidence of all: the official government seal had been faked. In short, the Limantour claim was a fraud. (Needless to say Limantour did not seek redress in the Supreme Court. He left the country.)

Richardson had gone before the Board not only on Garcia's behalf, but also on Limantour's. And, worse for Richardson, Limantour had returned the favor by testifying for him. By the time Richardson's case came up for appeal, he was directly downwind of Limantour's pettifoggery, causing the fussy District Court to go over the Richardson documents with maniacal meticulousness. The ink, the handwriting, both looked suspiciously like those on the counterfeit Limantour documents. And the signatures — good lord — the signatures had been verified by Limantour! Limantour the perjurer had stood up before the commissioners and had sworn to the authenticity of the signatures on these very documents Richardson was now asking the Court to accept. Nor could the court find any proof, whatsoever, that the Mexican government owed Richardson back pay. In fact, some people now came forward to accuse Richardson of dereliction of duty and relate how he had been unceremoniously discharged from his position as Captain of the Port of San Francisco. Richardson's claim went down in flames. His heirs pursued it to the Supreme Court twice, but the case was dismissed both times.

Now, for the first time the links between the Richardson and Garcia claims loomed up. The two *diseños* were obviously the work of one person. Why had no one noticed this before? Upon studying the matter further, officials of the court concluded that both sets of documents had been executed by the same hand and on the same paper as the bogus-seal Limantour document. Moreover, Garcia's seal looked for all the world like the fake seal on some of Richardson's papers.

The general flap and dither prior to the U.S. takeover had made it easy to monkey with Mexico's governmental archives. Did both Richardson and Garcia try something of the sort? Or was Richardson the scoundrel with artless Garcia simply standing too close when the dirt began to fly? And if either man, or both, diddled with the paperwork, was it a bald-faced attempt to filch resources? Or was it a last-ditch effort to hold onto what was rightfully theirs, something to be tried when they realized the normal legal channels were clogged?

I would dearly love to know if these two men were trying to pull a fast one, or if they were highjacked by a highhanded U.S. system. I yearn to see, precisely, how it all happened, but the past I peer into is obscured by patches of absent information.

Rafael Garcia tied up the land until after 1860. But that didn't slow the settlers. They came and carved out places for themselves before the land grant contest was resolved. Even after 1860 the land still was not legally available for settlement because it had not yet been surveyed. Government land distribution never kept up with the actuality of the land grab, and surveys notoriously lagged behind settlement. The U.S. General Land Office in charge of surveying, selling, and registering all public lands, got further and further behind. Citizens moaned and groaned. They complained to their Congressmen with expressions of discontent which sound thoroughly modern. The complainers had no patience for the ponderous process of dividing and platting. They had no tolerance for what they perceived to be the bureaucratic incompetence of the gal-durned Land Office. People in a lather to get on with their lives saw land lying there for the taking. Why should government paperwork stand in the way?

The making of our nation was a radical and noble experiment. The founding fathers planned a government untainted by individual self-interest. Their formula for how this was to be done was enlightened education allied with ownership of property, principally land, since land was the most long-lasting sort of property one could own. The model citizen was the self-sufficient, yeoman farmer, tilling and sowing the acres that simultaneously supported and anchored him. From Independence on, the U.S. government promoted settlement of its vast tracts of land, practically giving it away.

But the actuality of the land bore little resemblance to the simple Jeffersonian ideal. Between 1789 and 1834, Congress passed three hundred seventy-five different land laws in an attempt to get parcel size, cost per acre, method of payment, preemption rights all lined up in a manner that would make simple the business of getting people onto the land. It never became simple.

From 1820 on, the government sold land for $1.25 an acre at public auctions. But by the time a particular piece of land came up for sale, more often than not, it was already occupied and farmed by some impetuous settler. This settler, naturally, thought it confoundedly unfair that the land he or she had improved was now put on the block. Settling on government land without permission, squatting, was as old as the country itself, commencing as soon as emigrants headed west at the close of the Revolutionary War. Squatters began to insist on their rights. A whole series of temporary "I got here first, so it's mine" land laws was capped with the Preemption Act of 1841, the so-called Log Cabin Act. To settle land prior to buying it was no longer illegal, and squatters got the chance to purchase the land they occupied before it was offered for sale at auction. The actual settler was made safe from forcible eviction and loss of the value of improvements.

The Act of 1841 began to be applied to the lands of California and the other western states in 1853. Congress capitulated to the pressure of western frontier settlers, who, though they bitched and moaned about the inefficiency of the Land Office and the ineptness of government in general, had racked up a mighty sweet deal: as much as one hundred sixty acres of any unappropriated public land for a minimum price (usually at $1.25 an acre), no competing bids. The head of a family or widow or single person over twenty-one had merely to file a declaration of intention at the local land office within thirty days of taking possession of a parcel. After improving the place and building a house, and within a given period of time (usually twelve months), the new owner paid the purchase price. Then a certificate of preemption was issued, and later a U.S. patent.

But the sweet deal was not enough. Pretty soon minimum price with no competitive bids seemed too expensive. Squatters were crying out for free land. "Uncle Sam is rich enough to give us all a farm" was a hot political slogan before the Civil War. The first time Congress tried to give the people what they wanted, President Buchanan vetoed the bill, but when the brand new Republican Party came to power, homestead legislation was a lead-pipe cinch. The Homestead Act of 1862 gave one hundred sixty acres free, except for a nominal filing fee, to any qualified settler willing to live on and cultivate the land for five years (in 1912 the five years was reduced to three) then a certificate of patent was issued. The land reverted back to the government only if the settler didn't prove residence within six months of the filing date, or abandoned it for more than six months at any time.

The political dispute about the free land was peppery. From one standpoint, free land was a fair and just inducement for those willing to risk the wild unknown, possibly enduring great hardship and danger, in order to transform raw land into productive farms and ranches. From another point of view, giving away land was a tomfool impractical experiment destined to fritter away the public domain, which belonged to everyone, not just the would-be pioneers. The wrangling was further complicated by the claim that free land on the frontier would be a safety valve for the labor problems in the Eastern urban centers. In the Senate one supporter of the Homestead Act claimed the act would postpone for centuries, perhaps forever, "all serious conflict between capital and labor in the older free States, withdrawing their surplus population to create in greater abundance the means of subsistence."[3] It didn't work that way. In fact during the thirty years that followed the passage of the Homestead Act this country was rife with the most rancorous labor trouble it had ever experienced.

The Homestead Act did work to move vast amounts of land from the public domain to the private, complete with concomitant fraud by land-grabbing speculators. And yet many honest people who could not otherwise have afforded to buy a farm got the advantage of this radical legislation. Whatever history ultimately decides about the efficacy and rectitude of dealing the public domain out like so many poker hands, free land did mean opportunity for many deserving people. A fair number of people in my neighborhood still talk about the reality of homesteading.

Shortly before his death Al Gianoli said, "They came here from Italy. My uncles came here first in 1882 and my dad came here in 1890. They each got one hundred sixty acres apiece, that's what they were allowed. You had to settle and build a cabin and clear off the land. They had to plant a few trees. And if they were working someplace else on a better job they had to put a fire in the cabin once a week. That was the government. The government had already surveyed it off and you could go and pick out the land wherever it was. And most of them lived on the coast, worked in the mills and were glad to get a job. A dollar a day and they worked hard."[4]

And George Zeni explained, "When my father came here in 1892, at that time you could homestead property, 160 acres. It took five years to prove up on 160 acres. Prove up means that you have to build a cabin, build some fences, you got to show you're going to take care of it...what they call prove up on it, on your property. And you had to live there and this and that, which he did."[5]

The Homestead Act was subjected to several statutory tune-ups. Eventually it became possible to buy land outright for $1.25 an acre rather than waiting the five (or three or, later on, one) years to get it gratis. Various land laws followed to supplement the Homestead Act. Both the Timber Culture Act and the Timber and Stone Act — belated recognition of the fact that land on this part of the continent was timbered, steep, and generally ill-suited for farming — were designed to make the West Coast independent logger a counterpart of Jefferson's self-sufficient yeoman farmer. But the laws were easily manipulated by logging companies, and the Redwood Coast Point Arena abides now with the legacy of nineteenth-century land legislation. It isn't history book talk around here. It goes on; it is the stuff of our lives.

REFERENCE NOTES

1. United States District Court, Northern District of California, "Rafael Garcia v. the U.S." Land Case 96ND, Bancroft Library, Berkeley.

2. Spanish Archives volume T8, Bancroft Library, Berkeley.

3. Zinn, *The People's History of the United States.*

4. Alfred Gianoli, as told to Lucie Marshall, *Yesterday's News* (interview - ag01.spl).

5. George Zeni, as told to Lucie Marshall, *Yesterday's News* (interview - gza01.spl).

Chapter Six

WHERE HAVE ALL THE FARMERS GONE?

The land I now own was owned in the nineteenth century by the Thurman family. John Thurman, from Norway, was farming it as early as 1870, so I presumed he filed the original patent on it. But I came to discover Captain Niels Iversen, owner of Iversen Landing, originally claimed this property, selling it to Thurman when Thurman married the captain's niece. From the Thurmans it went briefly to Courtney Kendall, a cousin of Joe Halliday. Next it fell to Dutch Schrock who ran a dairy here, the Lake Street Dairy it was called inasmuch as back then access to the property was from Lake Street in Point Arena. Stepped-up regulation of Grade A dairies forced Dutch out of business, and he eventually sold most of the land to his niece, keeping for himself and wife the small Lake Street chunk with the farmhouse on it. Dutch's niece divided the property, and sold large parcels to the high school, to Peter and Anna Dobbins, and, finally, when she decided to leave town in a hurry, the piece she had meant to keep for herself, to me.

Since childhood, I've wanted to live on a farm, be a farmer, entirely self-sufficient, living off the land. When we moved to the eighty acres on Windy Hollow, I was well acquainted with vegetable growing and had a vegetable garden going before our belongings were unpacked. By the time our first summer was over, we had a small apple orchard planted, and a hen house stocked with a dozen Rhode Island Reds, an orphaned Muscovy/Mallard duckling, and a large beautiful Chinese goose named Genghis Khan.

My luck with waterfowl was not good, but the hens were a real success. All twelve looked exactly alike so I named each of them Dave after the Dr. Seuss book about a mother who named all her sons Dave then wished she hadn't. I thought my name a great joke, but no one was amused except Peter Dobbins who to this day refers to all Rhode Island Reds as Daves.

Our first four-leggers were Nubian goats to take care of our dairy needs. Then I bought three Romney sheep. Although I intended to be a dirt farmer, I wanted wool for hand spinning and weaving. Alan, though, saw the meat beneath the wool and began to increase my modest flock.

Until we got started, I hadn't realized how different Alan's goals were from mine. Where I saw orchards, he saw grazing cattle. Where I saw row crops, he saw waving fields of red oats. He knew as little as I about the particulars of farming, but, fitted out with his customary persistence and chutzpah, he undertook a crash course. He read books. He listened to Joe Halliday and the other experienced farmers. Whenever he saw anyone working in a field, he boldly strode over to ask questions. One afternoon when we had nearly finished building our house, he stopped his truck in the middle of Windy Hollow. For several days he had been watching a young man disking a piece of land across the road from us, and now he was going to interview him. The man was Nick Scanlon-Hill. The interview stretched into a series of palavers until pretty soon the two were partners.

Nick had begun his farm career with the Peace Corps. After his stint in Africa, he got married. In time he brought his wife and family to Point Arena where he found a job at Walt Stornetta's dairy ranch, but he got tired of working for someone else and decided to set out on his own. He knew what he was doing, but he owned no land. Alan had land, but no experience. It was a perfect match.

Nick's experience was primarily with cows, so at this point Alan's focus naturally turned bovine. Together they started by raising Stornetta drop calves — the unwanted male offspring of the dairy stock.

Alan loved to feed the little guys — some of which thought he was their mother. He suckled them on baby bottles of milk replacer, but, deprived of genuine mother's milk, drop calves tend to fall ill and die. More often than not, the powdered-milk substitute starts the infant animals scouring so badly they quickly become severely dehydrated. At the first sign of scouring, Alan began to feed them Vitrate, an electrolyte solution, mixed with sugar or molasses, a blend which helped douse their innards and give them energy enough to suck, and thus he was often able to save a beast otherwise headed for certain death.

Nick and Alan were both great vets. They nursed and nurtured with impressive zeal, rearing to maturity a remarkably high percentage of their animals.

They castrated the calves when they were quite young. On one occasion, however, they had missed a testicle, an oversight which went undetected until the animal was almost fully grown. I was furious with them, not because of the goof, but because of the remedy and their attitude toward it. They didn't seem to consider such an untimely surgery disagreeable in the least. Equipped with an old rusty utility knife, a threaded rug needle, and a quart of Betadine solution, they, in a state of semi-glee, advanced on a semi-grown, semi-bull. They showed not a soupçon of distaste. ("Not true," Alan protests. "Not true. That utility knife was not rusty. A little old, but not rusty.")

After the second surgery, Alan started supplementing the recovering animal's diet by bottle, just like when he was a wee calf. Miraculously the wretched beast pulled through. Now Alan was confronted with the dicey problem of weaning an assertive seven hundred pound steer!

Drop calves were too much work, so eventually we bought some breeding stock from Joe Halliday. Eighty acres wasn't enough for both grazing big animals and raising hay, so Alan and Nick began to lease land in exchange for work or for a portion of the crop. Pretty soon they were working between six and seven hundred acres, patches of it all over the place. Our herd increased until we were running eighty or so cows, heifers, and steers on a four hundred acre tract down by the river. Up at our place on Windy Hollow, where we had developed our own fields for permanent pasture, we kept a couple of dozen ewes. Then we were growing hay on several other people's land.

Plowing east, I see rows of forested hills, one behind another, behind another. Sometimes the sky is low above them. Sometimes the sky is high and blue, and from between the hills, tufts of white vapor rise up. I make the turn tight as I can, head west. Toward the western fence line I get a glimpse of the ocean. Turn again. Back and forth over the whole field, east and west. Then the whole field, north and south. Then again. Each field gets disked at least four times. Driving the tractor, I form a relationship with a plot of earth. During my first covering of the ground, the work requires undivided attention. The second pass allows for a little relaxing. By the third or fourth I am free to sing or recite poetry. Over the roar of the tractor engine, I declaim with great gusto. Romantic poets, Renaissance poets, Augustan poets, metaphysical poets, Victorian poets, modern poets. *The dead brood over Europe, the cloud and vision descends over cheerful France/ O cloud well appointed! Sick, sick, the Prince on his couch…* Immensely satisfying. I realize at last what a degree in English literature is for.

Every field has a different personality. I have favorites, but the only ones I genuinely dislike are the steep ones. They scare the piss out of me. When a seven thousand pound roofless tractor begins to heel over at an angle greater than about 15°, I start wanting to jump ship. Alan and Nick advise: "If you start to go over, just lower the disk. Boom. Everything's fine."

"Yeah, guys. Right. But what about the time I sat paralyzed with the disk cantilevered over a fifty foot cliff?"

This image makes them titter unchivalrously behind their hands.

Anxiety. The spring hay harvest is especially fraught with it: Will the equipment hold up through the mowing, the baling? Will it rain too little, or at the wrong time?

The harvesting is worrisome, but the planting is pure pleasure. Harvesting requires judgment but planting needs only the body, no mental calisthenics. We plant in the fall. After the first good rain, we disk-plow whatever field we plan to sow. The disk is a simple implement, innocent of bewildering, intricate mechanisms — an occasional whack with the hand sledge is about all that's ever wanted by way of repair. I love tractoring. In full or weak sunshine, in gray, bleak cold, in heat or wind, whatever the conditions, I love bouncing across those fields, turning up the rich-smelling dirt — the more acres the better. Sometimes I'll ride that noisy, jarring machine until I can scarcely walk afterwards.

Farm work is satisfying. "You mean for you," my sister corrects me. "You wouldn't recommend it for everybody." "No," I say, "No. We're all different." Dyed in the wool relativist that I am, I know that's the answer I'm supposed to give. But in my heart of hearts, I believe farm work to be the remedy for every ill, personal or social. Put aside what you're doing and head for the fields if you want to find yourself delivered from pettiness, from free-floating anxiety, from lack of self-esteem, from spiritual emptiness.

Though a family farm is certain to deliver you from several species of discontent, it is bound, as well, to deliver you from prosperity. Hard, if not impossible, to simply make ends meet. Alan and Nick put a minimum of thirty hours apiece per week into the cattle and the hay. Then there was upkeep on machinery and fencing, miles of fencing to be repaired over and over again. Along with all that, Alan and I had sheep work, and Nick and Laurie had a truck garden and a small dairy. In effect, Alan and Nick worked full time at what amounted to a part time job — part time in terms of take-home pay.

"Pasture Prime." That was the name Nick's retired father, a silent partner, gave to the business. Pasture Prime was ostensibly occupied with selling beef, but, truth to tell, what actually kept it afloat financially was the machinery.

The machinery's virtue wasn't in its labor-saving characteristics, but in its moneysaving characteristics. For one thing, we had approximately $80,000 invested in equipment, which allowed each family to take an income tax deduction on the depreciation of half the amount.

Tax saving was financial boon number one. But the more interesting godsend was Alan's and Nick's great genius for keeping old machinery running. Except for Alan's and my 47 horsepower Kubota tractor, nothing was new: Pasture Prime's third-hand 62 horsepower Ford tractor, disk, hay rake, sickle-bar mower, and ancient baler all were acquired, piece by piece, at bargain rates. During each haying season something — usually several somethings — broke down. Alan and Nick, squatting on their heels and scratching their heads, would study the problem, deliberate, speculate, diagnose. Then they would wire, weld, tie up, screw down, grease until, by guess or by gosh, the machine began to hum. Saving money with the purchase of less than mint-new equipment means big repair bills for many a farmer, but Alan and Nick, regular Galens of the motor pool, patched things by themselves — or with a smattering of help from Kentucky John the blacksmith.

All duded up like the foreigner he was, J.C. Halliday arrived from Nova Scotia in 1871. When he got to Point Arena, he opened his briefcase and began to do business. He ran a horse drawn stage line from Cazadero to Mendocino "...the finest carriage that is now or ever was in Point Arena." *P.A. Record*, July 14, 1893. And, in partnership with N.P. Howell, he set up a blacksmith shop with three forges.

The blacksmith shop shod horses, repaired equipment, made wagons and buggies. The partners also made sledges for the logging industry, and, before long, they began to make wedges to replace the ax heads that loggers were using to help them fell trees. (Native Americans had used elkhorn wedges.) Howell was exceptionally skillful at tempering steel, and pretty soon their excellent quality made Halliday and Howell sledges and wedges *de rigueur* in the coastal logging camps.

When logging slacked off, Halliday and Howell added a general merchandise store to the blacksmithing business. In time J.C. gave charge of the store to the one of his sons who would later become Joe's father. After Joe was born the family always expected him to take his father's place. But Joe was not at all attracted to the mercantile life. Over the years he had worked at an array of different jobs, but his love was for animals. He and his wife Dorothy have been doing, all their lives, what Nick and his wife Laurie, and Alan and I came here to do.

Hallidays know worlds more about ranching than we do, and they have been at it for three-quarters of a century. Even so their financial success has been no better than ours.

An ag expert from the University of California at Davis once studied the Halliday Ranch for his research project. He delivered his finished report in Russia at a World Wide Grass Symposium. The Halliday's Harris Ranch, he told the crowd of experts, was to be taken as a model of how to do things right. The quality of the stock and the ranch's general productivity were as good as they could possibly be.

"But we never made any money," laughs Dorothy. "We're real famous, but we never could make any money."

Why? Why didn't they ever make any money? Dorothy thinks it was simply bad luck. "For instance, when Joe's dad had the ranch, he got some of the best registered bulls he could get and raised the quality of milk cows to such an extent that they were some of the best cows in the county. Then the bottom went out of the cheese market so all of this went for nothing — there wasn't any money in it.So then Joe went into sheep and built up the sheep until he had the best flock in the whole shearing area. This was a great success but the dogs got into them, and we didn't make any money. We spent all this time and money and effort growing clover and grass and it looked real good. And we increased the capacity of the ranch and specially raised these calves that were half Holstein and half white-face. They were real good cows and gave us two calves apiece. The price went up on calf feed. And that market wasn't very good and we didn't make any money."[1]

Plain bad luck she says, and the same goes for Harris who owned the place before them. Trying to make a go in the horse business, he brought two extravagantly expensive studs all the way from France, only to discover that one was impotent.

"Like the rest of us, Harris had a dream that didn't come true."[2]

Maybe for Harris bad luck was the sole problem, but for the Hallidays — and even more so for the Scanlon-Hills and for Webb/Levine — inability to turn a profit with a small-scale stock farm was not merely a function of bad luck.

During the years bracketing the turn of the century, timber, potatoes and peas supported Point Arena. By the 1940s, though field crops were still grown, it was primarily the dairies which sustained the local economy. Practically every family had a small dairy; between Point Arena and Bridgeport there were at least twenty. By the time we moved here, only two dairies remained, the Biaggi brothers' and Walt Stornetta's, both big commercial enterprises. Today only Stornetta is still in the business.

An economically feasible dairy farm now requires a scale of operation far grander than most family farms can handle. Nick and Laurie tried to carry on a small family dairy, but found it impossible with all the regulations and inspection fees. Since two cows did not constitute a bona fide dairy, they found selling milk feasible only so long as they kept no more than two cows.

The low price of milk has done more than anything else to wipe out the small family dairy, just as low prices have wiped out the small family farm. Food is simply too cheap for small farmers to turn a profit. "Get big or get out," ultimatum of the U.S. Department of Agriculture. While population and number of acres under cultivation have gone up, the number of small farms in the U.S. has gone down, down, down.

A single farmer can now feed himself and fifty-six other people. The Department of Agriculture seems to consider that reckoning to be good news, something to crow about. But is it? Land is concentrated into larger and larger holdings. Land is abandoned if it can't be worked with monster-scale equipment. Good soil management is traded for monocrops, which are notorious fertilizer gluttons. Pesticides, herbicides go down in saturation bombings. Vast dung-mired feed lots run over with animals pickled in antibiotics, bulked up with growth hormones. A single farmer can now feed himself and fifty-six other people, but the land has not benefited, the farmers have not benefited. But then, it wasn't the farmers who engineered modern agribusiness. It was the specialists with the clean fingernails. They transfigured ploughers and sowers into industrialists and merchants.

"True agripower...generates agridollars through agricultural exports."[3] Governments, corporations, universities, bureaucrats and experts can congratulate themselves on their triumph only when they neglect to factor in all the expenses, only when they measure success in terms of marketable products without accounting the cost to air, water, soil, or the farming community.

Those farm families which cannot get bigger, eventually get out, and nobody, besides the displaced persons themselves, seems to consider it a problem, much less a tragedy. Yet hundreds of thousands of people every year leave farm country and head for the cities and suburbs, "a forced migration of people greater than any in history...," Wendell Berry calls it. Those who stay on the farm suffer from the schism between farming interests and business interests. When they risk too much money, they tend to become less heedful of husbandry. The best of them decide farming is properly the work of farmers not entrepreneurs. And these are the ones who go bust.

Many Point Arena farmers and ranchers have to work "day jobs" to support their animals. In Dorothy Halliday's memoir, *Coasting On Down*, she has entitled her section on ranching, "Ranching By Moonlight."

Nick, like Joe, plurally employed, wasn't bringing in enough farm money to support his family. Already a volunteer fireman and emergency medical technician, he studied to become a paramedic, and now he drives the local ambulance and teaches CPR. He no longer has time for farming, so our partnership had to be dissolved. Nick and Alan sold the old blue tractor, and Alan and I bought Nick's share of the rest of the equipment. We kept all the sheep and five of the brood cows. All the livestock graze on our eighty Windy Hollow acres, and we plant hay in three little fields south of us on the Dobbins place.

Periodically, Joe Halliday, too, decides to give up farming. The last time he resolved to give up his animals, he rounded up his cows, but: "He found he couldn't part with some of them," Dorothy told us, "They were his friends." In the end he put only half of the herd into the truck headed for auction, and it wasn't long before he'd bred the five back up to thirty-five. "Some retired men play golf, play the horses, play the stock market, or sit around and drink martinis.... This one raises cows and talks nice to the dog." But Joe knows he ought to cut back. He's not making any money, and he's not getting any younger. He'll try again to give it up and keep on trying until it finally takes.

Those who love farming don't give up without a struggle. Before the Scanlon-Hills quit, Laurie attended a conference on how to make a small farm commercially successful. She came home thoroughly disgusted.

"Ornamentals," she scoffed. "That's the best advice they could give me. I want to feed the multitudes, and the county farm advisor tells me to grow ornamentals!"

But what else? There is not much market for minor produce. A few restaurants serve locally grown vegetables and fruit, and Point Arena has a weekly farmer's market, vending surplus produce from family gardens. Only one fellow comes with the harvest of a really large truck garden. The problems and cost of transportation being what they are, small farmers' only hope of survival is in generating markets close by — local restaurants, grocery stores and al fresco markets like Point Arena's. Small scale farmers are going to have to convince consumers to buy locally, but to succeed, they will need to find ways to keep costs down. American consumers, for all their yammering about wanting carefully grown food, aren't yet willing to pay for it.

When the future of small scale agriculture seems doomed, I remind myself of George Zeni, up on Signal Ridge.

"You have to go with the times, you have to be diversified. Don't put all your eggs in one basket," George says.[4] His green thumb and persistent willingness to take risks have augmented the legacy of his father's vineyard.

"An old vineyard makes better wine than a young vineyard," he says with a wink. His father planted the first Zeni grapes a century ago. Signal Ridge has the same type of climate and the same sort of soil found in the region where the best Zinfandel grapes originated in Italy. Today George supplies grapes to a big wine maker who turns them into award-winning wine.

George grows chestnuts, too. "In this country right here, on this particular ranch, you could make ten times the money on a chestnut tree as you can on grapes. Because the grapes are old vines, and, you know, your tonnage is not there, your production is not there. But you take the chestnuts...you take one tree and you'll have 500 pounds on it. At $2 a pound, you know, just on one tree you can make quite a bit of money. I have sold as high as 14,000 pounds of chestnuts. People come from San Jose and the Bay Area and all over for chestnuts. That's getting to be a big thing now, chestnuts."

And the Christmas tree business. "It's been about thirty years ago. I was falling timber in the woods at that time. This fellow, Bob Lawson said, 'Let's start growing Christmas trees,' and I said, 'You must be out of your mind. Who's going to buy a Christmas tree? They can go out in the woods and cut them.' He says, 'They grow them up in Oregon - we ought to start growing Christmas trees.' I said, 'Okay, let's start planting them.' So we went down to the forestry and we bought seedlings and we planted three or four thousand trees over on Bob's property. So then I said, 'If you're going to do it, I'm going to do it, too.' So I planted three or four thousand trees up on the ranch. Well, then when you plant trees like that — we didn't know what we were going to do with them. How do you shear them, how do you culture them? How do you make them look like a Christmas tree...nice and symmetrical? We didn't know none of that, and nobody else could tell us because nobody else was raising Christmas trees. So, what we'd do is we'd go out and, kind of a wild looking tree, we'd take a picture of it. And then we would get hand shears and we'd get clippers and we'd just try to shape it. And throughout the next year we'd see what it looked like. How the top reacted, if it responded to the pruning. And we would compare it to the picture that we took of it before. Trial and error. In about seven or eight years we got the tree like we have now. And it's been a pretty good business. That's how we started, through trial and error because nobody knew anything about it. And right today Bob Lawson is the biggest Douglas fir Christmas tree grower in the state of California and I'm the second biggest."

George Zeni, even at this late stage in his life, is always open to new ventures, not all of which are equally successful. At one point he planted kiwi fruit. There was a market for it and it was easy to grow, perhaps too easy to grow, because, before long, everybody was growing kiwi and the price got sliced down to nothing. But George never waivers in his insistence that the key to agricultural success in this county is diversity. "The county is changing drastically and a farmer will never make it with just one crop."

Mendocino's major crops are grapes, timber and pears. They are quite profitable, too. The county's 1995 revenue from the three crops together, though down 10% from '94, was $236,000,000. But corporate investors, not the men and women doing the work, are the ones enjoying sizable returns from timber, grapes or pears, and these corporate investors are not generally Mendocino residents. Grass roots Mendocino squares its accounts with an illegal crop, *sinsemilla*, a potent marijuana, which fetches a fine price, yet can't be officially listed as a source of county revenue. "Marijuana farming is the perfect embodiment of a people's capitalism."[5]

Plenty of people around here grow marijuana. Twenty to thirty percent of them were born and raised in Mendocino County, local farmers who turned to the outlaw crop as the only way to save a failing farm. But the majority of growers came after 1970. When they arrived, most of them were young, mid-twenties to mid-forties. Most, but not all; approximately one in ten was a senior citizen.

It's an odd situation: you know and you don't know. Marijuana is a secret, but not a secret secret; concealed, but notorious; anonymous but conspicuous; criminal but commonplace; unseen but in the limelight. Dope growers fear getting caught, but they don't consider their occupation disgraceful. Indeed, some wear it as a badge of merit. It becomes an identity as well as a livelihood. Some growers are "raiders" who get in and get out quick as they can, but most are an integral part of the community, and the source of much of the money that drives our local economy.

And whether we approve of marijuana or not, we, all of us in Point Arena, live amidst the cogs of this illegal industry. Twenty percent of the county's population realizes a significant portion of its income directly from home-grown dope. In some areas of the county the percentage is as high as eighty. Of course, not all of those profiting from *sinsemilla* are actually cultivating it. Some sell materials for water systems, fences, implements for harvesting, trimming, drying the plants, equipment for backpacking (nobody grows on his own east meadow). Some are realizing a meaty profit by loaning money at a high rate of interest — 25% up to 80% or 100% if the crop is the only collateral. Some people get paid for providing land. If the grower gets caught, the landowner knows absolutely nothing about it.

Marijuana growers, like all tillers of the soil, work hard. When they don't lose a crop to either bandits or the law, they chalk up a substantial return, but by no means do they rake in a fortune. A good deal of their cash goes for the same day-to-day living expenses the rest of us have, thus marijuana money, constantly flowing through the system, finds its way into 40% of the county's billfolds and pocketbooks.

Living in Point Arena, I, in no way connected to the industry myself, never know for absolutely certain who grows and who doesn't. Over the years I've stopped even being curious.

REFERENCE NOTES

1. *Yesterday's News.* Joe Halliday's Story #3.
2. I have so many stories from Dorothy Halliday that I have lost track of where each came from. Her memoir, *Over the Dam*, taped interviews for *Yesterday's News* and for the school's Gifted and Talented classes, newspaper pieces she has written, and personal conversations — all sources, many repeating the same information, are mixed together in my notes.

3. Richard Bell, Assistant Secretary of Agriculture, speech to Fertilizer Institute Annual Meeting.

4. George Zeni, Interview with *Yesterday's News.*

5. Ray Rapheal, *Cash Crop,* p.171.

Chapter Seven

PREDATORS AND PAGANS

Lambing Season

When I woke up my hair was frozen. Lying on a mattress in the open back of the truck, I had zipped myself into a down sleeping bag and covered up with a quilt, so I slept warm, but a predawn cold snap crisped my hair.

Alan and I slept outdoors for a week, but they never came back. The dogs. Or dog. Our first night in the field was the worst. Disturbed, apprehensive, we were alert to every sound. The images were fresh on our mind: four ewes lying in their own blood, hindquarters ripped apart, seven dead and dying lambs.

Alan loaded his .22. What else could he do? The ewes' staring eyes were pitiful. After he put them out of their misery, I helped heave the carcasses onto the back of his truck. With my fingers deep in her silver wool, I recognized the bearer of our most magnificent fleece.

Alan doctored the surviving lamb, then, still greatly agitated, said, "I'm going into town." The .22 lay in the front seat.

"Do you expect to find the dog? How would you know him? Do you imagine he's still covered with gore? Or will he just look reprehensible?"

He drove around, looking, interviewing. Wandering dogs? Unattended dogs? He hunted up owners of big ill-mannered dogs. Had any of their animals been out last night? Everybody was sympathetic, but nobody knew a thing.

That first night in the field I felt too unsettled and anxious to sleep well. Moreover, I needed to go into the house every four hours to tend the lamb who had developed pneumonia. Alan was dosing her with antibiotics, and I was forcing milk-laced Vitrate down her throat. We bedded her in the living room beside a wood-burning stove where we kept a good hot fire going. Every time I opened the front door, I could hear her wheezing and gasping. She sounded like a locomotive. I would fix a baby bottle, hold her limp woolly little self on my lap, press the hinges of her jaw with my thumb and forefinger to force her mouth open, then, taking care not to drown her, I would squeeze in as many drops as she would swallow. Afterwards I would lay her in her nest of towels, throw another log into the stove, and go back to my bed under the tent of clear, cold, black sky.

After an eon of nighttime, the sky began to glow. Into the house. Utter silence. The gasping had stopped. "Well, that's that," I sighed. I had known the lamb wasn't going to make it, but her death made me downhearted anyway. When Alan came in, I gave him the bad news.

"I'll bury her before breakfast," he said, stooping to pick up the motionless body. Then, "Dammit all to hell, Nancy Kay! This animal isn't dead!" He was thoroughly disgusted with me, and spent the morning muttering to himself, "The animal stops breathing like an Allis Chalmers WC, so it's dead. Right? No other explanation. Can't possibly have gotten quiet because it's gotten well." Oh, me of little faith.

A couple of days later we noticed a ewe, mother of twins, suckling three lambs, two white and one black. It's rare for sheep to voluntarily adopt a lamb, but, as it turned out, this ewe had accepted the lamb because she was too weak to reject it. Examining her, we couldn't believe she was still on her feet. The Hell Hound had mangled her viciously. Starting with the opening of her vagina, he had worked his way in. The external parts of her genitalia were gone, as was much of the surrounding flesh. We put her into a small pen in the goat yard so we could doctor her and give her special feed. Every day we wrestled her to the ground, and Alan flushed out her wounded parts with two quarts of Betadine solution.

We left the male twin with her, but put the two females, along with the lamb from the house, in my vegetable garden where I patched together a small shelter for them. Now I had not one but three bummer lambs to feed. Six times a day I mixed powdered milk replacer with water and heated it in a big pot on the stove. Over the years I had done this repeatedly, but never with more than one animal at a time. At first the primary challenge was juggling three bottles, and making certain the lambs all finished more or less simultaneously, because if one got through too soon, especially if it was the big aggressive ex-adoptee, she would shoulder her way into another's share. I had to manipulate things so that the fastest sucker got the stiffest nipple with the smallest hole.

Later on, when they had grown and, though eating more, ate less frequently, I fed them through the fence, using the wire and my thighs to support the bottles. The challenge then was to keep the lambs from butting the bottles out of my grasp. The bigger they got, the harder they butted. Until the lambs were weaned, my thighs stayed black and blue. They also had a charming trick of grabbing the rubber nipples in their strong little teeth and tugging hard enough to pull the nipple off dousing them with a sudden face full of milk.

Getting Started

The first thing I wanted to get after we moved here was a milk goat. We had bought ourselves a farm, and now, by gosh, it was time to start raising some food. My girls, eleven and thirteen, did not want a goat. They were afraid I would make them drink goat's milk, which, of course, was exactly my intention. They said they would allow me to have a goat only if I would let them have kittens — a lady in front of Gilmore's Store had a box of them. Two more neurotic animals never existed than the two kittens the girls brought home. One of them is still with me sixteen years later, three-legged and half blind.

A month after she unloaded the cats on us, the woman from in front of Gilmore's Store telephoned to say she had a brand new baby Nubian goat, born of registered Nubian parents. Did I want it? It was not for sale — not for money. She wanted to make a trade of some sort. So for the price of one of my grandmother's small diamonds and a day's worth of my inept carpentry skills, I got two goats.

To produce milk, your animal first has to bring forth young from its womb. My initiation into goat midwifery was tense, however. With no help at all from me, the goat I bred managed to deliver healthy twins. I allowed them to suckle all day, but at night I separated them from their mother so I could milk her in the morning. The goat milk was very rich and good. We drank it, we cooked with it, and I learned to make cheese. I liked making cheese, and, after a time, I came to like milking the goat. Not at first, though. Getting up in the wee small hours of the morning was no problem, but tussling with a defiant goat was a real downer. Morning after morning she fought getting up on the milking stand. By trickery or blandishment I could eventually entice her into place, then quickly lever the stanchion closed. At this point she was supposed to casually munch her grain while I casually applied myself to her udder, but the minute I lay hands upon her teat, she began to kick, invariably hitting the bucket. My reaction time got fast, and pretty soon I brought her batting average down to about 250; but, damn it all to hell, I was the one who had gotten trained, not her. My heart set on being the one in charge, yet no amount of wheedling persuaded her to stand still, so I was obliged to fall back on cunning. I cut a broken leather bridle into two foot-long pieces, made a short lengthwise slice in one end of each one, and ran the other end through it to make a strong leather noose. Then I hammered fencing staples into the milking stand, sinking them in only part way, one on each side right below where the goat's back feet stood. Finally, I got me a handful 20-penny nails — I needed only two but a few extras wouldn't hurt — and after I noosed the goat's back hoof, I pulled the leather through the eye of the staple and inserted a nail through the slice. When the goat tried to lift her leg more than a couple of inches, the nail behaved like a toggle bolt, restraining the kick. One of these artful little snares on each side, and I was in the milking business.

After just a few weeks, she stopped balking at the stand, but never, never did she give up kicking. During all the years I milked her, I had to tether her back legs. None of her daughters was defiant. None of her daughters made as much milk as she did either, so she was the one I bred most often. Sometimes there was so much milk in our refrigerator nothing else would fit. Then it was time to make cheese, all kinds of cheese. When my children grew up and left home, I continued to milk, and Alan fed the surplus to drop calves he was raising.

Damage Control

After the dogs made a mess of our flock, the trapper set a couple of traps, but caught only a possum. We belled the ram and three of the ewes so we would be able hear them if they started to run, and I began to sleep with the window wide open and one ear wide awake. We've had no further trouble. No yet, anyway.

Predators are so prevalent and vexatious they have driven more than one sheep rancher into another business. George Zeni says his three greatest problems as a farmer have been insurance, environmentalists, and predators. He solved the predator problem by getting rid of all his livestock.

Authority for predator control is shared between county, state, and federal government. The feds get the birds, the state gets the wild mammals, and the county gets the dogs. Coyotes, classified as "non-game" animals, and domestic dogs do most of the damage, and ranchers are free to blast away any non-game animal they deem a threat to their stock. We also see some predation by lions and, even a little (very little) by bears, though bears, even grizzlies, used to be quite common here. In 1907 W.W. Fairbanks claimed, "Grizzly bears were so numerous that every bit of brush or jungle seemed to contain one or more and they had a bad habit of shuffling along the trails and roads in the day time scaring small boys into fits as the writer remembers." They appear now only rarely. Vern Kendall killed a three hundred pound black bear near his place five years ago, but I've heard of nothing since then.

Mountain lions, old timers call them panthers, though seldom seen, are numerous. In 1990 California voters passed an initiative designed to protect mountain lions. If a lion kills a domestic animal, or threatens human safety, it is to be destroyed by the trapper, a professional hunter employed by the U.S. Department of Agriculture. The landowner reports the lion (or bear, the rule applies to bears, too) to CA Department of Fish and Game, which investigates, and applies for a depredation permit. Often the feds will let Fish and Game do the hunting, and, occasionally, a landowner is allowed to do the job, if, and only if, authorities are sure the guy isn't going after the big cat for fun — the point of the legislation is to stop sport hunting of mountain lions. The law deeply rankled a number of folks who consider hunting predators a normal and natural, even useful, human activity, more gratifying than going to heaven. George Zeni told me about clubs that competed each year for which could bag the most predators, either avian or mammal. Those who miss their sport say the predator populations are out of control now.

The trapper has an official bureaucratic title: Animal Damage Control Specialist. There used to be five in the County, but the number gradually diminished to three. Last year Mendocino County was so impoverished it couldn't afford its share of the salary for any of its trappers, who are paid by county with matching funds from the federal government. Several private organizations — Woolgrowers Association, Cattlemen's Association, and Farm Bureau — came up with $16,500 for two inland trappers. Without enough money to pay him, the coast trapper, who lives in Manchester, chose to continue on a volunteer basis rather than stay on the payroll by moving to another county. When time runs out on the year of private funds, everybody hopes the Board of Supervisors will be able get the trapper back in the budget.

Harvest Moon

Now it is lambing season again. Our pasture is alive with lambs jumping all over it like sand fleas. New lambs mean last year's crop go into the freezer. Alan and Nick slaughter, doing five or six at a time. They hang the meat in

Vick Soldani's locker. After four or five days of hanging, Vick butchers for us. Today is butchering day.

A heavy sliding door lets us into Vick's shop. The smell — not a dead animal smell, but a healthy, cold, fresh meat smell — greets us. Over our heads, all around the walls, hang deer antlers, faceless mounted horns, several wearing loops of used saw blades. The big room has a concrete floor and three windows, large but dusty. No view, yet plenty of light falls on the ten half-lambs. Pure ivory and coral, they lie side by side, slightly overlapping with their straight hoofless legs pointing at the band saw.

Vick Soldani is small and gentle with white hair and stooped shoulders, but despite his age Vick cuts so fast that, wrapping, I can't keep up with him. Loin chops, rib chops, shoulder chops. I wrap. White paper ripped from the roll, two sheets per package, an inner wrap then the outer wrap, tape. With a black marker I write: 5 lb. leg 3/96, 3 lb. half-leg 3/96, Rack of Lamb '96. Alan works with a set of very sharp knives, boning out the shanks, trimming the stew. Periodically a customer shows up to lend a hand or simply make choices. How many chops to each package? Shoulder roast or should Vick cut it up? Shanks, stew or ground?

"Worthy is the lamb that was slain to receive power, and riches, and wisdom, and strength, and honor, and glory, and blessing." *Revelations* 5:12. Strength is by way of garlic or sometimes rosemary. Riches are by way of sauce. And the glory takes place between the palate and the tongue. Every reunion with one of the honored and blessed of our flock confirms its delectability. One sybaritic reunion, a celebration of the harvest moon, fell on the autumnal equinox. The party was at Raven and Lucinda's place up on the Ridge, where autumn evenings are warm and crickety. Children swam in the pond while their parents, barefoot, and drinking wine, enjoyed the dregs of a summer season.

Guests had brought salads, vegetable dishes, breads, and sweets to fill the vast outdoor table. In a nearby stand of tall trees, a cast-iron bathtub held a colossal quantity of glowing coals. Cooking the meat took patience, a special barbecue patience paired with the gift for gab, the sweet banquet of the mind. Wit, laughter, flirtation mixed with the fine rich gamy smell of sizzling lamb.

After the food, came drums. Harmonicas, guitars, too, but chiefly drums. We danced under the round moon. We danced until the last drummer begged us to set him free. Next morning my feet were bruised and scraped, but that night they stamped and pounded the damp grass with painless joy.

Chapter Eight

COME TO STAY

"The westering myth is the nearest thing to a national myth we can ever create."[1]

Edward Abbey

I did not know him well. When we arrived he had already been banished, like the Levitical goat, to the periphery of the circle. Everybody in town turned out for his funeral, though. The church filled, respectable citizens intercalated among his trailer park cronies, who were recognizable by the any-age look that comes with protracted drug and alcohol use.

The musty-sweet atmosphere of the old United Methodist Church was tense with a heartache rung on paired themes of Waste and Woe — the dead man, young and highly intelligent, the widow, pale and calm, her towhead twin sons, bewildered. The rest of us were uneasy. What could the preacher say? What would be fitting?

"Friends. We are gathered here this afternoon to mourn the death…"

("*rrarmmm…armm…*") A sound behind me, only half noticed at first, like the buzz of an insect, or the passing, far overhead of a plane.

"We mourn the loss not only of a human life, but the loss of…"

But the unintelligible mutterings grew audible, then louder and louder, until they could no longer be ignored. "…*aaarmmmm!*" I turned to glare at the fellow. My glare, which usually worked on my kids, had no effect.

"*No. Harm,*" he said, putting greater effort into his enunciation. "*No. No haaarm.*"

Pale and bleary-eyed with a chin neither unshaven nor bearded, the man finally managed to bring the solemn young Methodist preacher to a full stop. The silent preacher waited until the mutterer went silent.

Then the preacher resumed, "We mourn the loss not only of a human life, but the loss of…"

"*No harm. No. He never meant no harm. Schweetest guy in the world. Never meant harm…*"

"…the loss of hope."

"*My buddy…ne'r hurt…*"

Seriously embarrassed by the duel of rival eulogies, the congregation sat dead still, trying to ignore each parry from the interloper, but the authorized preacher wasn't holding up well. He began stammering while the seated man, ever more strident, gave way to weeping.

"*He loved ev'rybody. Ne'r wanted to hurt any-goddamned-body in the goddamned world.*"

Mercifully, a large, freshly scrubbed logger, got up and whispered something in the fellow's ear. Afterwards the ranting diminished to an occasional inarticulate muttering, a vague antiphon, to the properly decorous service.

The extempore mourner was a stranger to me that day, but after the funeral I saw him around a lot. He was Paul, son of Myrna Scott. Myrna was a frail poet with bent shoulders and bad teeth. One night, not long after her son came to town for what was supposed to be a visit, she fell ill and died. She was a Quaker and her Society of Friends funeral, held on a hillside at Schooner Gulch, embodied considerable stretches of quiet. Paul, memorably voluble at his friend's funeral, was mute as a stone at his mother's. When the crowd of Myrna's friends had sat silent for a sufficient space of time, Paul took his mother's ashes to a cliff to fling them into the sea.

carry me seawind
where I need no name…
carry me seawind
to the starlit dream and salty blood.[2]

Paul was beyond our view for a long time. A very long time. Lolling on the grass in the sunshine, we waited, speaking of Myrna, whom everyone admired, in hushed tones. After a while conversation relaxed and broadened. We had almost forgotten we were there for a funeral, when, bearing the empty urn, a pale and sober Paul came back to us. That day he offered no explanation what had kept him so long, but several weeks later, watching a Monday night football game at the local bar, he spilled the tale to Alan.

"It was the most horrifying thing that ever happened to me in my life," he said. "I went up there with her — her ashes, I mean. It's what she wanted. Everybody knew she wanted to be —her ashes to be — scattered into the sea. I was doing just exactly what she asked. Anyway, there I stood on that cliff. At first I tried to think of something to say. I couldn't, but I tried. Then

I opened up the urn and threw her — the ashes — as hard as I could, but they didn't go out to sea. "They came right back at me. Hit me right in the goddamned face. Some heavy chunks, bone and stuff, dropped straight down, but most of her just stuck to me. Filled up my eyes and my ears. Stuck all over the front of my goddamned shirt…oh, christ, it was awful. Some of her was even on my teeth."

Alan didn't know what to say, but it was plain to him that Paul was asking for a response of some kind, so he said, "I guess your mother isn't an easy kind of person to get rid of."

"Something like that." Gloomy, Paul proceeded to drink himself into a stupor.

He's still here in Point Arena. Like a lot of people, he came for a visit and never left.

I took a Sunday stroll across three pastures, over the highway, and down the narrow road to the lighthouse, and was standing at the edge of the bluff admiring the breakers, when a beat-up car with an east coast license plate stopped and a woman got out. She stood beside me sighing loudly.

"I guess this is as far as I can go then," she said. "I've been headed toward California for six years. I've driven and driven and driven. Six years. Now…" she gestured vaguely toward the sparkling waves, "I can't go any farther."

"No," I said. "Not in your Volvo."

"So!?"

"You could turn around and start driving back the other way."

I had said the wrong thing, and the woman stared at me as though I were a jabbering gull. She's still here, too.

America has always traveled west. West was the course along which Europeans moved when they crossed the Atlantic. Then the U.S. settlers, going west, spread across the continent. The complacent ones followed the malcontents, and as population filled in, the restless moved again —always west. The West meant opportunity, and when the latest western frontier, California, revealed its vast treasure trove of natural resources, the West became El Dorado.

Point Arena was just about as far west as they could go in the lower forty-eight. The land was virgin, untouched, unspoiled. To the Euro-American settlers the western landscape was synonymous with "raw material." The economy of the U.S. West didn't evolve, it boomed into existence.

Even after the days of wide-open venture were over, Point Arena failed to outgrow a romantic nineteenth-century notion of itself. The people who had been coming here to stay for the past hundred and forty-five years, all had desired (to varying degrees and for varying reasons) to escape urban or suburban life. Myrna Scott came for solitude and the sea. I came for affordable land. Many have been drawn by woods work. Nowadays the big-money hopefuls come to develop a comparatively underpopulated region. Others come to seek their fortunes as outlaws. An increasing number of retirees are settling now on this coast. And vacationers —some who come on holiday find they simply can't bear to leave despite the fact that jobs here are hard to come by.

Individuals and couples, families, then clans, of newcomers evolve. A surfer cruises into town to catch a few of Point Arena's legendary waves, and never gets around to leaving. His mother or brother comes for a visit, ends up buying land, is joined by another relative who has volunteered to help build the new house. Or a retired couple attracts kids and grandkids who want to live close by. Nick Scanlon-Hill came to work on a dairy farm. Now he and Laurie and their three children share one sprawling house with Nick's sister and Laurie's brother, who are married to each other and have two children. Nick's mother bought the adjacent property and built a house.

Many recent arrivals, but the demographic backbone of the community was established by the core clans begotten by nineteenth-century settlers. Many of the settlers' descendants stuck around, and, as in the Greek myths, intermarried so often it's hard to keep the genealogies straight. A tangle of ever-spreading old clans, some, like the Iversens— two brothers named Iversen married two sisters named Iversen who, themselves, had two brothers named, of course, Iversen— is nigh impossible to unravel.

Isolated by geography, static in population size, Point Arena, became a place ignored by time. The town's institutions and industries, concoctions of the nineteenth century, managed to retain — or failed to shed —their nineteenth century stripes. Founded on diverse population and vigorous nineteenth-century capitalism, Point Arena became the ideal site for struggles between old forces and new.

For the more than three centuries after Europe discovered the Americas, its globe-girdlers sailed past the Redwood Coast, blinking at it through occasional chinks in the fog. The Spanish used reaches of the Redwood Coast for navigation, and, in 1594, Sebastion Rodriguez Cermeno, returning to Spain from Manila, described it as "mountainous and heavily forested with trees that could not be distinguished." A shore to pass on the way to somewhere else, rather than a shore to make for. Fifty years earlier, Juan Rodriguez Cabrillo's expedition left several place names, like forsaken laundry, draped on salient landmarks. In 1579 an English outrider, Francis Drake, anchored somewhere in these latitudes. The location is hotly disputed, but wherever it was, Drake stayed there only long enough to refit his ship and speak his bit about claiming the place for Queen Elizabeth, etc. before going on his way. Neither he nor anyone else from Europe showed interest in a protracted stay until the Russians in the eighteenth century discovered the sea otter's pelt of "soft gold." The Russians pursued *Enhydra lutris* from Alaska all the way down the California coast. In 1811 the Russian-American Company sent twenty-five Russians and eighty native Alaskans from Kodiak Island to establish an outpost. This band built Fort Ross, thirty-five miles south of Point Arena, and periodically sent parties trekking into the Garcia watershed to cut tall timber for ship masts.

Russian Fort Ross burrowed like a chigger into the flank of the vast Spanish Empire. It rankled, but Spain wasn't strong enough on her northern frontier to rid itself of the trespassers. New Spain had no missions north of San Francisco. Its center of gravity was firmly fixed in the south, so the pesky Russians not only got away with thumbing their noses at Spanish autonomy, but worse, they were able to hog the lucrative sea otter trade. From her rudimentary presidio at San Francisco, Spain tried to intimidate the trespassers by marching soldiers, in full armor, north along the coast. Though the spectacle scared the wits out of the indigenous peoples, it had no effect on the Russians. Issuing restrictions and hurling threats, New Spain managed to keep the Russians north of San Francisco, but couldn't shake them loose altogether.

The long-drawn-out revolution that severed Mexico's tie to Spain in 1821 kept the new government or, more accurately, new governments — a fair series of them — vulnerable. Anxious to secure the northern frontier, Mexico added a Sonoma mission to the twenty-mission string: Mission San Francisco Solano, where Lieutenant Mariano Vallejo established a garrison and a pueblo. But the Russians' 1841 departure from California had nothing to do with threats from Mexico. The Russians left because the supply of sea otters, with its lusty boodle of rubles, was used up.

Scarcely was Mexico rid of the Russian *moscos* than from the Sierras issued the buzzing of a far more vexatious pest: U.S. pioneers. The very year the Russians shipped out, the first wagon train from Missouri pulled in. Settlers, with no allegiance whatsoever to the Mexican government, were on their way. In an urgent attempt to increase the number of her own citizens, Mexico, in lieu of wages, dished out chunks of northern California to sundry public servants — a double expediency since the new republic was chronically short of cash.

In 1844, fifty-three-year old Rafael Garcia, a Mexican soldier distinguished by "valiant service against the Indians" at Mission San Rafael, asked for a grant in the future Mendocino County. Eight years earlier he had accepted, in lieu of back pay, two square leagues in Marin County; but now, he claimed, his Marin *Rancho Tomales y Baulenes* was too small to support all the livestock he owned. So north he came with the governor's passport in his soldierly hand. "You are hereby authorized to present this to the Military Commandant of the line of that frontier, that in view of the same you may go in search of a tract of land asked for as a compensation for your services to the charter. In case you should select a tract of land, you may at once occupy it with your stock and take possession of the same, while the necessary proceeding are being taken and the map presented."[3]

Whether or not Garcia was ever bona fide owner of all those forty-thousand acres between Mal Paso and the Gualala River, his claim to them left at least one legacy: a river bearing his name. On the north side of the river, Garcia built a small wooden house near the present intersection of Highway 1 and Mountain View Road. His foreman stayed on the property, while Garcia came north only often enough to satisfy the terms for occupation. He adequately fulfilled two other preconditions of permanent ownership with his "summer home" and with his cattle grazing on the fertile bottom lands. But his efforts were wanting with regard to a further requirement — the education of the local native population. Mexican colonists were expected to indoctrinate natives into a Spanish/Mexican way of life. Although *Rancho del Norte* had rounded up a number of Pomos and set them to work, the only thing they learned was to loath Garcia's steward enough to try to poison him. They were not drawn to the strange newcomer's culture and persisted with the way of life they had known for centuries.

By a series of quick bold strokes, the U.S.A. scaled down the sprawling and mighty Mexico. First, prior to tackling the great Rocky Mountains, U.S. settlers expended their westward-ho enthusiasm, filling gaps in Mexico's skimpily populated Texas. Unfortunately for the Mexican Republic, it had tried to staunch the flow with restrictions which proved unconstitutional. Mexico's violation of her own brand-new constitution gave the wily Texicans a perfect excuse to declare their independence. Eighteen thirty-six was the year of the Alamo. General Santa Ana won the battle but lost the war. Defeated, captured, released, Santa Ana turned his back on the Texas problem, as did everyone else in the Mexican government. Ridiculous gringos. Let them proclaim until they get hoarse in the voice, but they are part of Mexico. *Punto.*

Meanwhile in the United States a gratifying but factitious notion advanced, gathering strength: Manifest Destiny was on the march. An unsigned editorial in an 1845 expansionist paper warned of foreign governments trying to check "...the fulfillment of our manifest destiny to overspread the continent allotted by Providence for the free development of our yearly multiplying millions." Dastardly foreigners daring to obstruct westward expansion. The urge to expand into every undeveloped nook and cranny of North America was deemed proper and legitimate despite the fact that such an urge was putting us in hot water with Mexico over the southwest, with Russia over Alaska, with England over Oregon. In no time at all Manifest Destiny flung its net ever wider, becoming the excuse for annexing various Caribbean and Pacific islands including Hawai'i.

When in 1845 the United States annexed Texas, it claimed a wedge of land between the Nueces and the Rio Grande rivers, a region not previously occupied by Texicans. The Mexican Republic had easily ignored Texas's assertion of independence, but this new challenge, this arrogant affront by its powerful northern neighbor provoked Mexico to sever diplomatic relations with the USA. Blandly, President Polk offered to settle the Texas boundary dispute, and, at the same time, buy California (where a few settlers had already raised the U.S. flag, though neither Mexican nor the U.S. government yet knew it.) Mexico was too indignant even to respond to Polk's insolent proposal. So Polk, calmly and deliberately, ordered troops into the disputed part of Texas. When the inevitable clash occurred, he calmly and deliberately declared a national outrage: *American blood has been shed on American soil!* Uncle Sam marched, easily capturing New Mexico and California (Upper California only; useless Lower California was left to Mexico).

From the middle of the nineteenth century to its end, the shaping of the American West was a three-ring circus. One thing lead so swiftly to another, so much happened in so many different arenas, that it was hard to keep up with the action…even without the surprises.

March 3, 1848. Mexico City. At the banquet of Guadalupe Hidalgo, which closed the Mexican-American War, the U.S. of A. happily agreed to pay Mexico fifteen-million dollars, as well as pay off three million dollars to U.S. citizens with civil claims against the Mexican government. Mexico, less happily, ceded all its territory north of the Rio Grande and Gila rivers, and west across the Colorado to the Pacific Ocean — a piece of underpopulated, unexploited real estate, which already billeted a handful of U.S. citizens.

Two of these U.S. citizens, bushwhackers seeking their fortunes in California, had recently hit on a harebrained scheme. They planned to raft sawed lumber down the American River. They had finished building their mill and were ready to go into business, when a problem turned up. The end of the tailrace proved to be too shallow. Water backed up, preventing the flutter wheel from turning. Two months before the signing of the Treaty of Guadalupe Hidalgo, which would give the American River, mill and all, to the U.S., one of the harebrained bushwhackers, an impractical carpenter, closed a gate, stopped the flow of river water, and squatted down. Pondering his tailrace predicament, he casually scooped up a handful of wet sand. His mind was so busy trying on and rejecting a series of solutions that several minutes passed before it registered: his palm was full of 23 karat gold.

Carpenter and partner tried to keep the gold a secret, but, not surprisingly, news leaked out. Initially, however, no one showed the slightest interest! Did the taletellers lack credibility? Or had the news not been properly presented? In May the situation changed abruptly. A store owner galloped through the streets of San Francisco waving his hat and whooping, "Gold!" He for one knew how to recognize a lollapalooza. The word proved mightier than a stone in the hand, because the very same men who, a few weeks earlier, sat thoroughly unimpressed by hard evidence of a gold, now leapt to action. Within days twenty-five percent of the city's male population was on its way to the American River.

John Archibald Hamilton, a New Hampshire lad, was bored at Harvard College, so he quit school and took a job with a Massachusetts shipping company. Supervising the purchase and transportation of South American nuts, hides and tallow, he sailed back and forth between many ports, foreign and domestic. One afternoon in 1849 he disembarked in the ramshackle frontier town of San Francisco. The town consisted of about three dozen wooden buildings, some of them nothing more than the hulls of old ships, but people were pouring into town faster than roofs could be built to shelter them. Gold brought them west in droves. Hamilton abandoned the shipping company and took up work in San Francisco as a ship builder. In four months he was ready to head for the mines.

A year and a half on the Yuba River. It was rough, really rough and still Hamilton was empty handed. Broke, he was forced to go back to carpentry, but gold fever is hard to cure and pretty soon he was mining again, this time on the Feather River. As before, nothing panned out. Discouraged and impatient, Hamilton decided to make a major leap. He'd try stock farming in Yolo County. He was in the process of acquiring cattle when, in 1855, he chance to meet a Mexican national named Jose Leandro Luco. Luco owned a vast land which was tied up in a long litigation which was not settled for five more years, but Luco was peddling it nonetheless, and Hamilton, then and there, bought a portion of Rancho Del Norte in Mendocino County.

Twenty-five years later a Mendocino County chronicler wrote, "At this remote distance, it is impossible to determine who was the first permanent settler in the township. It would seem, that in 1855, J.A. Hamilton, Joseph Sheppard and William Olive[r] came from Yolo county with a drove of cattle, and settled on claims on the Garcia river bottom, and to them doubtless belongs the honor of being the first settlers outside of the grant overseers, as no traces of any previous settlers can be found." (This must have astonished any of the local Native Americans who read his book.)

John Hamilton came to Point Arena in a pack train with his wife Helen, a small daughter, and a ten-day-old baby boy. With them came Helen's brother William Oliver, and two hundred eighty-four head of cattle. They built their home near Garcia's house. Joseph Sheppard took a place nearby. Another newcomer, William Shoemake, purchased six hundred forty acres of Rancho Del Norte on Brush Creek, just spitting distance north of the Garcia. The first marriage recorded in the neighborhood was in 1858 between William Oliver and Lavinia Shoemake, William Shoemake's daughter. William Shoemake's son claimed the honor of the first recorded death.

In 1858 Mart (a.k.a. Mark) T. Smith and Julius Garwood Morse, M.D. showed up in Point Arena as agents of Luco, current owner of Raphael Garcia's forty-thousand acres. When the U.S. Supreme Court invalidated the grant, it stripped Luco of most of his holding, but he had realized some profit by selling portions of it when the title was as yet undecided. To protect people like the Hamiltons, Sheppards and Shoemakes — U.S. citizens, who, in good faith had bought Mexican or Spanish land-grant property, then occupied and improved it — Congress whipped up some hasty legislation. Through the Conness Act, such settlers were allowed to retain the very large tracts they had claimed prior to the Homestead Act.

In 1860 when Luco lost his land, he no longer needed his agents, Morse and Smith. Dr. Morse liked it here, so he stayed on the Garcia River to become Point Arena's first postmaster. Mart T. Smith, still looking to strike it rich, shifted around a bit. He bought a shipping port at Fish Rock but sold it a year later and left the area. He returned in 1865 with a franchise to build a wharf at Point Arena. Today more than a century and a quarter has passed since Smith built his wharf, but Smith's ghost haunts the records. A handwritten entry in the county's Miscellaneous Book records the "Memorandum of Agreement between M. T. Smith, and H.M. Whitmore and R. Stevens," notarized and dated April 26, 1869. The faded ink and spidery script goes on for several pages, describing Smith's original contract to ship lumber from the Garcia Mill.

On their five-hundred acres, John and Helen Hamilton and William Oliver ran cattle, raised grains to feed the animals, and grew a cash crop of potatoes. To get the cattle to market, they had to drive them all the way up to Shelter Cove in Humboldt County. During their 1862 drive William Oliver was killed.

John Biaggi, an Oliver descendent, tells it like this: "They were driving cattle up to Shelter Cove, just south of Eureka, and it was during the Indian Wars. Either somebody paid the Indians, or something, to do this. Anyway, they shot my great-grandfather and scalped him and stole the cattle. It was in all the papers and I have an account of it. It was in 1862. So then my great-great-grandfather rode up there and they sewed him into a series of canvas bags and brought him back here to be buried at the Evergreen Cemetery."[4]

Unable to verify the account, I nevertheless find it credible. Hungry and desperate to check the flow of white-skinned interlopers, natives began to kill livestock. In retaliation, stock owners began to kill natives. The U.S. Army marched into the fray, but the onset of the Civil War pulled most of the troops to the battlefields back east. More and more Native Americans managed to arm themselves, and, though the odds still favored the whites, bloodshed became less one sided. Poor William Oliver was one of the casualties.

Along with his brother-in-law, John Hamilton lost a good percentage of his cattle, so the next year he went back again to boat building. A year after his schooner *Helen* was launched at Point Arena, the fifteen-ton vessel went down in almost the exact spot where she had been set afloat.

A succession of larger schooners, produced by his builders Walworth and Reimers, followed the *Helen* to the bottom of the sea, one by one, taking first Hamilton's money and then his ranch. By the time his granddaughters, Hazel and Irma, came into the world, the Hamilton family was decidedly out of pocket. Rather than scions of landed gentry, the girls judged themselves poorer than most children they knew. They remember their grandfather as a crotchety old misanthrope.

John and Helen had six children who survived to adulthood and several more who died in childhood or infancy — Evergreen Cemetery is well populated with Hamiltons. The name, Hamilton, has been phased out since neither of the sisters, nor any of their three other siblings had children.

Hazel and Irma, the only descendants still here, are widows who quilt, go to church, and get their hair done at the beauty shop (perfect stereotypes of sweet little old ladies, except that when my friend Lucie invited them to the elementary school to be interviewed by students for an oral history project, they exclaimed, "Oh, my, no. We don't care for children!" which I loved because stereotypical little old ladies love children, and I don't care for stereotypes).

The sisters describe their dad, Arch, as a poor but gentle, hardworking man, a farm laborer who hired himself out to other farmers while working his own twenty acres in Manchester. His five children drove the family ducks to Brush Creek, as they walked to school. In the afternoon they shooed the flock back home.

When not working on school assignments or home chores, the children played on the grounds of the ill-fated Eagle Paper Company mill on Brush Creek. Only the straw barn and two excavations, one for the mill and one for the fire room, remained, but below the abandoned site the Hamilton girls found hundreds and hundreds of buttons cut from rags on the way to becoming paper.

John Biaggi, a distant cousin of Irma and Hazel, is a descendent on his mother's side, of The First Wedding, the Oliver-Shoemake match. Unlike the Hamiltons, John's family increased its wealth and strove to maintain the genteel manners the Shoemakes and Olivers brought to a raw and isolated locale. John Biaggi, who lives on the old family place, remembers a sheltered childhood and a loving mother, father, and grandmother who strictly enforced patrician standards of etiquette.

His family's large dairy ranch, the Shoemake chunk of *Rancho Del Norte*, supported another household in San Francisco and still another in Healdsburg. On the coast the family claimed a position of social superiority. They socialized only with certain, select families, yet John and his sister were always allowed to play with the native Pomo children, even to visit in their homes.

John's mother was considered the best dressed woman in the county. She shared her parents' attitude toward wealth and status, but her "expectations" didn't prevent her from falling in love with the family's ranch foreman, a young Italian Swiss immigrant. She was a strong-willed woman who usually got what she aimed for, and, if her people objected to her marriage, no evidence remains. She took John senior and, by the strength of her personality and position, promoted him to her own level, from which proud height he henceforth shunned the rest of his Biaggi kin.

From 1607 until 1840 fewer than a million people immigrated to the United States. In the second half of the nineteenth century, thirty million poured into the country. Nova Scotians, Irish, Scots, Germans, Russians, Scandinavians, pushed on west to the Redwood Coast along with homegrown U.S. settlers. At the turn of the century, a second wave from Europe brought to Arena Township Italians and Italian-speaking Swiss with their lilting multisyllabic surnames —Scaramella, Soldani, Gianoli, Biaggi, Stornetta, Giacomini. Today these families own most of the good agricultural land, including Hamilton, Sheppard and Shoemake's big farms.

Joe Scaramella: "How my father wound up here, specifically, I cannot tell you. But I can tell you this: for all these pioneers, somebody come first. Somebody had come here long before he did. How that somebody got here or why, I don't know. The business of survival then took all your time. There was very little left for anything else. If you were going to survive, that was it. So they come up here and letters would get back saying, 'Come on out here, I think you can get a job and this is what they pay and compared to what they have there, it's so much better.' And so they just naturally shifted."[5]

At first the forests of redwood, Douglas fir and tan bark were the big draw. But enterprising white settlers quickly elaborated on initial resources.

They built mills. They organized cooperative creameries. They established a flourishing tannery. A few made a living from commercial fishing.

All this activity called for shipping. Once begun, the shipping business expanded steadily and in the long run turned out to be the biggest industry around. From the wharf at Arena Cove passengers came and went on a regular schedule. Passengers, though, were a minor cargo. A schooner's primary business was bringing in supplies for the settlers and carrying away what the settlers had to sell — lumber, paper, posts, shakes, railroad ties, vegetables, meat, and dairy products, especially the good butter. When Point Arena's long-time newspaper editor, William Hanen, told people in San Francisco where he lived, they immediately responded, "Point Arena? Ah! that is where the butter comes from."[6]

A population of working folk and their families needed stores, hotels, entertainment, a blacksmith, a newspaper, churches. Schools sprang up like wildflowers. A lighthouse was erected on the point. Within a brief space a time, a population transfigured a wilderness.

REFERENCE NOTES

1. Edward Abbey in an interview with James Hepworth from *Resist Much, Obey Little.*
2. Myrna Scott, "Seawind," *Driftwood Shores*, Spendrift Press, Berkeley, CA, 1981.
3. Spanish Archives volume T6, p.270, via Sullenberger, Bancroft Library, Berkeley, CA.
4. John Biaggi, *Yesterday's News*, SPL p. 23.
5. Joe Scaramella quoted in Bruce Levene et al., *Mendocino County Remembered: An Oral History*
6. William Hanen, writing in the *Northern Crown*, 1907.

Chapter Nine

FIRST

With little prompting my imagination runs to the early settlers. I like to pick them up out of the tired dirt of their nineteenth-century eastern farms or up from the increasing clamor of their nineteenth-century cities, then shepherd them across the face of the continent or around its edge, setting them, finally, on their feet in wild Mendocino mountains hemmed with gullies, valleys, thick virgin forests, or depositing them on the bank of a roiling river verged with willows, berries, sedges, rushes, game, flowers, or, sometimes, simply fetching them up, awed, before the magnificent Pacific Ocean. My imagination quivers to ruminate on what these newcomers must have beheld in the days before this land, this plum of a place, was squatted, patented, utilized and domesticated.

But my quivering imagination swoons well-nigh to witlessness when I squint backward through the next door in the enfilade of history, a creakier door jammed nearly fast for want of pen-and-ink lubrication. A glimpse through this farther, and far less accessible, door to pre-European North America would reveal a land ripe and wild, but a land furnished already with a human culture. White settlers dubbed each other "the first this" and "the first that," yet they were not first at all; were, in fact, trespassers on a thoroughly established population. And, whether the newly arrived persons knew it or not, whether they gave a tinker's damn or not, the ancestors of the already established population had been here for no fewer than ten thousand years. *Ten thousand!* And the white settlers? How long have they been here? A hundred and fifty years? Two hundred?

As late as 1769 no non-natives lived in Upper California. Though Spain considered California a chunk of its own vast empire, Spain's claims would have been news to the three hundred thousand plus people living here. The natives who made the Garcia watershed their home are known as the Pomo. Spread across present Sonoma, Lake, and southern Mendocino counties (plus a small offshoot in Glenn County), these indigenous peoples of the north central California coast had never considered themselves part of a unit. However the conquerors, as was general policy, found a "tribe" and gave it a name: "Pomo."

When the white invasion began in earnest, the so-called Pomos were (so-called) California's second most populous native group, numbering around eight thousand, but the Pomos never secured great notoriety in the annals of the West. When known to the outside world, they are usually associated with baskets. The Pomos of Mendocino County are among the most celebrated basket weavers on earth. Beautiful as well as practical, Pomoan baskets are highly valued works of art. Museums around the world exhibit them. Leningrad has an especially large collection, acquired in the nineteenth century when the Pomo helped the Russians build Fort Ross.

During the 1890s, Carl Purdy, "the Dean of Wildflowers", became so enamored by the beauty of Pomoan baskets that he contrived to live among the Pomoan people for a time, studying and collecting. He wrote, "Into the life of a Pomo, baskets entered every day from his birth to his death. He was cradled in a papoose basket, and in it, hung by a broad band on his mother's brow, he made his early journey. His home was a great thatched basket, his toys were baskets modeled after the large ones that he saw. He ate from a 'da-là,' or flat basket, and drank from a round 'tci-mà.'"[1] The seeds from which his meal was made were ground in a 'mu-tci,' or mortar basket, and his fish and meat were cooked in large mush bowls or 'tci-mas,' and a large 'tci-mà' was his water-bucket. His fish were caught in a fish net basket, his meal was winnowed in winnowing baskets and screened in a sieve basket. When he traveled, his belongings were carried in a 'bu-gi,' the conical burden basket, and these answered for every purpose for which we use a wheelbarrow or wagon. If he gardened, his fences were of wickerwork, and he trapped birds and game in long cylindrical baskets. On Clear Lake the art of basketry applied to tules was used in making canoes…There was a name for each weave and other names according to the use.

"Until long after the white man came, their winter homes were domes of wickerwork, thatched heavily with grass or tules…In such a house three generations of a family lived and stored their food…Great storage baskets filled with acorns were stacked on the sides, fish hung on string on the walls. The summer house was also of wickerwork covered with boughs, and the tribe often moved several times a year, as acorns, fish or game, or dry quarters were the desiderata."

Though they came in wide variety of sizes — baskets four feet high to ones less than an eighth of an inch in diameter — all were made with the same materials, primarily willow twigs and sedge roots, and were formed by one of two methods, twining or coiling. The coiled variety could be woven tightly enough to hold water.

The special treasure of collectors were, and continue to be, the intricately designed, exquisitely decorated gift baskets. In the Pomoan culture, to receive a gift basket from its maker was considered the greatest possible honor.

Men made some types of baskets, the traps, for instance, but the expert weavers who pursued the craft with a patience and care involving not only artistic resources but spiritual values as well were the women. Women continue to be the guardians of Pomoan basket weaving, and the teachers of the distinctive weaving methods. Sad to say, though, not many of the younger generation are interested in learning. The task is too quaint, too time-consuming. It's not modern. Yet enough weavers still exercise the skill to keep it from going the way of the elk, the grizzly, or the Pomoan language.

Pomoan languages have all but disappeared. Only about sixty-five people alive today speak any of them fluently. All have complex grammars and rich vocabularies composed of words which are hard to pronounce. Hard to comprehend, too — or so I've been told — because single words have many different meanings. Densely textured, these languages are pleasing to the ear. I met a ninety-something Pomoan woman who spoke almost no English. Even though I hadn't the vaguest notion of what she was saying, I loved to listen to her talk. Her native tongue sounded intriguing and like nothing I had ever before heard.

The various Pomoan groups did not speak dialects of the same language, as early investigators of Pomoan cultures claimed. They actually spoke separate languages so distinct, one from the other, that a Pomo living on the Garcia would not be able to understand a Kashaya Pomo from Annapolis only thirty miles away. The invading investigators were misled by the fact that the separate languages — seven in all — derived from the Hokan language family.

This shared linguistic kinship furnished the invaders with their reason for lumping the diverse peoples into one tribe. Then, having identified a "tribe," the experts sorted the seven "dialects" into geographical regions, assigning to each a name based on its location relative to the Russian River — Northern, Northeastern, Central, Southern, Southwestern (Kashaya), Eastern, and Southeastern. Thus each designation referred to three things: a geographical location, a language, and the group who spoke it.

The Pomoan people consisted of several dozen independent bands, tribelets which were small but politically equivalent to minuscule nations, each with its own territory and its own leader. A mini-nation might number one hundred or fifteen-hundred members, occupying territory scaled by nature's formula: the character of the land — how many mouths it could feed — balanced with the size of the band. The smallest of these domains encompassed twenty square miles while the largest covered three hundred square miles.

A band's territory was at the disposal of every one of its members. Within their own territory the people freely ranged to hunt, gather food, visit, trade, always returning to the fixed settlement for winter. No individual Pomos owned property, but property lines between separate communities were strictly held, and only with permission could a member of one mini-nation hunt in another's territory.

Each territory contained one or more fixed settlements, a "winter village," which was used year round and was peppered with semi-permanent settlements to be used seasonally.

Though few communities made the coast their home, inland dwellers trekked regularly to the coast, but the Pomo were an unnavigating people. They gleaned a wealth of provender from the sea, but obtained most of it from the shore. The only boats they possessed were rudimentary, inelegant rafts, assembled from a few rough logs, and used to reach offshore rocks rich with mussels or sea lions.

The Clear Lake Pomos wove wickerwork canoes, crafts practical for paddling around in lakes, not seaworthy. The few scholars who have studied the Coast Pomos seem perplexed by Pomo boatlessness. They scratch their heads and say it's "remarkable that a shore people, deriving much of their sustenance from the ocean and with the best an easiest of all canoe materials — the redwood — at hand in superabundance, should have been entirely boatless,"[2] while simultaneously identifying the Pomoan language as Hokan-Souian, a linguistic family of the Great Plains. Doesn't origin on the Great Plains explain a preference for terra firma? To me it looks as simple as two plus two, but I'm no anthropologist so I may be missing something.

Whatever the cause, the indigenous population of the Redwood Coast was definitely not a crowd of old salt-sea dogs. Even "coast" settlements were located far enough inland, often three or four miles from the beach, for protection from the Pacific's fiercest weather.

Pomos settled beside rivers, usually along north and east banks where thicker vegetation held moisture throughout the dry summer months. An archaeologist working for the California Department of Forestry tells me they practiced aquaculture. He says he has found evidence of such in the Garcia watershed.

The Garcia band was of the Central Pomo group. From its territory near the coast, its members wore a trail up the river toward the inland valley where most of the other Central Pomos lived. The Garcia settlement called, *Pda'hau*, meaning "at the river mouth," was on the Garcia's northern bank. Modern archaeologists write with confidence of a second settlement, called *Kodalau*, on Brush Creek, but no nineteenth century sources mention it, and John Biaggi, whose family lands have encompassed the Garcia River settlement since the earliest days of U.S. stewardship, believes the Brush Creek artifacts indicate nothing more than an abandoned camp of the *Pda'hau* community.

"They shifted around a lot. Whenever one place got too muddy or a particular food source got depleted or there got to be too many fleas, they just moved camp," he says.[3]

John grew up in the company of Pomos. He visited native homes, sampled native foods. He and his younger sister attended the one-room Brush Creek School, and, later, the Dorrington School. In both schools the white Biaggi children were in the minority. But the students all got along well together.

Many employees of the large Biaggi dairy ranch were Pomos, as were all the house help. "You never, *never* called them servants. That simply wouldn't do. When I was very young, Florence Silva's grandmother took care of us, my sister and me. I remember one time she was rocking me and — she didn't know it, but I had a little pair of scissors — and while she was rocking me I cut out the front of her dress! That's the only time I saw her mad."

John says he and Martin Laiwa, young scion of a powerful Pomo family, squabbled in the seventh grade. "Martin would complain that my family had stolen his family's land." John insists these disputes were thoroughly good-natured. By then, John's forebears had deeded a small portion of the land in question back to its original owners. His mother's great-grandparents granted to the local Pomo band — with legal provision against its ever being sold — the fifty acres beside the Garcia the band had been living on since 1877. Later, in 1909, the federal government added to the holding some of the adjacent land up the hill and established the whole parcel as a ranchería.

Until a hundred and fifty or sixty years ago, the little settlement on the Garcia River lived undisturbed. Rumors of white intruders probably reached it from the south in 1811 when Russians built Fort Ross as outpost for otter hunting and for provisioning Russia's Alaskan colonies. Members of the *Pda'hau* band may even have encountered some of the fort's fur traders who periodically traveled to the Garcia watershed to cut timber for ship masts.

The Russians came with their own labor force, the skillful otter hunting Aleuts, shanghaied from Alaska, so these first white-skinned newcomers had no reason to trouble California's native populations.

In 1833 another bevy of foreigners paused briefly in the vicinity. A Hudson's Bay Company trapping party of a hundred men, French and English, with their children and Indian wives, camped on Noyo River not far to the north of the Garcia where several days of heavy rain brought them to a standstill. Local natives delivered the strangers from their watery blockade by helping them build rafts to cross the swollen river.

The Hudson's Bay trappers never came back (not enough beavers here), and Pomoan life on the Mendocino Coast continued undisturbed, except for an occasional and unsettling report from Clear Lake of murdered Pomos and Wappos: one hundred fifty victims in 1839, one hundred seventy in 1841. Mexico was the culprit, but all outsiders — Mexicans, Russians, English, Spanish, Americans — were probably the same to the uninitiated natives.

In the middle of the 1840s life was finally well-and-truly interrupted when Rafael Garcia appeared on the Garcia to claim his land grant. He, in the person of his steward, immediately began to herd neighboring Pomoan groups into the *Pda'hau* settlement where he put everybody to work.

Soon governmental authority shifted. In charge now of Upper California, the United States redoubled the disruption of native life by sweeping everyone living at *Pda'hau* into a herd with four or five thousand other Pomos, Yukis, Wappos, Coast and Lake Miwoks — peoples from as far off as Eureka and Chico — and relocating them in 1856 to a new reservation between the Noyo and Ten Mile rivers. Some of the displaced natives resisted, escaping into the hills with armed soldiers at their heels.

The U.S. government considered the Fort Bragg reservation a means of preserving the natives, an uprooting to forestall annihilation since many white settlers were determined to get rid of their indigenous neighbors one way or another. But the twenty-five thousand acre reservation was a resounding failure. From its inception it dwindled steadily until officially discontinued in 1866. By then most of the residents had been relocated to an inland reservation at Round Valley, a site of racial wrangles and social unrest from the time of its inception to this very day.

After the Fort Bragg reservation closed, a few people lingered on while the land was sold off a piece at a time, but the majority of those not taken already to Round Valley headed for places which might be home. A handful of Pomos, some hailing from *Pda'hau*, some exiled from other places, made their way forty-five miles down the coast to the Garcia. They set a permanent winter village on the bank of the river. Later, sometime around the year 1877, they moved it four miles upstream to the site of what is now the Manchester Ranchería.

Despite their first encounter with the invaders, the Pomos on the Garcia were inclined to be friendly and, by all accounts, the U.S. settlers at Point Arena were rarely ill-treated by the Pomos. Yet by appropriating all the land, white settlers prevented the natives from wandering freely as their way of life prescribed. Whenever a Pomo roamed, somebody with pale skin invariably popped up to say, "Get off my land."

Indigenous peoples managed as best they could throughout California, but as a rule they had a rough time of it in most parts of the state. After 1860 any native not on a reservation or under some citizen's protection was considered a "wild Indian" to be hunted down by soldiers. California was admitted to the union as a free state, but the free state status failed to protect California natives, who, according to the terms of the 1850 Act for the Government Protection of Indians, became the property of the settler upon whose land they were living.

Ranchers and farmers took unfair advantage of this legislation before it was repealed in 1868. After it was repealed, they still needed cheap (free?) labor so they began setting aside a few acres for native peoples to live on in exchange for work. "Rancherías," these parcels came to be called, and the term ranchería is synonymous now with a small reservation, usually big enough only for the residents' homes and tiny garden plots.

Nestled deep into the north bank of the Garcia River valley, the Manchester Ranchería, originally named the Dorrington Ranchería in honor of some Indian agent or other, was established in 1909. Today its older dwellings, patrolled by wandering poultry, are small and of a ramshackle architecture. Traditional Pomoan homes, the building style John Biaggi's mid-nineteenth century ancestors first beheld, were cones of thick redwood bark strips supported in the center by a tall, forked pole. Long willows were leaned against the pole, then slabs of redwood bark were piled on until all holes, except one at the top for smoke, were covered. The temporary shelters of the summer camps were casual constructions of brush.

Every Pomoan settlement had a community house, the roundhouse. John's mother described the local community house, a big round affair with a fire in the middle. Circling the fire, people danced to the beat of hollow log drums. During John's childhood the Manchester roundhouse remained the physical center of the settlement with the separate family dwellings arranged around it, but now the roundhouse sits beside the river at the farthest extent of the ranchería's crumbling road. In very bad repair, it is rarely used.

Another traditional locus of activity, though limited to males, was the communal sweathouse, conducive of health and hygiene, as well as camaraderie. From a shallow pit, crowned with brush or redwood bark cones similar to houses, a fire or pile of hot stones generated heat. The remains of two sweathouses are still discernible on a hillside near the Manchester ranchería. John Biaggi recently sold the particular piece of land upon which they once stood, but he says the last time he walked there the pits were still perfectly apparent. The ranchería's present-day sweathouse is right on the bank of the river.

In 1937 the federal government bought Sam Iversen's Ranch on the south side of the river and turned it into a second ranchería accessible via Windy Hollow Road. The ranch consisted of two hundred sixty acres (some of it prime agricultural bottomland), thirty cows, and a modern dairy equipped with a cooling system. The government built eight new five-room houses, and by 1940, a crew, including local Pomos who would be living there, had begun to fence the perimeter. These men drove fourteen-thousand redwood pickets and five-hundred-fifty redwood posts "so close together a jackrabbit couldn't get through," or so said the Mendocino Village newspaper."[4]

Without boats to cross to the Manchester side, the residents of the second ranchería planned to lay a road so they could get their milk to the Manchester Creamery. They also devised a plan for controlling the river's course. The winter of 1939 had brought exceedingly heavy rains, swelling the river to a mighty size and washing away much of the ranchería's good bottom land.

Neither the road nor the river project was ever completed. In fact, as a business venture, the new reservation was a disaster. The feds had envisioned a tidy arrangement with some of the ranchería population planting and tending crops, while others milked the cows and operated the dairy, the proceeds of which would pay for the land. Things did not work as the government planned, and everyone has a different theory about what went wrong.

John Biaggi insists the dairy was a modest success until old man Laiwa realized he was doing all the work. As soon as he balked at doing more than his fair share, the business fell apart. Pretty soon the erstwhile Pomo dairy farmers had eaten all their cows.

Longtime tribal chairperson, Florence Silva's version is simple. She says that "certain factions" used all the money and wrecked the dairy. She goes on to explain that the government officials who set up the second ranchería assumed everybody would want to move there and were surprised when a good many members of the band chose to stay on at the old place. Florence believes the damaging influence of that long-ago split persists: "Factions. They interfere with the smooth running of things right up to today."

Even to an outsider it is apparent the ranchería suffers a contentious split, but I find myself wondering if the line is the clear and simple fault line of the river, a rivalry between the two discrete segments of what is, administratively and historically, a single reservation? Or is the clash between families or other hubs of power configured beyond family ties? I try to find out more, but answers are guarded by a reticent people whose society is complex and perpetually in flux.

Though local white ranchers disagree about what, exactly, thwarted the Pomo dairy, they are unanimous in their scorn concerning the fate of the cows: "That was their brood stock, for crying out loud! That was the whole damned *investment*!" A legitimate appraisal, but one which fails to take into account the historical Pomo way of life, a deep-rooted culture of hunting and gathering with no tradition of husbandry.

When people are our neighbors, when we see them every day, wearing clothes like our own, involved in activities similar to ours, we tend to forget about cultural differences. Yet those cultural differences, authentic and fundamental, exist often prompting misunderstanding.

One example: I helped care for a woman on the Manchester side of the ranchería when she was dying of cancer. She lived with her husband in a tidy little house, two big rooms built onto a travel trailer. Toward the end of her life, when she could no longer get out of bed, I brought her a pretty blue hospital gown which opened up the back, making things easier for me and the nurse. Besides being practical, I was hoping something new with a bit of lace would please her.

Her husband, Jewitt, unwrapped the box and pulled out the nightgown. While I urged Frieda to put it on right then, Jewitt insisted she should wait. Next time I came she was not wearing it, so I searched and finally found it in the top of the closet, still folded in its box. I quizzed Jewitt, and he admitted he was planning to take it back to the store. Piqued by what seemed to be pure stinginess — presumably he intended to exchange the gown for the money — I made it impossible for him to return the present: when Jewitt left the house, I bathed Frieda and dressed her in the gown.

After she died, her niece helped me clear out all the hospital things. As we worked, the niece told me stories of her aunt, things she remembered from her childhood. She described the beautiful Kleenex dolls Frieda once made and wondering what had become of them, said, "I guess the dolls were gone even before Mamma and Uncle Jewitt took away all the things they couldn't bear to burn."

"Burn? Why burn anything?" I asked, and she explained her people's ancient custom of burning, or otherwise destroying, all belongings of one who dies. This surprising information gave me a different insight into Jewitt's reticence about "wasting" a brand new garment, and I felt contrite about my harsh judgment. (This sudden repentance so preoccupied me, I neglected to ask the niece what in the world a Kleenex doll was.)

Though I came to be sorry I had gotten into such huff with Jewitt, I was never sorry I had sabotaged his plan. The dying woman deserved to enjoy that powder-blue and lace nightgown, even if for no longer than two or three days. Maybe she had agreed with her husband about the waste, if waste it was, but she made no protest as I unwrapped the tissue paper and put her arms into the soft blue batiste sleeves.

I was fond of Frieda. I liked Jewitt, too. Usually. He was intelligent and charming. But he was manipulative and not entirely dependable. One day he asked me to sit with his wife while he drove to Ukiah to get some new bed sheets. The hours passed. It got late and I needed go home to my family. Finally, I called Frieda's sister, Mabel, from next door to replace me. After dinner Jewitt still was not back, and Mabel needed to take care of her family.

Frieda absolutely could not be left alone. What was to be done? I sighed, rolled up my sleeping bag, and I drove back to the ranchería.

Frieda's hospital bed stood in the middle of the living room. I made a pallet on the floor beside it, and slept so soundly that once, when she needed some pain medication, she had to throw a Kleenex box at me to wake me up.

At dawn Jewitt came home. My makeshift bed lay directly in front of the door, so he had to step over me to get in. He tiptoed to his room and shut the door.

Everyone on the ranchería knew I was there and why. Next morning the first caller who strolled up the front walk was Uncle Hector, leaning on his cane, his small black mustache and short black hair perfectly groomed. After a cordial, formal greeting, he took a chair and a cup of tea. (Frieda said I was the only person she knew, Indian or white, who could make a decent cup of tea.) Soon Mabel arrived with her mother. Before long half the residents of the ranchería — all of them Frieda's relatives — were sitting in Frieda's living room. No one asked me any questions. In fact, no one said much of anything. Silently, they lined the room as if waiting for a show.

Early morning birds twittered. Dogs barked. Frieda's roosters crowed. Outside the windows Elvin, too shy to come in, walked back and forth. I smiled politely.

Jewitt stayed hidden in the back of the house until everyone had gone. He emerged with no bed linen, nor any explanation for his absence. I did not press him for information but never again did I allow him leave without a firm commitment as to what time he would return.

One afternoon Mabel and I sat by her sister's sickbed talking about the Garcia River. "So many fish in the old days," she said. "What has become of them?"

I asked her to tell me more about the old days, expecting to hear a lament for pre-white existence as poignant as her lament for the missing fish. But, no.

"Bad! Conditions were very bad back then. Sickness of the stomach. Infection of the eyes. Very bad. No lights. No running water. Water had to be carried up from the river in a bucket. Very heavy. And the mud! Winter time was the worst." She then proceeded to catalogue, down through the generations, the many wonderful things certain white families had done for her family, and I thought: Well, so much for my political correctness.

At the time I had assumed Mabel was talking about Pomoan life before the white invasion, but I now suspect she was referring to the hardships of her own young life when she lived with her parents and five siblings in a very small house beside the river. After the family moved to a larger house on higher ground, one with electricity, gas, indoor plumbing and a telephone, life must have become enormously easier. When she became an adult, Mabel stayed on in that same trim, red house taking care of her mother, her own children, her children's children. Her sister Frieda moved into a trailer next door.

John Biaggi's family was proud of its benevolence toward the Pomo, a people deprived of their traditional means of livelihood, and thus thrown upon the mercy of government and charity. John laughs when he tells of the San Francisco missionaries who periodically sent barrels of clothes to the ranchería. The recipients of the missionary largess refused to wear the hand-me-downs until each garment had been soaked and scrubbed, scrubbed and soaked. "The Indians had so little that they were glad to get what they could, but *they hated the smell of whites*."

Prior to the invasion, Pomos were obliged to spend the most of their waking hours gleaning necessities from the woods, rivers and sea — not an easy way of life, but apparently they managed well enough since their tales, myths, and lore reflect no chronic scarcity. Though occasionally one band forbade another to hunt or gather acorns within its territory, it would have instituted such a ban because of a quarrel rather than because of a paucity of resource.

Describing the old way of life, Florence Silva — descendent of a mixed union between a Pomoan woman and Bodega townsman Stephen Smith — says, "It was a free and easy type of living." Owing to a diverse food supply, her ancestors could venture out and, depending on the season, bring back any number of good things to eat. And they valued their tradition of generosity. "Acquiring and processing your own food meant sharing both the food and the experience."

Acorns were the primary staple. Many Pomos still eat acorns, even though they require a long process of preparation. First the raw acorns must be ground. Originally this was done in a basket mortar with a stone pestle, but Florence grinds her acorns with a hand mill. Next they must be dried. "You must dry them very, very well. Then you leech them. Soak them, and keep changing the water until there is no more bitter taste. And last of all, you boil them." She keeps the finished product in screw top jars or plastic containers. "It can be eaten as a mush, or baked into a bread." She writes out her favorite acorn bread recipe for anyone who wants it.

Along with acorns the Pomos ate seeds, roots, bulbs, seaweed, sea lions, mussels, abalone, fish, and game. Many of these foods remain on the Pomo menu, even kelp and seaweed, eaten either fried or baked. Florence says the secret is, "You've got to get it when its green and tender." Sea lion is no longer popular, but fish, abalone, sea snails, periwinkles, and game (a category which, now and then, might include a neighbor's steer) are.

Martin Laiwa was born in 1922. He grew up on the Manchester side of the river, but his family moved to the other side when the new ranchería was built. His earliest memories are of gathering and preserving food, and he believes that, even as recently as the days of his childhood, the residents of the ranchería were self-sufficient. The dozen or so households raised potatoes, beans, and corn, trading what they didn't consume for salt and sugar in town.

Ranchería residents dried and smoked large quantities of abalone and fish. As Native Americans they have been granted the right to fish without regulation by the game warden. The Laiwas began their fishing season each year directly after the first rains and they fished on through March. Martin's father and grandfather would launch their boat upstream and, drifting, fish the river down to the ranchería where young Martin waited with the team and wagon to haul the catch home. Each day the men brought in at least a dozen fine, big fish — ten to sixteen pounders. What they didn't eat right away was preserved to last the year.

Nick King asked Martin Laiwa if his family ever sold fish, ever turned any of their catch into money. The question made Martin laugh. "No," he said, "we'd never make any money anyhow — we're not 'smart' like the white man. If we'd had to sell anything, we'd have starved to death first. We used what we caught for food. That's what it's for."[5]

"One thing I was very struck by in talking to Martin was his lack of jealousy towards us whites," said Nick. "He is disgusted, angry and bitter that he has lost his way of life. But he is not jealous of what we have...He doesn't want to be like us. He just wants to be himself...to have his own life back."

But Martin Laiwa isn't going to get his own life back. It is too late for that.

⚜

The smaller Manchester portion of the ranchería is tucked down in a shady valley on an elbow of the river. On the south side, and a half mile downstream, the Point Arena site sits atop a terrace of Pacific Plate terrain with a panoramic view across wide acres of cultivated bench land all the way to the lighthouse. Throughout both reservations a gaggle of older homes are scattered to which a recent crop of brand-new tract-style houses have been added. But the old dwellings on the Manchester side have a more haphazard appearance than the old homes on Windy Hollow, built to encircle a grassy play area. Manchester has the history, the roundhouse, the river frontage. Point Arena has the health clinic and the modern-day problems.

To get the new housing the local Tribal Council negotiated a block grant, and by the middle of 1988 HUD homes were going up on both sides of the river. To be eligible for one of the new houses, an applicant had to be registered on the tribal roll. Anyone whose parents or grandparents lived on the ranchería in 1935 is automatically, via the official government census, a member of the Manchester-Point Band of Pomo Indians. Not everyone on the tribal roll lives on the ranchería, but many who left were lured back by the new, cheap houses, and their arrival brought troubles.

"We are a close-knit community and it's hard," says Eloisa Oropeza, a young teacher and school board member. "We've had new buildings come in and homes come up and people coming in from the cities and they come in with a different attitude. We got along fine when we were raised together because we're country kids. We got along with everyone. Native and non-native. Everybody just sort of worked together. And now I feel that there is a division."[6]

"On a reservation — and we've had problems, there's been a lot — the native community all lives together, so people are more aware. Whereas if we were scattered, I don't think there would be a big deal made of it — as much as there is."

Tensions are greater on the Point Arena Ranchería than on the sleepier side of the river, but the tensions don't stay corralled within the Native American community. They escape.

TWO HURT IN POINT ARENA STREET ATTACK

City Council reacts to violence

> The specter of urban-style gang violence in their streets brought an overflow crowd of Point Arena residents to the City Council meeting Tuesday night when a group of Indian men assaulted two Point Arena men, both white, on Main Street. The victims, Abel Mouton and Keith Abrams, both required medical attention after the attack.

> Abrams, who had numerous facial injuries, was the first to address the meeting on the subject.
>
> "Last Saturday night I was attacked by a group of young men wearing Raiders and Kings jackets who asked if we wanted to get shot and brandished a knife," he began.
>
> "I'm aware that there are deep-seated problems in the Indian community that have been going on for 120 years when Pomos were shot on sight here. I feel bad about that but I wanted to say that no one wants to live in a community where this happens…
>
> The second victim of Saturday's attack, Abel Mouton who sustained a broken jaw, spoke next.
>
> "I don't think this is a problem that can be solved just by law enforcement, 10 p.m. curfews or banning Raiders jackets."
>
> The statement of the next speaker, Ed Christensen, drew heated response from Councilman Steve Oliff, Mouton's employer.
>
> "I went to school with these guys," Christensen said, "and I think somebody said something and got their ass kicked."
>
> "That's the stupidest thing I've ever heard!" retorted an angry Oliff…
>
> "How can we make it abundantly clear that as a community we will not tolerate this kind of behavior?" asked Councilman Raven Earlygrow.
>
> Oliff also expressed concern that the incident not take on racist overtones…
>
> Arena Elementary Schoolboard member Eloisa Oropeza spoke about the concerns of the Indian community.
>
> "I live on the reservation and I don't carry a knife or gun. I'm afraid myself out there….We're your neighbors. Pomo people aren't uncivilized. You can talk to us. We are not all like this. We are not all bad."
>
> *Independent Coast Observer*, January 17, 1992

The town exploded, but, unlike clashes in the past, this one exploded in dialogue rather than violent retaliation and repression. Raven was mayor by now and he told the tribal chairman that ignorance feeds fear which feeds into racism. What was needed was better communication, so Point Arena City Council members attended Tribal Council meetings where, for each grievance aired, a constructive solution was proposed. A good sign, demonstrating that racial issues were not as precarious as they used to be.

Eloisa Oropeza: "The problem of racism is a lot better nowadays. If people just communicate, I think that's the biggest problem...a lot of people think that if you're a Native American and you're living on the reservation, the government pays you and everything is free. And if you're a Native American you have to drink and you do this and that. There are stereotypes, but we're working real hard to clear those up. To let people know that we are normal. We're like everyone else. We feel just as everyone does. Not everyone drinks and fights and has a knife and things like that. Yeah, there are stereotypes in the community, but with the effort we're trying to make I think we'll be okay. We've got a new generation of people who want to use their voices and they are using their voices to be heard."

REFERENCE NOTES

1. Carl Purdy, *Pomo Indian Baskets And Their Makers*, Mendocino County Historical Society.
2. A. L. Kroeber, *Handbook of the Indians of California*, p. 243
3. Quotes from John Biaggi are taken from conversations I have had with him over the years I have known him.
4. *Mendocino Beacon*, June 22, 1940.
5. Personal interviews with Garcia Community members. GRV Enterprises, 1991, Point Arena, CA.
6. Eloisa Oropeza, *Yesterday's News,* interview e007mr.

Chapter Ten

WILD, WILD WEST: CARRIE POTTER

Sophie closed the "Gorilla Bar" early. She had no more energy for wrangling with Chava and his three cronies. All evening they had been giving her a hard time. At one point Chava, drunk, was cheeky enough to reach behind the bar and try to lift a six pack from the refrigerator. Sophie could handle them, of course. All those years at the wharf cafe had trained her for just about anything. But this was Thursday, supposed to be a quiet night. She was tired of the tussle. Every time she kicked them out, they came back.

Before Sophie got the men out for the last time, Carrie and Irma arrived at the Gorilla Bar. Trying to ignore the barrage of suggestive remarks from the four feisty young Latinos, the women bought their beer, but their presence escalated the hubbub.

"Go on. Get on out of here," Sophie told the men who just laughed. Carrie grabbed a broom and helped Sophie drive her tormentors out door.

Carrie and Irma planned to take Charmaine and little Darrin to the Point Arena Ranchería, before driving down to the river to drink the six-pack, but on the way Charmaine woke up. She whined. She didn't want to go home. So all four sat in Irma's Camaro in the foggy dark beside the river.

It wasn't long before Chava and his compadres showed up. Afterwards they would say they had been invited, but, "Bullshit," says Carrie, "we hadn't even talked to them before they followed us to the river." Yet Chava's cronies insist they were invited, otherwise they never would have come. They were invited, and that, of course, meant…

Straight off, Ismael asked Carrie if she wanted to have sex. Carrie admits she didn't say no. "But I didn't say yes, either." The guys hung around, drinking beer, listening to the car stereo and chatting, even though they were beginners at English and none of the women knew a single word of Spanish. Things were amicable for awhile; then they began to go awry.

"Chava climbed into our car," Irma says. "Right through the window. It's broken, the window on the passenger side. It won't roll up, and he just came right through it. He started shining his flashlight around." Which made Carrie snappish. Darrin, her two-year-old son, was asleep in the back seat. The noise and the flashlight were going to bother him.

The other guys began to pester for sex. "One of them touched my butt," Charmaine says, "and I told him to get his fucking hands off me." This was the last straw for Carrie. Charmaine was just a kid. Carrie had been out of high school nearly four years but her sister was just a schoolgirl. Carrie defended Charmaine, and Jaime feinted punching Carrie in the face. A shoving match ensued. It was definitely time to leave.

Irma tried to back the Camero out, but the other vehicle blocked her. She asked the driver to move, four or five times she asked before, furious, she jumped out of her car and tried to push his old black jalopy out of the way. But Jaime was too fast for her. Starting his engine, he drove forward, shoving the Camaro, with its sleeping passenger, to within a few feet of the river. Irma opened her trunk. She was beside herself with rage. Was there anything in there she could use for a weapon?

"You looking for a gun? Huh?" asked Jaime. "Well, I got one too."

The women were as scared now as they were mad. Irma maneuvered the Camero onto the road and hastily left the river. Oh, how the women wished they still had Elvin's gun. Only that very morning they had returned it. On their way to Darrin's doctor's appointment in Ukiah, Carrie, Charmaine, Irma and with half of Irma's family packed into one car, had stopped at the Manchester Ranchería to give Elvin back his rusty .22 Ruger. Never had Irma actually used it, but she borrowed it now and then. They'd had prowlers at her mother's house where the back door was broken so it couldn't be locked. But worse than prowlers, for the past two years, ever since Irma's brother had shot Martin Laiwa, Jr., she had been afraid of the Laiwas. Martin, recovered from the wound, later killed Irma's step-brother. So Irma had gotten into the habit of borrowing the gun whenever she was especially nervous.

Irma and Carrie set a course to the Manchester Ranchería now. The distance from the Point Arena side to the Manchester side of the ranchería is less than a half a mile along the river, but by road it's a pretty fair piece — eight miles when the summer crossing on Windy Hollow is out, as it was this first week in March.

Behind them in the dark they caught sight of a black car. "They followed us," Carrie says, "with the headlights out. They got real close. A time or two they even bumped us. We pulled way ahead, but they kept on following, flashing their headlights."

The guys say they never meant any harm. They may have driven a little too close to the Camaro — a car's length away at the closest — but there was definitely no bumping. It was all in fun. In fact, they hadn't given up on getting some sex. When the chase led into the ranchería, though, chary of male relatives, the men backed away.

Elvin didn't take kindly to being waked up at this ungodly hour — it was nearly two a.m. But when Carrie told him there was a problem with some prowlers, he let her have the rifle. "The magazine was loaded when she took it," he says, "but there wasn't a round in the chamber. I gave her some extra ammunition." Carrie laid the gun in the car alongside a tire jack. She left little Darrin with Elvin.

All day, ever since they got home from Ukiah, Carrie had been looking for her boyfriend. She wanted to see him now worse than ever, but he lived in Gualala, and Irma refused to drive that far. She was willing, though, to drive back to Point Arena so Carrie could check his friend's apartment again. The apartment overlooked the General Store parking lot which Irma entered by way of the back alley. Carrie was just about to get out of the car and climb the wooden stairs when she saw Chava leaning against a white van. She stayed in the car.

Irma aimed a few choice words at Chava, who replied in kind. With her attention directed at Chava, she didn't notice Carrie lifting the .22 and pointing it out the window. "I just wanted him to see it," Carrie claims, "but when I pulled it back in the window, it went off."

Within the white van — they were living in it these days — Chava's two friends had turned in for the night, but were still awake when Chava, speaking through the vehicle's wall, told them he could hear the Camaro coming into the parking lot. Though they couldn't make out precisely what was said, the two men in the van heard the verbal exchange, followed by a single shot.

The bullet hit Chava under his left arm, passed through his lungs and heart. He took two or three steps before he fell down dead.

The gun had discharged right next to Irma's face. Horrified, she stepped on the gas and lit out for home, but Carrie begged her to turn around. This time Irma submitted; the boyfriend's house didn't seem so far away now that panic had ousted any hope of sleep. En route, Carrie threw the gun and ammunition out the window. Carrie was in shock, but she didn't know she had hit Chava, much less that she had killed him. She had no idea what she had done until she was arrested.

That she had hit him at all was a perverse and tragic sort of miracle. The weapon — an average weight, semiautomatic .22 caliber rifle with a trigger pull — was in very terrible condition. And, although Elvin had demonstrated how to use it, how to draw back the bolt first, she had never before fired it. In fact she had never in her life before fired any rifle.

At first she told the deputies a pack of lies and half-truths. Finally, she made a full statement. Why did she lie at first, the authorities now want to know? She was scared, she says. She wanted to protect the other people involved.

Why hadn't she called the sheriff when the problem with the men first started? This question might make Carrie laugh if she weren't so distraught. Why, indeed! "For one thing the sheriff is a long way away. Twenty minutes to an hour away. For another thing I'm an Indian. A woman and an Indian." Was it necessary to say more?

REFERENCE NOTES

Though a dramatized account, all information in WILD, WILD WEST: CARRIE POTTER was taken from court records and depositions in Case CR07238, The People vs. Carrie Anne Potter.

Chapter Eleven

NEWCOMERS

In a country where all men were once adventurers, the difference of a few years in their arrival could not make them less American. Thomas Paine, 1778

"The swimming hole. It's nice enough now, but it used to be better." Kate is entertaining me with tales of the Land's early days. "It was deeper back then. When the kids were little, we all hung out there whenever it was warm. Remember Fernando? Or was he before your time? He was a visitor, one of those long-term visitors. The Land had a lot of them. It wasn't cool to turn anybody away, and sometimes we had whole families — sometimes all at once, sometimes one at a time — for *loooooong* periods of time. One afternoon at the swimming hole, Fernando picked up this huge rock and walked into the water. He kept walking, straight across the river and out on the other side. The swimming hole was deep then, and he just disappeared by inches, was completely underwater for a while — you could still see him walking under the water — then he reappeared by inches. The kids went wild. Fernando was a real favorite with the kids."

I've come to see her new room, a studio, light-filled and simple, built of stucco and wood from trees felled on the Land for one reason or another. They were just lying on the ground when Kate needed wood, so she had them milled. Spending time at Kate's place tends to make me peevish, discontent with the clutter and confusion of my own household. Her cabin is a small one she built in the late '60s. Rough-timbered, rustic, everything looks handmade — most of it is. Recently she experimented with bent willow furniture. Her love seats and chairs turned out so well a local gallery decided to sell them. Everything about Kate's life is aesthetically pleasing: the way she arranges fruit on a wooden plate; the way she waters potted plants with a pug-nosed, bubble-laced, blown-glass pitcher; the way she cuts a hunk of bread and cheese for her lunch.

Although PG&E eventually brought electricity to the Land, Kate eschews it, preferring her combination solar and hydro-power. "I have everything I want. Why complicate things?" Ah, for the simplicity...eat your heart out N.K.

Kate was one of the first people I met when we moved here. Kid friendships brought us together — her children, both adopted, are the age of my two adopted daughters. I never manage to get much time with her, though. Her schedule is dense. She travels, she gets involved with political causes and with helping people, she draws and makes prints. Her *Madrugadora* hangs in our living room right above Nick King's salmon photograph.

Kate and Nick were a married couple before the Land helped undo the ties. When she left Nick, Kate built the cabin with one of the other Land owners, a bachelor. Nick built his house on his and Kate's site. The late '60s back-to-the-land trend was hell on marriages. Of the six original couple-owners of the Land (two owners were single), only one is still a couple. Leaving the city set a lavish and unexpected mixing and matching of mates into motion, a rearranging which, in a few cases, hasn't yet played itself out.

The California Center For Rural Design. That was the legal name of the 160 acres which came to be known as the "Land." "We're going to the Land." "We're moving to the Land." "We're staying out at the Land." The year was 1967, three friends from Bay Area, looking for a place in the country, found a farm on the Garcia River just upstream from Eureka Hill Road. They made a bid. Not enough. Nick and Kate were recruited to the partnership. Their added money was still not enough. Another partner came into the deal, and so on, until, at $65,000, their offer was accepted. Eight partners each put up $2,000 cash, then committed to monthly payments for ten years.

In no way did this cluster of folks begin as a conscious group. Degrees of acquaintance between and among them varied, but they had one important thing in common: a deep and instantaneous love for the 160 acres on the Garcia River. Buying it, they formed a corporation, drew up bylaws to cover all problems and conflicts their imaginations could conjure, and hired an attorney to draw up the proper documents. With six of the eight partners being couples, the corporation added up to fourteen people. The actual community was even bigger, embracing a great many children and hangers-on. Potential for conflict was considerable. Young and idealistic, the group initially expected to make all choices by consensus, but a city lawyer with horse sense convinced them to settle for a three-quarter majority, a policy which, over the long haul, has saved them an immense amount of aggravation and bother.

Each owner was to have a separate domicile, so they drew lots for building sites. Collectively they devised a water system, and provided for sanitation, garbage disposal, and fire protection. They extended the unpaved road and worked — continue to work — keeping it in good condition. They constructed a sauna. In winter, with a tractor, they drag it to high ground to prevent its being swept away by floods. They used the old farm house as a community house until it burned down. They planted a community garden, which didn't last, and serves now as Nick King's Garcia River Nursery orchard.

The Land-ers weren't trying to prove anything. All they wanted was a life simpler than seemed possible in the city. They shared a fantasy of living outside the system, of providing for their own needs by growing vegetables, catching fish, shooting deer, building houses. A connection with sources — that is what they yearned for.

From the start they held regular meetings several times a month; and, although over the years problems have arisen, none has proven insuperable. The Land experiment has been a success. Many of the original owners still live there; others, who eventually moved from the Land, chose to stay in the larger Point Arena community.

The Land's urban dropouts were sophisticated and educated, as were the founders of Oz. Oz was located on the river downstream from the Land, five or six miles if you measure as the salmon go. If you measure by road, the distance is a looping 15 miles.

In 1971 Redwood Kroll, a math professor, bought from John Biaggi, 160 acres directly upstream from the Manchester Ranchería. The place had nothing on it but a barn. The following year four dozen people, eager to embark on an idyllic planned community, followed Kroll and his family to the Garcia. They spent the summer in tents and pickup trucks. They wanted pretty much what the Land people wanted, and by the end of the summer most of them had decided to stay.

As I sit writing these words, my phone rings. It's Peter Reimuller calling to coax me to do a newsletter for the movie theater restoration project. "Uncanny to hear your voice," I say. "I'm just now writing about Oz."

"What wild times," he laughs.

"You've told me that before, but tell me more. Something specific. Give me some juicy details."

More laughter. "I don't remember a thing, and my dog ain't talking."

Even without getting Peter to incriminate himself, I have formed a pretty good picture of things. Outrageous clothes. Long-haired men. Half-naked women. An unruly pack of children. Rock and roll. Dope. Blatant sexuality. In short, injudicious behavior which scandalized a plain-speaking, small-town community. Signs went up in shop windows: "No Hippies Or Dogs Allowed In Here." Louie Frazer, of the Land, said the owners of the Manchester store went so far as to chase him and his wife out of their place with a can of bug spray!

But he remembers kindness, too. Kindness from the McMillans, owners of Point Arena's general store, an old-fashioned store where you handed over your shopping list and the person behind the counter collected the items. "The McMillans. Those people didn't just treat you okay, they solved all your problems. One time I mentioned I was looking for a bathtub and Ralph McMillan told me about one that was out in the horse pasture and if I wanted it I could have it. A beautiful tub, it's one of those really big, long ones. I still got it. They were just a resource place. They found everything we needed. They told us how to… we didn't know anything!"[1] The McMillans and the Gilmores, who owned the other general merchandise store in Point Arena, and Don Stuart, and Roy Fox, proprietor of the wharf restaurant. Many of their new neighbors were kind and friendly, and some, who on a day-to-day basis were neither neighborly nor hostile, stood up for the newcomers when occasion rose.

The denizens of Oz built cabins, tree houses, yurts, and pyramids. They put in a composting privy and a community garden. They acquired goats and cows. Adjacent to the barn, Redwood and his family built themselves a big house with a community kitchen. Later they turned the building over to their new summer camp, the Village of Oz Growth Center, and the Krolls moved into a huge double dome on the south side of the river, accessible only by foot on a suspension bridge.

A mighty wonderful experience, according to Peter R. Yet, unlike the Land, Oz didn't last. The community fell apart, and in 1989 the Krolls sold the property to John Hooper. Why did Oz fail to jell?

"It was supposed to be a commune," says Peter, "and a commune should be self-supporting if it ever is going to be self-sustaining. We had great dreams, but never, from day one, were we self-supporting. Only infusions of money from elsewhere kept the place going."[2]

Another problem, perhaps the primary one, is that a single individual, Redwood Kroll, was in charge. He was the owner, and Oz was his domain. The sense of sharing, the sense of democracy, always a matter-of-course at the Land, was missing at Oz.

Oz made quite a stir in the fixed community with doings which flabbergasted even the most tolerant locals. In the early days of Oz, Redwood hired Don Sorensen to do some work. Don told me, "All morning I saw people walking up a path to the top of a hill. A well-worn path, like a sheep trail. I wondered what was going on. Working the backhoe, I'd look up there, but I couldn't see any buildings or nothing. But they kept on going up — a fellow or a gal. Pretty soon down he'd come. What the heck was going on?" No buildings, nothing planted. When he was able to back off far enough, he saw people sitting on the top of the hill, scattered about, not all together. What, what were they doing? He mulled the situation over until it finally came to him: those people, male and female alike, were sitting on cans, and that the hill was nothing less than an alfresco latrine! "Oh, god…I sure was glad that…I, I could never, never…" The ever-articulate Don Sorensen, fumbled for words, but I understood. He was thanking his lucky stars he hadn't been born to the counterculture.

When Oz installed a wind generator, Dorothy Halliday's nephew at UC Davis wanted to see it. Dorothy and Joe were interested in Oz's organic gardens so, with the nephew, they visited Oz. A gardener greeted them with deferent hospitality. He was easygoing, courteous, and buck-naked. Dorothy was greatly amused. "A polite young man. Naked as the day he was born… No, no," she corrects herself, "he had on his boots." Broad-minded and rather earthy herself, Dorothy wasn't offended by the gardener's nudity, but she was contemptuous of the bravado: to garden without any protective covering was a tom-fool thing to do. She was willing, open to learning something from the New Age farmers, but how was she to trust a fellow willing to hazard so much?

Change comes hard, especially in quiet backwaters where strangers with strange habits can scare an entrenched population determined to protect its way of life. Some members of the entrenched population found change congenial. John Biaggi, for instance. John loves newcomers. Scion of a proud and aloof family, John, is, nevertheless, thoroughly egalitarian. All fresh additions to the local society — hippies, Coast Guard, lighthouse employees, Air Force personnel, surfers — all, in his opinion, are good for the neighborhood. "Not so much class division," says this classiest of men.

The hippies never irked Dorothy Halliday, but the Air Force invasion made her mad as a hornet. In 1950 the Air Force installed a radar station at the top of Eureka Hill Road. During World War II, the government required civilians on the coast to take turns at one of several lookout cabins watching, around the clock, for enemy planes. Wartime Plane Watch Calls — mandatory volunteer participation.

Observation posts were to report anything which appeared in the sky, its height, its position, all pertinent information. Dorothy found the duty dangerous, especially the night slots — driving around in the blackout without headlights. For some people the duty was a hard burden. And unnecessary. "All four stations — one at Elk, one up Mountain View just northwest of the ranchería, one on the lighthouse road, and one south of town near Bill Hay's gate — all reported the same thing at the same time. So did the Coast Guard. It was redundant." Dorothy is convinced the only real purpose of the Watch was to keep civilians aware of the war. "It was busy-work for people already too busy."

So Dorothy was already miffed with the military when the Air Force came to Point Arena to track planes. "Placing the Radar Station in this community should have required an Environmental Impact Study," she says. She had a couple of adolescent sons at the time. Suddenly Point Arena was full of restless young men in uniform, driving cars, spending money, completely disrupting normal life, especially the normal lives of families containing adolescent sons. Not enough girls to go around as it was, but now! Local boys just didn't have a chance. Refusing to adapt gracefully to the situation, the boys got into all kinds of mischief.

The base employed one hundred eighty men, military and civilian, until a new radar station near Sacramento — an over-the-horizon radar that bends along the curve of the earth, able, alone, to oversee the entire west coast — eliminated the need for all the little radar stations like the one on Eureka Hill. The government has been in the process of dismantling the Point Arena base for twenty years. Though a small civilian staff still lives there for the time being, the military personnel have been gone since 1980.

Throughout her life Dorothy has been in a position to watch the comings and the goings within her community. She has experienced local changes from a series of vantage points: one year at the telephone company, nine years at the Manchester Creamery, twenty-four years, two months, and eighteen days at the Point Arena Post Office. Dorothy has seen it all. Air Force, surfers, urchin divers, "alternative" communities, the retirees. Never in favor of barring or banishing, she, nevertheless, has a complaint or two. "I've respected their abilities, but I haven't appreciated *all* the changes," she says about the city slickers who moved to the country without wanting to leave their accustomed amenities and facilities behind. They insist on the same goods and services — especially services — their suburban or urban lives included. To provide these services, the county has to raise property taxes. Dorothy and Joe and their kin managed to live here for eight generations without ambulances, libraries, sanitary landfills and the like. "We were willing to go without — heck, I'd *still* just as soon go without. But, like it or not, now we've got to pay."

And she's nettled by newfangled, mawkish susceptibilities. At a Planning Commission hearing Dorothy sat dumbfounded, listening to a bleeding heart newcomer try to ax a proposed housing project by claiming sunlight reflected off windows would disturb migrating whales!

The Land and the Oz ex-urbanites had much to learn if they intended to "live off the land." The ones willing to take advice fared better in the community than the know-it-alls. The locals were happy to instruct, glad to have their skills acknowledged and valued. In return, the newcomers brought fresh things to town. Purchasing real estate, shopping in town, they brought in hard cash. Enlightened parents enriched the education system by getting involved in the local schools. To the community at large, the ex-urbanites introduced plays, a reader's theater, dancing, choirs — music, much good music. Some brought their art, and some became active in community services. Among them were a couple of genuine entrepreneurs, who — when the adventure of being a dropout began to pall — infused the business community with new life.

The '70s newcomers made a permanent impact on the neighborhood they invaded. Peter Reimuller left Oz, but didn't go far. He is everywhere present, a mover and shaker, working in the community, working on the river, developing — then selling — one successful business after another. An Oz couple who opened a cafe back in the '70s are now the proprietors of Bookends, Point Arena's popular bookstore/coffeehouse. Nick King still lives at the Land. A professional photographer in his former life, he chronicles Point Arena's activities with his camera. He also operates a nursery specializing in antique varieties of apple trees. Whenever I buy a tree from him, I get a detailed genealogy. Another ex-Lander is director of the local hospice. Louie, a Land recluse, redesigned the exterior of Point Arena's crown jewel, Pangaea Restaurant. And he and Peter Dobbins built a gem of a sail boat, a fishing boat, they named the *Roy Fox*. Redwood and his family continued to live at Oz for many years after the Oz community disintegrated, but when their youngest daughter was ready for high school, they moved to San Francisco. The last time I saw their daughter, a good friend of Emily's, she had purple hair and was headed for Yale.

The '70s newcomers were outriders. Many followed, including a large number of retired persons. The entrenched attitude that anybody not born and raised here is an interloper, though it persists in some quarters, is diminishing. In truth, we are all elements of the same community. The more homogeneity, the less conflict, and our population is so nicely varied that we, more often than not, enjoy the exhilaration of discord. But discord, if it can be held in check enough to prevent blowing the head gasket, helps fuel the engine. A complicated dynamic. Consider the municipal park:

Point Arena was in a tizzy about Bill Hay's rock crusher and proposed asphalt plant. Those opposed to it — a muster heavily favored by the so-called newcomers — pleaded for protection from noise, air pollution, increased traffic. Those in favor — a coterie, which, though it by no means represented the entire old guard, included no newcomers whatsoever — exclaimed against infringements on private property rights, and cried out for the jobs and prosperity that seemed ever to evade their fair city.

Feelings were running high when voting day rolled around. The general sentiment about the municipal elections was, "Well, now, we shall see what we shall see," because every seat but one, on the City Council was up for grabs. No political battle, anywhere or for any stakes, was ever besmeared with more mud or waged with more heat. The pro-crushers were more confident of success than the keep-it-clean-and-quieters, who, nevertheless, defended their ground with admirable zeal. Keep-it-clean-and-quieters need not have fretted. Their victory was a rout, a sweep, with their candidates winning by a landslide. Obviously pro-crushers had misjudged their constituency. (They delivered to the polls several carloads of voters who, even as they smiled and said, "Thanks for the ride," were planning to pull the wrong lever.)

The election is currently referred to as, When the Hippies Took Over the Town. Some of the losers took it better than others. A few turned sullen and hid; one deposed incumbent was not seen for several months. But some of the pro-crushers joined the new mayor in a grand reunifying plan: the city would create a new park.

The project began and proceeded, punctuated by small wrinkles and winsome complications.

"Let's have nothing but the picnic tables, a barbecue and a playground?"

"But what about volleyball courts?"

"An outdoor amphitheater?"

"You promised us a teen center!"

"What we most need is a city government building."

"No, a library."

"Where's all this money to come from? We absolutely have to stick with just the picnic tables, playground and barbecue…"

Throughout the weeks of debate, volunteers continued to work on the park, doing whatever tasks were conclusively squared away. The community is used to doing things for itself. All our fire fighters and emergency medical technicians are volunteers. Local hospice is staffed by volunteers, as is the library, which acquires all reading materials and operating expenses exclusively through donations. Most of the services other communities take for granted, we secure by our own endeavor. As individuals, we pay property taxes and bed taxes, but coast money goes to Ukiah, never to return, so we keep our hammers and shovels at the ready; and, every fortnight or so, we, appropriately attired, attend a picnic, a banquet, a concert For The Benefit Of _______.

Saturday morning. Twelve or fifteen of us set to work. Up on the rise, Alan shouldered his tractor to the job of scraping and flattening a patch of ground for the picnic tables and fire pit. Accompanying the noise of the tractor, a generator roared in a different key. A power saw chimed in at intervals as a City Council member measured and cut lumber.

A hundred yards down the slope the rest of us scuttled back and forth between what was left of an old barn and a large bonfire — a large and rather abstract bonfire which now and then crawled into the dry grass, so that, with whoops and mad arm waving, we summoned the tractor to come at a gallop to restrain the blaze.

Toilers pried off rotten pieces of barn, bits that would definitely give the building inspector apoplexy. Others rooted up several decades of accumulated trash. Eric wrestled with the nastiest job of all, ripping out the miles of tangled blackberry vines hugging everything. I, arms piled high, toted and burned.

It might look like four scraggly, unused acres lying between the back side of the laundromat and the east flank of Point Arena's new low-income housing. But it wasn't. No. This patch of earth was a park, Point Arena's first municipal park.

Richie, a member of the City Council (once the newcomer who built St. Orres Inn, now a tourist legend), worked to salvage a four-foot length of old-growth redwood 2 x 12. The behemoth plank had been marred with dozens of 20d nails to a rotting slab of timber. Richie called me over to jump down on one end of one crowbar, while he pried up with the other. Slowly, slowly the redwood came away with a deep organic tearing noise. All things here seem to have grown together. Wood on the ground was in a state of decomposition advanced enough to undermine the distinction between "wood" and "ground". Humus to humus…

Somebody's little daughter took an indignant stand against the graffiti chalked on a remaining fragment of wall. With a can of blue enamel paint she was carefully covering up obscene and subversive words. Loading my arms with a pile of planks that he jimmied loose from the studs, the mayor said, "Watch out for the wet paint." Apparently the adults were prying off the boards even as the child painted them.

My library crony, heaving a sour and moldy mass into the blaze, complained, "It would be easier to burn the thing down and start over." Contrariwise, Richie, every time he passed by, beamed with pride saying, "Isn't this big old barn a beauty?"

REFERENCE NOTES

1. *Yesterday's News* interview, lf6.spl.

2. *Yesterday's News* interview.

In General: I have gleaned so much information from Dorothy Halliday that I have lost track of precisely where some of her words came from. Her memoir, *Over the Dam*, taped interviews for *Yesterday's News*, talks to the school's Gifted and Talented classes, newspaper pieces she has written, and personal conversations — all sources, many repeating the same information, are mixed together in my notes.

Chapter Twelve

FORTUNE SEEKERS

Thus on the northern coast,
In the echo of teamsters' calls and the clinking of chains,
and the music of choppers' axes,
The falling trunk and limbs, the crash, the muffled shriek, the groan,
Such words combined from the redwood-tree, as of voices ecstatic,
ancient and rustling,
The century-lasting, unseen dryads, singing, withdrawing,
All their recesses of forests and mountains leaving,
To the deities of the modern henceforth yielding,
The chorus and indications, the vistas of coming humanity,
the settlements, features all,
In the Mendocino woods I caught.

Walt Whitman, "Song of the Redwood Tree"

When Euro-American and European settlers arrived in the Pacific Northwest in the late 1850s, their jaws dropped in awe. They were looking at the densest stands of marketable timber in the world. This land-of-milk-and-honey is going to provide amply for everybody's needs with enough extra to make some of them really fat.

Of the many trees they found, none was as remarkable as the redwood: *Sequoiadendron giganteum* and *Sequoia sempervirens*. *S. giganteum*, giant sequoia of Yosemite and Sequoia National Forest, the larger of the two species, proved to have little commercial value. Not so *S. sempervirens*, the coast redwood, inhabiting the lower Coast Ranges. The habitat of *S. sempervirens* stretches from eight miles north of the Oregon border south to San Francisco, popping up again briefly in the Santa Cruz and Santa Lucia mountains. Except at Big Sur where it grows right down to the sea, the coast redwood range begins about one mile inland spreading thirty miles to the east — forty in some sections of Mendocino County. In fact, fifty percent of the world's redwood habitat is in Mendocino County where growth is the tallest, stands are the densest.

Precipitation in Mendocino is high, rain in the winter and, in rainless summer, heavy fog, which condenses on branches then drips to the ground, keeping things wet. Swathed in fog, protected from intense wind, coast redwoods cluster close together, making their own weather.

Bark three inches to one foot thick protects the tree against insects, disease, and fire. If a circle of bark is stripped all the way around the trunk, the tree dies. Otherwise, if allowed to, it stands for a long time. A very, very long time. An individual coast redwood's life expectancy is 1000 to 1500 years. *Sempervirens* means "everliving," but the species was named by a taxonomist who had given no thought to the commercial value of the tree. The tree's virtues have just about wiped it out.

The redwood is easy to work with. Close-grained, straight-grained, knot-free, it splits neatly. And it is durable. Water won't corrupt it — fresh water, saltwater gives it some trouble. Redwood has little tendency to either shrink or swell, it resists termites, it holds onto paint. A light wood which, though not strong in an absolute measure, is strong relative to its weight. And the trees are huge, the tallest plants on earth with diameters greater than any other timber tree. The nineteenth-century newcomers had stumbled on a treasure, acres upon acres of it.

July 5, 1850. It was starting to get dark when Captain Edward Faucon saw the breakers on the rocks outside the little cove at Point Cabrillo. He ordered the helm turned hard to port, but his maneuver was too late and the *Frolic* hit, stern on, and immediately began to fill with water. Edward Faucon, was the same Captain Faucon of *Two Years Before The Mast* fame. Richard Henry Dana had admired the man: "... a sailor, every inch of him. He knew what a ship was, and was as much at home in one as a cobbler in his stall. I wanted no better proof of this than the opinion of the ship's crew, for they had been six months under his command, and knew him thoroughly, and if sailors allow their captain to be a good seaman, you may be sure he is one, for that is a thing they are not usually ready to admit. To find fault with the seamanship of the captain is a crew's reserved store for grumbling." Dana had adventured with Captain Faucon fifteen years before the wreck of the *Frolic*, but the good captain obviously had remained competent since he managed to get himself and most of the crew — six refused to leave the ship — safely ashore in the *Frolic's* two lifeboats. Finding no aid at his landing, he left eleven crew members on the beach at Big River and ordered the two boats to continue south. Against southerly winds and coastal fogs, they rowed south for ten days until they reached San Francisco.

Here and there, Mendocino history intersects with the doings of the wider world. This is one of them. A decade or so before the United States began to settle the Redwood Coast, China, way across the Pacific Ocean, was resisting Great Britain's persistent attempt to trade Bengal opium for Chinese goods. The first Opium War began in 1839, and the United States promptly ferreted out a way to take advantage of the situation. While Britain was ostracized from Chinese ports, the U.S. built several ships especially for the opium trade. The *Frolic,* a classic Baltimore clipper, was one of them. (The *Frolic* was constructed in a shipyard where a slave named Frederick Douglas worked, another history intersection, and I find myself wondering if the combined ramifications of any one story, set any place on the face of the globe, ultimately add up to the story of everything on the face of the globe?) Three times a year the *Frolic* sailed to Bombay, picked up 100,000 pounds of opium, delivered the cargo to Canton, then returned to North America with 17,000 to 24,000 pounds of silver.

All the while, Yankee ingenuity, busy with everything everywhere, came up with a new boat, one powered by a steam engine. The steamship was considerably faster than the clipper ship, so, all in a stroke, the *Frolic* was outmoded as an opium runner at which point it was set to transporting a more condign, if less lucrative, cargo. Thus it was that in 1850 Captain Faucon, bound for San Francisco where fortune seekers of another ilk were going mad about gold, was driven onto the Mendocino rocks with crew of Lascars, from western India, and Malays, and a hold full of silk, paintings, lacquered ware, scales and weights, stoneware, silverware, camphor trunks, furniture, ivory fans, combs, umbrellas, porcelain beads, gold filigree jewelry, sweetmeats, twenty-four hogsheads of beer and other merchandise including "101 packages comprising 1 House."

Faucon and his officers, rowing toward San Francisco, had spent their nights ashore. The fifth night they partook of the hospitality of Stephen Smith of Bodega Bay, who had just sold his mill to Henry Meiggs of San Francisco. The Gold Rush was pumping up the lumber market, and Meiggs could see right away the mill was too small for his aspirations. He was trying to figure out how to expand his enterprise when he heard about the *Frolic.* Fortune seeker supreme, Meiggs immediately sent his mill superintendent to see if he might turn a buck salvaging the clipper ship's cargo.

But when the superintendent got to Big River, he found nothing to retrieve. Instead of sinking, the *Frolic* had drifted into the cove and washed ashore. The men on board along with those left ashore, had taken all they could carry and began to walk, advertising their loot to everyone they encountered, including the local native population. Who knows how many helped themselves to the *Frolic's* booty by the spring of 1851, when Meigg's superintendent traveled to Big River. It didn't matter though, because he found something else, something far better than salvage: colossal timber stands, a gold mine of redwoods. Without missing a beat, Meiggs loaded an assortment of sailors and carpenters and other workers, many of them disappointed gold miners, onto a schooner along with a complete steam sawmill and shipped the lot north to Big River, while he and his colleagues set up the California Lumber Manufacturing Company with Meiggs as president. Around the same time, William Richardson began construction of a mill on the Albion River a few miles south of Big River. The year was 1852, and the history of the timber industry on the Mendocino Coast was off and running.

A major depression in California in 1854 inhibited the growth of the local lumber industry. But within a few years the economy improved enough for Point Arena to sprout a crop of mills. By the late 1870s a dozen saw and shingle mills were operating in the surrounding area. The Garcia River alone boasted four. The first was at Allen Gulch. It was probably the one built by Raphael Garcia, taken over now by an American family who operated the small water powered mill to produce shingles. The three other Garcia mills were Doe's Mill on a tributary of the South Fork, Riverside Mill built by J.C. Halliday and Neils Iverson at Ellis Gulch, and the crown jewel of the watershed, the Garcia Mill, erected five miles east of Point Arena, and eight miles up the river, just above the North Fork confluence. Built in 1869, the Garcia Mill was averaging 50,000 board feet a day in 1881, and a mill community of ten or more families with a store, a school, and a hotel all adjacent to the mill building.

Early redwood logging was a challenge. It called for ingenuity. The size and distinctive characteristics of the redwood tree made new methods of hewing, milling, and moving necessary. The distinctive characteristics of the land made new methods of transportation necessary. But to confront a challenge, to rise to a challenge, is immensely satisfying, a dividend beyond the paycheck, a rake-off for ego and soul. The modern notion that "easy is best" robs an endeavor of its measure of the sort of glee enjoyed during logging's halcyon days. The men trying to start the Garcia Mill faced "problems that would have seemed insurmountable even to the average lumberman of these days," according to Thomas Moungovan, long time mill employee.[1]

The first problem was exactly where to put the mill. Mill owners Stevens and Whitmore knew they could count on the river to bring them the timber, but they would need a dam to keep the logs from floating on by. But a dam wasn't going to be easy on this river. The first spot they found sufficiently buttressed on both banks was at the confluence of the North Fork, eight miles from the river's mouth, which meant eight long miles from the closest shipping point. But never mind; a few short miles of railroad track would get the lumber to the wharf. So they began both to build the mill while they surveyed for the railway.

The lay of the land proved ideal for railroad track. However things didn't go as well for the purchasing agent as they had for the engineer. When the agent set forth on his quest to obtain rights-of-way across the properties lying between the mill and the wharf, he ran into trouble. Six property owners were happy to oblige, but a seventh held out for an immense sum, far more money than Stevens and Whitmore were willing to pay. Since there was no way to go around this land, the mill owners had to scrap their railroad plan. But the mill was well underway! What could they do? Plan #2: a wagon and team of horses. They had already erected a bridge to get the teams across the river when somebody with a pencil and scrap of paper figured out it was going to take more than fifty horses to pull one day's output up the steep hill behind the mill. Any more suggestions? Much head scratching before the company engineer rose to the challenge with a wild idea. What about a flume all the way to the ocean?

"After some quick and snappy arguments, the plans were approved and work was started the same day," said Moungovan. "A temporary survey was run down the open river channel. The line was run down the river to eliminate brush cutting along the bank. This was completed in one day. The following day the final survey started, and the lumber for the construction of the flume was ordered."

The mill paid each riverfront land owner along the route a dollar for right-of-way, and the flume was erected in a hurry. Whenever the building crew got to a spot needing to be graded or cut, another crew was run in without delay. They found it was easier to go under than over the county road, now Windy

Hollow, so two crews began to tunnel, one from each end, "and as the survey reached its lower end, the blueprints were on the drawing board."

The flume was seven miles long, two and a half feet wide, sixteen inches deep, with a twelve-inch catwalk on one side. Another flume a mile and a half long was built from the mill up the North Fork. Suspended by cables, it fed the larger flume. The flume was an outlandish project. That it was seriously considered, then eagerly carried out, off in the back of nowhere with little capital and no sophisticated technology is a testimonial to nineteenth-century gumption. That the venture was successful is a testimonial to the audacity which was making America "great." The flume operated until 1912. Afterwards pieces of it remained in place for many years, long enough for some of the older Point Arenans to remember it.

Lumber went straight from saw or planer into the flume. Dropping about ten feet per mile, the lumber floated from what is now Buckridge Road to right above the river's estuary. At the base of a 300 foot bluff, workers removed the wood from the flume and loaded it onto a bank of rollers equipped with pointed steel brads devised to keep the wood from slipping backward. Water spilling onto an enormous wheel, working a system of gears, powered the rollers which hauled the wood to the bluff top. Sorted and dried, it later traveled by wagon across the bluff and down the precipitously steep Devil's Cutoff to the wharf. The empty wagon returned to hoisting work at Rollerville through town, a longer drive which avoided the steep incline. Pretty soon the wagon was replaced by a short railroad line which ran right alongside the existing wagon track. The railroad bed is still visible beside Highway 1 with a segment of it lying a few hundred feet from the corner of my south pasture.

REFERENCE NOTES

1. T. Moungovan, "Where There's A Will There's A Way," Mendocino County Historical Society, 1968.

Chapter Thirteen

PRAGMATIC VISIONARIES

But more in you than these, lands of the Western shore,
(These but the means, the implements, the standing-ground,)
I see in you, certain to come, the promise of thousands
till now deferr'd,

Promis'd to be fulfill'd, our common kind, the race.

The new society at last, proportionate to Nature,
In man of you, more than your mountain peaks or stalwart trees
Imperial,

In woman more, far more, than all your gold or vines, or even
vital air.

Fresh come, to a new world indeed, yet long prepared,
I see the genius of the modern, child of the real and ideal,
Clearing the ground for broad humanity, the true America, heir
of the past so grand,
To build a grander future.

Walt Whitman, "Song of the Redwood Tree"

They came, and it was grand, and everything was big. They came, and they kept on coming to a land in its glory, with rivers running wild and free, and untouched forest, ripe for the picking: tanoak, sugar pine, spruce, Douglas fir and redwood. They cut all kinds and marketed them with varying rates of profit. They sold tanoak bark for tanning hides and it fetched a very nice price. They harvested Douglas fir. It was strong but subject to rot. Not so the redwood. No other tree had the commercial appeal of the coast redwood. Virgin redwood. That was what they came here for.

But redwood wasn't a tree you just swaggered up to and chopped down. Its size and special characteristics exacted a huge fee in time, energy, skill, cleverness. These trees were so massive they could be destroyed in the felling, so choppers spent considerable time preparing the ground to receive them. Existing mill equipment was the wrong scale for the immense and often contorted root swells, so choppers had to lob off their trees well above the ground — sometimes as much as twenty feet. To work that high up the trunk, loggers erected a scaffolding. First they incised a notch as high as they could reach. If this was not high enough, a man climbed to the notch and reached again, and again, as many times as was necessary. When they got up to where they wanted to cut, they drove iron-fortified ends of several six-foot wood planks into the trunk.These they braced with posts thrust into the ground before connecting them with loose boards. Voila! a scaffolding. Now the actual felling work could begin.

With a double-bitted ax, two choppers made the undercut on the side toward which they wanted the tree to fall. They had to make absolutely certain both sides of the undercut were equal distances from the center and that the center was in line with the direction of the fall, otherwise the tree would take an unwanted course on its way down. The undercut complete, the choppers incised a ring through the bark all the way around the tree and drove in wedges to take pressure off the saw, as well as to help direct the fall.

Now they commenced sawing through the trunk with either an eight-, ten-, twelve-, fourteen-or sixteen-foot saw. One man held one end and another held the other with a harness around it. As the cut went deeper, they kept introducing more wedges until the giant finally toppled.

After they removed all the branches and sliced the prone tree into logs, peelers came along with flattened iron bars to remove the bark. Redwood bark, like no other bark in the world, was so thick and tough and stringy that it played hell with the mill machinery.

Moving the monster logs was the next tussle. To float them down a watercourse was the easiest way, but where loggers lacked a river, they brought in teams of oxen or horses hitched to great, cumbersome trucks. Hauling with beasts was slow, and, pretty soon, somebody eyeing the problem devised a way to corrugate the road with half-buried logs laid crosswise. A major innovation, a skid road, they called it, and they began to grease it to make it work even better. Skid roads eliminated the need for trucks, and the animals were able to drag the logs, three to seven at a time, right along the ground. Everything went faster, including the incidence of serious accidents. If the wood could be made to slide more easily, men and animals would get hurt less often, so a "water packer" began dousing the road just ahead of the lead log.

The redwood kept everybody busy figuring. Every difficulty exacted headwork. A fellow up near Shelter Cove tried mounting a steam winch, like the ones used on ships, on skids. When he brought his invention to the woods, the loggers called it a donkey engine. Beginning as nothing more than an upright boiler with horizontal cylinder and gypsy drum on a horizontal shaft, the donkey engine perpetually mutated until, all up and down the coast, a wide assortment of donkey engines were hauling logs.

Yankee ingenuity accepted no dead ends. Every dilemma had its solution, every stoppage its clearup, every snag its unraveling. Logging methods improved steadily, as did milling equipment. The water wheel used to lever the vertical, single blade "muley" saw, was replaced by a steam engine. Then the saw itself was bettered by the new sash-gang saw. A circular saw, like the ones used for laths and shingles, would have been even better, but the average redwood's diameter was too great to fit under the hub of the head rig, so further brain work eventually contrived a double circular head rig with a cable-feed carriage. Two circular blades running in opposite directions, one above the other, worked twice as fast as the perpendicular muley saw. Muley, sash-gang, double circular — the line culminated in the band saw, capable of smoothly handling any size log.

Improvement followed improvement. And not only in the timber industry. Nineteenth-century America was as dogged as it was optimistic. Throughout the nation, visionary pragmatists were grappling with how to do things better, cheaper, easier, faster. While Redwood Coast determination deliberated on how to increase the diameter of circular saw blades, Great Plains determination focused on how to fence a vast open range. Urban determination focused on how to manufacture clothing faster than with two hands pulling a threaded needle and how to electrically transmit voice communications over long distances. Throughout the nation, resolute begetters sweated over their history-making brainchildren. Barbed wire, the sewing machine, the telephone, a multi-shot pistol, the incandescent lamp, the phonograph — all were invented in the United States during one forty-year stretch of the nineteenth century.

Early loggers were not conservation minded. They suffered no particular appreciation of the consequences of overharvesting. Their goal was to cut trees and sell them. But they were careful. Because the early mills, unlike mills of today, were unable to utilize any and every scrap and sliver brought in, a logger got paid only to the first break in the tree. If he ruined the tree in the felling, he didn't make much money. "The men that felled timber in those days were artists. We had one gentleman by the name of Rasmasson. Bob Rasmasson. A marvelous guy. And he was an artist. He would go out and he would make a bed for the tree. He would cut the stuff out of the way — the little brush and things that might break it you know. And he would pick the spot where he wanted to put it and he would go out and take a 2 x 4 about a hundred or a hundred and fifty feet from the base of the tree. And he would put the 2 x 4 in the ground and let it stick up about that much and he would put the tree right down and drive that 2 x 4 in the ground with the tree. I said, 'Why do you go out and put the 2 x 4 down?' 'It's my mark. I know I'm going to put it right there.' He was one exceptional chopper."[1]

And then there was the legendary Long Walker, famous in the logging and tie camps between Gualala and Point Arena. He made his own handles out of live oak and fitted them with the heaviest heads available. Even after everyone else switched to the felling saws, Long Walker wouldn't give up his ax, yet he could put down more timber than two men using the most modern tools available at the turn of the century. "He chopped all week, but never let a tree fall until Saturday afternoon, when he chopped one so that it fell...and hit the next tree, and so on," taking all the trees he had partially cut with big undercuts and small uppercuts.[2]

The internal combustion engine changed the whole show. Instead of artists honing their skills in the woods for many years, loggers became semi-trained chainsaw-toting tree reapers. The chainsaw and the Caterpillar bulldozer made a one-man logging operation possible; a one-man logging operation undermined the unit of a cooperating crew. The logger was divested, too, of his mythic dimensions, his cowboy status. Now instead of a burly guy in a red flannel shirt living in a camp with a crew of other burly guys in red flannel shirts, eating loads of flapjacks and coffee, the logger was a burly guy in a sweatshirt driving his car to work every morning, then driving home to his wife and children at night, just like a bank clerk or a carpet salesman. Woods life was gone. Esprit de corps was gone. Poetry was gone.

The comely simplicity, the prosaic splendor of a yoke of six or ten Brindle Durham oxen, fourteen hundred or more pounds each, geeing and hawing their cortege of mammoth logs, arranged largest to smallest and all followed by a twelve-foot hollowed-out fir full of equipment was supplanted by a noisy smelly bulldozer, which readily and without skids, dragged big timber across the loose bark and slippery mud of the naked forest floor, raking away the slash as it went.

The timber industry had always cut trees as fast as it could, but, in the beginning, the pace was necessarily slow. Methods were ponderous. Parts of the forest were inaccessible. Those who arrived first had taken the trees easiest to get. Steam power took more and more trees from farther and farther away.

The inventing, the quest for solutions, never slowed. By the second quarter of the 20th century the internal combustion engine was on the job. Chainsaws, logging trucks, and bulldozers were felling trees considerably faster than the forest was growing them. There was no place for a tree to hide from the dynamic duo of Caterpillar and logging truck. New technology threatened to improve the redwood industry right out of existence. Overharvesting was not the only problem. The internal combustion engine made a mess of the landscape. Logging had always been destructive. Early loggers clear cut, interfered with rivers, denuded hillsides by burning bark and slash, but their pace was moderate enough to keep damage within the bounds of remedy. Logging crews sliced roads out of the earth, but road building took so much effort that logging outfits contrived to keep road lengths at a bare minimum. The Caterpillar, though, could cut a road in two shakes of a dead bull's tail. Nothing got in its way. It moved natural barriers. It dozed away slopes, setting whole hillsides into motion. The good old D8 Cat could make a mess without even trying. It altered the very physiognomy of the ground merely moving itself from place to place. Heroic innovation had put the timber industry's future in jeopardy.

Commercial redwood was felled as early as 1840 in Santa Cruz, but most lumber used in California before 1849 had come from Oregon and Hawaii. Then, all in a stroke, the California Gold Rush whipped up a lusty attack on *Sequoia sempervirens*. Redwood shored up mines. It built the gold-driven expansion of San Francisco and rebuilt it after each of the many devastating fires. Thirty years after the California Gold Rush, the Alaska Gold Rush called on redwood again.

The railroads demanded redwood. In 1869 the last spike in the transcontinental line linking the Central Pacific to the Union Pacific was driven near Salt Lake City, Utah. Spur lines rapidly meshed far flung points on the map. A multitude of discontinuous short lines were laid, too. Wood began riding out of the forest on a rail. Railroad companies were significant consumers of Mendocino timber. They wanted redwood for ties, and not just any old redwood, either; they wanted the very best.

Mendocino railroad ties went abroad, too. Twenty years after opening his mill in Mendocino County, good old Harry Meiggs, land developer, entrepreneur, investor and builder, found himself in a financial embarrassment. After embezzling from the city of San Francisco, he fled with his family in 1854 to Chile, where he set up business building railroads. In the 70s he convinced the Peruvian government it needed a railroad through the Andes to break Peru's isolation from the rest of the South America. When all was said and done, Meiggs had constructed two railroad lines, securing for himself an immense fortune. Castigated for buying millions of feet of redwood and Douglas fir from his own California Lumber Company at Big River to make his South American ties, he swore up and down the contract bidding had been done by the rules. Although the deal looked mighty suspicious, nothing could be proven. Harry Meiggs's grandiose railroad project, which succeeded in diminishing only slightly Peru's isolation, augmented enormously Peru's national debt.

The Redwood Coast timber business was launched with a bang. Redwood went for railroad ties, building material for houses and barns and fences, shingles, curbs, gutters, siding, beams, flooring, doors, newels, columns, moldings. It was essential for wharves, piers, bridges aqueducts, flumes. Yet despite the enthusiasm, the demand for redwood began to dwindle. Transportation costs were already too high when a national financial crisis culminating in the Depression of 1893 quenched the California building boom. The market eventually recovered, but cutthroat production continued to drive prices down.

The long downward trend enjoyed occasional upward blips, such as in 1906 when San Francisco, suddenly and unexpectedly, needed to do a lot of rebuilding. After the earth had stopped shaking and the flames were put out, a survey revealed that most structures still standing were made of, or sided with, redwood. In 1906 Redwood Coast mills cut six million board feet, an all-time record, but in two years the market was sagging again.[3]

A couple of years after they built it, Stevens and Whitmore sold the Garcia Mill to R. Nickerson and S. Baker, who, in 1891, sold it again to L.E. White and Company, based a few miles north in Greenwood (now Elk). Following the Depression of 1893, L.E. White and Company converted the Garcia Mill to tie making. The market for building materials had hit bottom, but demand for railroad ties had kept on climbing, and the Garcia flume could carry twice as many ties as it could board feet of lumber. When the mill burned down in

1894, the company didn't rebuild, since tie production could easily be sustained by the tie camps all up and down the river. The company converted a skid road at Hutton Gulch to a railroad. Horses pulled empty cars up the tracks to a landing where they took on ties. Gravity, held in check by a brakeman, brought the loaded cars down to the water and off to the flume.

Alas, the reigning spirit of innovation and improvement eventually introduced the railroad companies to creosote, altering forever the railroad's relationship to redwood. Creosote-treated Douglas fir was strong and impervious to rot. When treated with creosote, soft redwood got softer, unusably softer. Obviously, creosoted Douglas fir ties would outlast redwood ties.

The last tie scudded down the Garcia in 1912. The company sold all its land as small ranches and farms. Logging in the Garcia watershed, heyday's grand shows, were reduced to modest family pursuits. Point Arena, once supported largely by timber, fell back on its farming and dairying.

After World War I, woods work picked up a little. Point Arena talks about the big post-World War I boom, but the boom doesn't look very big on paper. Those mills which held out over the years were shipping rough, green lumber to San Francisco. The post-World War I market was on the east coast, where the demand was for dry, finished lumber. The largest mills on the Redwood Coast expanded to include planing mills and drying kilns, but few small mills could afford to expand and so were forced to close or consolidate. In 1913 thirteen mills operated in Mendocino County; in 1920, nine; after the Great Depression and the longshoremen's strikes of the '30s, only three mills remained.

The longshoremen's victory was the mills' grim reaper. Before the longshoremen secured exclusive rights to the loading and unloading of schooners, the job had been done by an informal muster of sailors, mill workers, and various passersby. The expense of paying longshoremen to load lumber sunk the last of the small mills.[4]

REFERENCE NOTES

1. William Allen, *Yesterday's News* interview. WA18log.ind.
2. T. Moungovan, "Where There's A Will, There's a Way," Mendocino County Historical Society, 1968.
3. Jack McNairn and Jerry MacMullen, *Ships of the Redwood Coast*, 1945.
4. Collins interview, Melendy, unpublished dissertation.

Chapter Fourteen

THE FALLING GIANT

"Farewell my brethren,
Farewell O earth and sky, farewell ye neighboring waters,
My time has ended, my term has come."

Along the northern coast,
Just back from the rock-bound shore and the caves,
In the saline air from the sea in the Mendocino country,
With the surge for base and accompaniment low and hoarse,
With crackling blows of axes sounding musically driven by strong arms,
Riven deep by the sharp tongues of the axes, there in the redwood forest dense,
I heard the mighty tree its death-chant chanting;
The choppers heard not, the camp shanties echoed not,
The quick-ear'd teamsters and chain and jack-screw men heard not,
As the wood-spirits came from their haunts of a thousand years to join the refrain,
But in my soul I plainly heard.

Walt Whitman, "Song of the Redwood Tree"

The closing of the flume in 1912 marked the end of an era on the Garcia River. Logging never ceased altogether, but it wasn't until after the Second World War that the industry expanded to another genuine boom. A nationwide postwar demand for housing set off a jamboree. Modern timber merchants, armed with chainsaws, galloped into the Garcia watershed with a remuda of Caterpillars and logging trucks. Few mills remained in the immediate vicinity so most of the wood cut here was hauled inland for milling, depriving Point Arena of as hefty a share of the new prosperity as it had enjoyed in the halcyon days.

The upper tributaries of the Garcia were intact before the logging of the 1950s. The only roads were a few trails leading to old homesteads and ranches. Within a decade the watershed was scotched with shoddily engineered, unmaintained roads — six and a half miles of road and twenty-seven miles of skid trails for every square mile of the Garcia watershed. Roads became open wounds draining soil into the river. Landslides diverted water. Nasty gouges appeared, more and worse where the land was burned after it was logged.

Slash slid, or was dumped, into streams. Cats used the river and its tributaries as roads and skid trails. The timber industry could not have mauled the river more thoroughly if it had come in on purpose to scour, rip and generally disfigure the ground. It couldn't have played more havoc with the fishery if it had deliberately thrown up mud baffles and a fretwork of snares.

The heaviest logging of the Garcia watershed was done between 1954 and 1961. First time through, the timber companies took the best trees and left the low quality timber standing — highgrading, they call it. The U.S. was hungry for wood, so in the 1960s and 1970s the companies logged the same areas again, this time taking everything they could sell.

The watershed was brutally mangled. With few regulations and even fewer agencies to enforce them, California's timber industry was left to supervise itself until in 1973 the state legislature passed the Z'Berg-Njedly Forest Practice Act to "end resource depletion and restore the forest to maximum sustained productivity." A Board of Forestry was appointed to make rules based on the act, and the California Department of Forestry was in charge of implementing those rules. Yet twenty-five years later Mendocino County's timber continues to be harvested two to three times faster than it grows.

The West has never taken well to regulation. In the nineteenth century, citizens began to settle well in advance of officially sanctioned procedures for laying claim to a homestead. Settlers on the Redwood Coast had no choice but to begin as squatters; it was impossible, legally, to buy land not yet surveyed. In the words of one historian, the West was "settled before it was discovered."

The survey took a long time. Before it was completed, the common practice of the timber industry on the Mendocino Coast was to locate a stand of trees, log it, and move on. Technically, both surveyed and unsurveyed land not held by the state or private grant holders, was the property of the federal government. While Washington diddled with how best to dispose of its seemingly endless acreage, timber, in effect, was free to anybody who wanted to take it.

In late 1869 the area surrounding the Garcia River finally was surveyed and officially opened for settlement. By then the Homestead Act was in place allowing a citizen, after living on the land and cultivating it for five years, to file for title to 160 acres. Homesteaders complained about the long "proving up" time, so Congress added to the Homestead Act, a clause allowing purchase in a mere six months. This "commutation clause" aided homesteaders but simultaneously made it easy for the lumber companies to carry on as before.

Moreover, the Homestead Act was designed for east coast agriculture. Pacific Northwest land, even cleared, was unfit for farming. In 1873 Congress passed the Timber Culture Act giving a homesteader the chance to add 160 acres to an existing claim by agreeing to grow trees on 40 of the new acres. This new legislation, even revised, redrafted, reworked, rewritten, reorganized, revamped and amended, didn't protect forestland from speculators.

The laws were easy to exploit, but the ideal persisted: the independent logger was to be the counterpart of the happy, hardworking, democratic farmer. Together they would form the backbone of a Great Nation. To that end the Timber and Stone Act was passed giving any U.S. citizens living in a West Coast state the right to buy, for personal use only, 160 acres of timberland at $2.50 per acre. Logging companies simply hired people to buy timberland, then turn the deeds over to the company. Sometimes an unscrupulous lumber merchant hired "cruisers" to determine the value of heavily timbered tracts. Then he put out word he was prepared to buy this or that subdivision from anybody able acquire it under the Timber and Stone Act. Companies were known to bring in shiploads of their own employees, furnished with the necessary funds, to get the land they wanted. Three quarters of the transactions made under the Timber and Stone Act were fraudulent. Worse still, though fraudulent titles were easy enough to come by, some timber companies didn't even try to look legal; they just set up shop and began to slaughter trees, moving on as soon as they were done.

Rapacity was not the only cause of land-deal tomfoolery. The redwood tree itself complicated matters. The redwood was mighty big — 490,000 board feet of lumber in a single tree. And these giants lived on a taxing terrain. Alone, a logger had trouble getting his timber to market. Legislators Back East did not fully grasp the situation Out West. Their hopes for a quota of firmly entrenched, independent loggers was quixotic. They failed to see that large, well organized crews were needed to harvest, move, and mill the redwoods.

Nor did the lawmakers tumble to the fact that 160 acres was a woefully undersized holding for a logging operation. Small plots were subject to such banes of nature as fire and disease. And nobody was going to go to the trouble and expense of setting up a logging operation and establishing a mill without several years' supply of timber to work on.

Timber and Stone Act remained on the books. Congress tried to curtail fraud by repealing the early Preemption Act and by amending the Homestead Act to make sure claimants lived on and cultivated their land for no less than

14 months before gaining title to it. The means to these reforms, the General Revision Act, passed in 1891, were established the same year Congress passed the Federal Reserve Act to protect forests by taking them off the public land rolls. As usual, neither law did much to change logging habits in Mendocino County.

> "1893 - less than 5% of Mendocino County timberland had been cut over
> 1906 - 20%
> 1912 - 32% (1,085,886 acres)
> 1976 - 92% of all virgin timber had been logged."[1]

Even as early as the 1920s lumbermen could see the supply of redwoods was running low. Little old growth remained, what with clearcutting and genetic degradation from highgrading, and second growth timber didn't look too promising either. Worried companies started planting seedlings, but they were too little and too late. The supply of redwoods — the supply of all coniferous timber in the region — was bankrupt.

One winter day in 1910, Thomas Moungovan stood beside the rain-swollen Garcia River talking business with the company superintendent. To young Moungovan the land looked like a field of grain spreading out from Chute Hill. The biggest tree on the hill grew at a tilt, and had done so for as long as anybody at the mill could remember. Today, though, Moungovan thought the angle looked different. He kept up his end of the palaver, but his eye kept returning to the giant tree. Finally he interrupted the superintendent to ask if the tree's slant seemed awry to him. The older man advised him, "If you watch any one object in the woods long enough, Tom, your imagination runs away with you and even the trees move." Unconvinced, Moungovan was sighting it on two other trees when abruptly, from the ground beneath his feet, he felt a heavy, dull thud. To their horror the two men saw the earth in front of them opening up. Moungovan shouted, "If ever you made a desperate attempt to run for safety, you better double it now." By the time they got to the fissure, it was five feet wide. They jumped. When they looked back, the spreading gap was nearly twenty feet across. They could see the tree falling over now, and realized the thud had been the sound of its root parting deep down in the earth. Slowly, slowly the giant toppled until finally, with a great cascade of soil and rock, it crashed into the river creating a mighty upstream wave, then it was traveling downstream at a pace faster than the two men had thought possible. "That tree's moving as fast as a man can walk," the supervisor said. "We'd better step on it or we'll never get over the tie flume catwalk before the roots on that monster take it out."

Again they began to sprint. They had to cross the flooded river on a springy Douglas fir somebody had laid there years before. The crossing was a slow, single file affair during which the two men watched the redwood giant, patulous limbs and roots splayed every whichaway, gaining on them. Then on they ran toward the tie flume.

"We won't make it any farther than halfway across the catwalk," Moungovan said, but the superintendent pressed on, faster and faster.[2] With the giant well in the lead, they still had about a thousand feet to go when, when suddenly and unexpectedly, the tree rolled onto its side and, slipping into a deep pool, passed safely just beneath the flume. Then it rolled back into its former position and kept on going. Thomas Moungovan was enormously relieved, and for the rest of his days, he pondered the mystery of why that tree so conveniently turned at that particular spot.

Without meaning to, Moungovan and his colleagues at the L.E. White Company played merry hell with the river. They were merely trying to wrest a good living from the woods, but by 1900 the volume of water was so low they had to bring in a booster donkey to aid the water wheel. The mill dam and the temporary splash dams were blocking fish migration. Logging practices were making hash of the ground. Soil washed into the river and its tributaries, choking salmonid spawning grounds. One winter the pond behind the mill dam at Buckridge was so full of silt that mill workers had to add temporary summer dams to keep the logs afloat.

But the nineteenth-century entrepreneurs were innocent because they were ignorant; they did not recognize the long-term consequences of what they were doing. Products of their age, they acted, for better or worse, on what they believed. And who's to say what we would have done had we been there ourselves. With no notion of what we don't know, we, if we be honorable, behave honorably only in the context of what we do know.

"Gone," laments Moungovan, "gone is the most beautiful timber of the Garcia river basin, the redwood. Gone, also, are the sugar pines, the only ones that grew near the coast…They were as large and as tall as any sugar pines that have ever been known.

"Silent are the saws, axes, and the cry of 'timber' on the Garcia, but the memories still linger in the minds of those who remember the flying logs of Chute Hill, the ties scurrying down the flume to Rollerville, and the ships loading from the long wire chute in Arena Cove."[3]

Late in his life, he bemoans the loss of the trees. I want to say: "Dammit all to hell, Tom. You and your cronies are the ones who took them all away!" But scrutinizing his sentiments more closely, I realize Moungovan regrets the loss of the trees not merely for themselves, for their coniferous splendor, but also for what he has to give up. He can never again go out there and cut them down. He misses the old logging days. His sorrow isn't for what he did, but for the fact that those days are over.

It is easy in 1998 to predict the future for 1898. A hundred years from now it will be easy for our successors to call us idiots or villains. We act according to what we believe to be true. Today's responsible citizens cannot behave as those guys did. Seeking a fortune, or making a living, is no longer a free-for-all. For better or worse, it has become struggle among disciplined forces. As I write, my husband sits in a florescent-lit office at the California Department of Forestry, combing through timber harvest plans, one by one, gleaning information for a legal action he hopes will save trees. He acts according to his idea of a responsible citizen. Yet — may the archdruids forgive him — I bet he'd rather be outdoors beside a roiling river, huffing and puffing with two astonished men trying to outrace the falling giant.

REFERENCE NOTES

1. H.H. Markham, *Resources of California*, (Sacramento: State Printing Office, 1893) pp. 39-40; California State Board of Forestry, Fourth Biennial Report, 1912, p. 17; Anthrop Donald F. Redwood National and State Parks. Happy Camp CA; Naturgraph Publisher, Inc. 1977.

2. Tale of the leaning giant from "Where There's A Will, There's A Way," Monograph #2 in a series on Logging in Mendocino Count by Thomas Moungovan, Julia Moungovan, Nanie Escola; copyrighted 1968 by the Mendocino County Historical Society

3. Thomas Moungovan, Julia Moungovan, Nanie Escola, "Where There's A Will, There's A Way," Monograph #2 in a series on Logging in Mendocino County; copyrighted 1968 by the Mendocino County Historical Society.

Chapter Fifteen

ACRONYMS

Raise the question of water use, and the situation resembles an old-fashioned showdown, but with the rivals converging from ten different directions instead of the more traditional two.

Patricia Nelson Limerick, *Legacy Of Conquest*

After a wholly satisfying baked, grilled, scrambled, and toasted breakfast, we walked up the river from Oz to the Connor Hole. The hydrologist Graham Matthews drove his truck loaded with tool boxes, meters, cables, wood posts, rebar, twenty-foot lengths of galvanized pipe, surveying equipment, hammers, shovels, a post-hole digger, a sledge hammer, and a hefty metal box. The rest of us, his seven votaries, full of enthusiasm and strong coffee, marched up to where he ran out of dirt road and began to unload. With more zeal than prudence, we bucked and lugged the quarter mile through the redwoods, over downed logs, around a stump, across a soggy hole back to the river. We dumped armloads full of paraphernalia at the work site, then trudged back for more. Back and forth, single file, like a column of army ants passing one another in a loop. Graham supervised, but he couldn't be everywhere at once and before he noticed it, we had completely emptied the pickup, stripped it of everything — his personal gear, his tools for other jobs, extra channel iron. So, while Peter Dobbins and Peter Reimuller surveyed for the first of the three staff gauges and Alan and Eric began to dig a hole for the pressure transducer, a trio of us carted the unwanted overmuchness back to the truck. I, small but determined, had singlehandedly transported the heaviest section of channel iron down the hill. Now I had to haul it back up. (Before the day was over, Graham decided we needed this particular chunk of metal after all, and, since I was so well acquainted with it, I got to schlep it down again.)

"A continuous record of information about the river is the basic tool for making any long term assessments," Graham had told us at breakfast.

The Friends of the Garcia, FrOG, was establishing two continuous stream height — "stage" is what hydrologists call stream height — and temperature monitoring stations on the lower Garcia and planned to add a third one later. Each station would include one BDR320-B 4-channel data logger, one Keller Series-169 5psi pressure transducer, one 107B-L50 temperature probe, plus two or three staff gauges to measure the river's height.

The first monitoring station was set up at Connor Hole. "A hell of a hole. A long, long hole that had a lot of depth to it. A hundred yards long. The flow came from the east there and had to turn sharp towards the ocean and that kept rooting the hole out. Ten to twelve feet deep. Always a good fishing hole," Don Stuart told Nick King, and Nick heard the same thing from all the other old-timers he interviewed.[1] Connor Hole once ranked high on a river chock-full of first-rate fishing holes: Bishop Hole, Mitchell Hole, Miner Hole, Summer Crossing Hole, Indian Hole, Redwood Hole…the list goes on.

"After the first rains in the fall, those salmon would be going up by the dozens … you know … on the riffles. They'd hang out in the holes during the day and would move on up the next night… and so forth. And there was fish in every one of these holes … you know, 15 to 20 fish in every hole," Vern Kendall had said.[1] Large coho salmon, an occasional chinook, as well as an abundance of steelhead trout, so many fish it didn't really matter where you went or how you fished — lines, spears, traps — you were bound to come home with a good catch.

By the seventies the numbers of fish had definitely declined. Chinook, or king salmon, vanished first, along with chum and pink salmon. The fishery went down fast until the anadromous fish population was all but nonexistent and the sighting of even one coho salmon was big news. Everybody agreed the problem was spawning habitat — the river was no longer deep, dark and cold with lots of places to hide — but no one agreed about why the water was muddy and warm, or why the gravel was choked with silt. Fishermen, farmers, ranchers, environmentalists, the timber industry, gravel miners, recreational boater, hikers — diverse claims with a stake in this fragile coastal stream, loudly debated the cause of the spoiled spawning habitat.

Our river is in trouble, but not yet past hope, and much of the community is determined to protect and restore it. FrOG — "your local environmental watchdog along the river," (confounded taxonomies all the way back to sub-phyla, but no one but me seems to care) managed, through John Hooper's influence, to persuade a private foundation to fund a monitoring program. The gauging station at Connor Hole in September 1992 was the first step in a fairly ambitious project.

A sunny Sunday, a calm clear day for the FrOG-marshaled crew to work in the wet shade of a redwood grove. Connor Hole was once a USGS site, so Peter Dobbins used the old USGS marker on the opposite bank to survey for the staff gauges. "Down … down …" looking through the dumpy level, he instructed Peter Reimuller, who was planting the staff gauge. "Down … ooops. Up. Uuup. Okay, down about a millimeter … gentle it down with the top of the sledge."

Eric sat on the damp ground unpacking a growing heap of apparatus. He would pick up an item, look it over, scratch his head, then leaf through one of the numerous manuals. When he saw me watching him he grinned and said, "Some assembly required."

The data logger was set in a custom-welded steel box we mounted high on a large tree trunk. After doing that, we took turns digging in the river, deepening the hole where the pressure transducer and the temperature probe were to be sunk. When they judged it deep enough, Alan, Leslie and Eric ran a pipe from the pressure transducer to the data logger, then spent the next hour feeding wires through the pipe, inch by inch.

A pressure transducer ascertains stream height — stage — by measuring the amount of water above it. To gauge the velocity someone will have to come down to the river several times a year with a velocity meter, carry it out into the river and, from several carefully spaced points, measure the flow. The water moves in varying rates across the river. By gauging velocity from a series of spots, we'll get a cross section of the flow. Someone, also, will have to visit each of the data loggers to download the computer's stored information.

Late afternoon found me on my knees in the damp humus beside a young man I'd never laid eyes on before breakfast at Oz, a junior-college student who wanted to become a fishery biologist. The two of us faced an upright spear of channel iron. In identical positions across from us, knelt the two Peters. Tired and cold, we had run into a minor but frustrating problem. Pondering, muttering, we circled the channel. Graham saw us and walked over.

"How many white men does it take to plant a Style C staff gauge?" he asked, laughing.

"Don't know," said Peter R, not laughing. "We haven't figured it out yet."

Within the next couple of days FrOG discovered it had committed an expensive goof when it bought the 107B-L50 temperature probe. Misled by the (perfidious!) claims of a salesman. The monitoring station had to turn all four of the data logger's channels over to the press-trans, and FrOG had to spend more of its precious grant on a different sort of temperature probe from another company. But other than that, the kickoff was a success, and in the ensuing months FrOG installed two more stage stations and inserted twenty-five little "Hobo" temperature probes into the river, up and down the mainstem, as well as certain tributaries.

FrOG is gleaning worlds of hydrologic information and FrOG likes to share. Anyone who asks — even logging companies and gravel miners — is welcome to facts and figures. Last fall the National Oceanic and Atmospheric Administration asked to attach a modem to the Eureka Hill Bridge data logger, the only one of the FrOG stations with a rain gauge. Now, by telephone, the federal agency collects information to help it predict flooding.

FrOG, started in 1989, was spawned by Nick King three years earlier when some friends of his learned Bill Hay had applied for a permit to mine gravel in the river near their Buckridge Road home. Worried about what a gravel plant would do to their quiet existence, they lobbied against the permit. Nick, who lived up river from the proposed gravel mine, was a great friend of the river and, if not a great friend of Billy's, was at least on friendly terms with him. They shared a constitutional distaste for bureaucrats. "Hippie and red neck," said Nick, "we'd sit around and plot about how to keep the agencies out of here so locals could control the river." Having as little stomach for nasty or protracted wars as for agencies, Nick went straight to Billy and asked him what his plans were. Billy insisted the thing was going to be small, run at a loss, most likely, just a little something to leave his sons. Nick thought maybe it was a good idea to get some of the gravel out of the river. Moreover, he liked the way Billy did things — the jobs always looked tidy. Although Nick recognized, even admired, Billy's brash ambitiousness, he took at face value Bill's vow to keep the mining operation small, and ultimately went to bat for the permit. As soon as his Bed Rock, Inc., was legally settled on the river, Billy, as Nick puts it, "started grabbing." He tried to expand his permit — make official what he was already doing. The business was getting out of hand, and, feeling responsible for the mess, Nick canvassed the neighborhood and found a number of people willing to fight against the new permit. To raise money for legal action, he formed a group and formalized it with a name: Friends of the Garcia=FrOG. "I had no particular vision," said Nick, "but I had a verity, an unassailable truth. It was simply this: you can't just go in and screw up a river."

During the time Nick and Billy were still buddies, conspiring against the mandarins, Billy let Nick photograph his gravel plant and mining sites. When the two locked horns, Nick refused to use the photographs to further FrOG's cause. He was pissed, but not pissed enough to betray a trust. He still believed things would get fixed. The row would end and FrOG would pass from existence along with any lingering rancor. Everybody would gather for a big farewell-to-FrOG barbecue, Billy and litigants sitting side by side on the picnic benches.

Billy, too, figured FrOG's life would be short and toothless. A stubborn and wealthy man, Bill Hay was not used to things getting in his way.

"The fish're gone because their spawning areas got all messed up."

"They're gone because of overfishing."

"It's the goddamn otters. Used to be not so many, and now they're taking over, the voracious little sons of bitches."

"It's the mergansers and blue herons … "

"It's the sea lions and seals at the river mouth …"

"It's the drought. Nothing but the drought. Leave things alone. Soon as it rains the river will be the same as it used to be."

"Too much rock in the river. All that gravel is an industrial spill from logging practices of a hundred years ago."

"The river's so choked with gravel the fish can't get up to spawn. Our big problem is we got a lot of people who think they're ecologists telling us not to clear up the mess — that is, take the gravel out."

"Too much gravel? Maybe yes, maybe no," said FrOG. "But Gravel mining doesn't dig gravel from the bottom of the river. It skims it off the bars, and without bars, a river loses its curves and stops cutting the deep holes necessary for spawning."

Armed with facts and figures, FrOG had no doubt about where to put the blame: "The damage is caused by decades of intensive logging and, more recently, instream gravel mining." Logging takes away the shade, leaving water too warm for salmon eggs. Logging cuts roads, roads mean erosion, and erosion means sediment which smothers the eggs. Gravel mining eats up the bars and the riparian growth that anchors the bars, keeping them from washing away.

Nick King is no longer a FrOG. Not an active one. "Overdose, burnout, whatever you want to call it. One day I just knew, 'That's it. I'm finished.'" He's annoyed with FrOG for opening the door to the agencies. "Now you can't spit in the river without a permit."

When FrOG emerged to take on the mighty Bed Rock, Inc., it came up against another, more formidable foe: the timber industry. At the time of FrOG's lawsuit, California Department of Forestry had just okayed a timber harvest plan in a woefully overcut section of the Garcia's North Fork. California Regional Water Quality Control Board criticized the plan: "Prior to current timber harvest rules, this area was tractor logged without regard to stream protection, road and landing stabilization, etc. As a result there are still slides and other wounds that bleed sediment into the North Fork and its tributaries …. When evaluated independently, THP 1-89-105 MEN is not considered to present a significant environmental threat. However, when we consider that the THP is the tenth plan to be submitted on this watershed in the last ten or eleven months and recognize that the previous nine adopted plans cover 72% of the watershed then this plan becomes a potentially serious problem."

Despite advice to the contrary, CDF approved R&J Timber's plan, and Nick King prepared FrOG to sue CDF and the timber company. Unlike the gravel lawsuit, the timber suit was resolved out of court. Nick worked with the timber company's watershed consultant — "a real good guy," says Nick, "a hippie just like me" — to draft a settlement. They determined to bring all sides together. Monitoring. Mitigation. Much optimism.

"A specialist shall be employed by R&J for the purpose of preparing a comprehensive watershed restoration plan for the Garcia River system…. Both R&J Timber and FrOG agree to cooperate in seeking funding for implementation of said plan from private and public funding sources." From the settlement of the THP-1-89-105 lawsuit, something new sprang, fully formed like Athena from the head of Zeus: the Watershed Advisory Group (WAG).

"If it's not WAG, it's subject to an EIR. And anything that hasn't got a neg. dec. is gonna have to come up with an EIR because I'm just not comfortable with big holes being dug all up and down the river…. Plant. CDF loves planting… I know, I know. The RCD knew about it, but nobody else. SCS wasn't even notified. Craig doesn't like public input. Everybody in FrOG is thoroughly pissed. WAG is a public entity funded with public funds. FrOG should have been notified."

Compliments of the telephone, I share my breakfast with a lot of demi-conversations, which would be bad enough if the conversations were conducted in a language I understood instead of a cryptic alphabet soup dialect. For Friends of the Garcia you say FrOG, National Oceanic Atmospheric Administration becomes Noah, the acronym for Sierra Club Legal Defense Fund sounds something like "skull death." Surprisingly, though, MOU, memorandum of understanding remains M.O.U. rather than moue, as in "the consulting fisheries biologist made a little moue of displeasure."

The alphabet soup bubbles and swells with new additions. For a while it was the WAG that kept tongues wagging. Funds for the WAG came from the Mendocino County Resource Conservation District, the RCD, which assists private landowners and government agencies with voluntary soil and water conservation projects. The RCD is administered by property owners appointed by the County Board of Supervisors and staffed with employees paid by SCS, i.e., the federal Soil Conservation Service.

In 1990 the California Coastal Conservancy granted the WAG funds to gather information and develop a resource enhancement plan for the Garcia River Watershed. The RCD massed a small delegation representing every conceivable interest on the river: agriculture, commercial fishing, gravel mining, the timber industry, sports fishing, the Pomo ranchería, the environmentalists. Participants from interested agencies joined the local membership: County Water Agency, Soil Conservation Service, Department of Fish and Game, the California Coastal Conservancy, North Coast Regional Water Quality Control Board, the Bureau of Indian Affairs, a Farm Advisor, a member of the RCD, a watershed consultant (the lawsuit specialist who was to be "employed for the purpose of preparing a comprehensive watershed restoration plan for the Garcia River system….") and a paid project manager. The WAG would treat everyone with equal consideration while devising a plan that could be collectively supported and easily understood by everyone — even those who had not acquired acronym as a second language.

Debra Caldon grew up on a ranch, went to law school, then decided she was not cut out to be a lawyer and declined to take the bar exam. Instead she went back to the university to be schooled in forestry and watershed management. After working for the EPA for seven years, she took a position with a private consulting firm. Intelligent, educated, experienced, worldly wise, dynamic, attractive and every inch the professional, Debra was, nevertheless, unprepared for what awaited her in Point Arena when she came up from Berkeley to act as project manager of the WAG.

Her first surprise was the sheer numbers of her watershed roundup. The WAG membership included twelve voting members and fifteen or so advisory participants, but the public was invited as well. Debra scheduled the first meeting for 7:30, July 30, 1991, at the Coast Community Library in Point Arena. By 7:00 the place was full. By 7:15 it was more than full, and people continued to come. Debra watched all these people crowd into her orderly, businesslike meeting and wondered what she had gotten herself into. And the size of the assembly wasn't her biggest surprise. The bushwhacked zeal — raw, factionalized, unencumbered by the restrictions of decorum — threw her for a loop.

"At least nobody was armed." she said at breakfast, joking. But instead of laughing, I told her Pete Giannini always attended City Council meetings with a .38 in his belt. Her eyes got bigger but kept on laughing. In fact she never lost her good humor throughout her series of missions to her Mendocino Coast outpost, which she came to enjoy as one enjoys a chunky, inelegant novel. After the first night, she changed the meeting place to the spacious VFW Hall, and she started them an hour earlier, but she never did manage to get her mob under control.

Billy tried to pack that first meeting. He rallied a cohort of toughs who owed him allegiance for one reason or another. They came, expecting I don't know what, but by the time the protracted debate about the cobble-embeddedness on the North Fork segued into a detailed report on fish disease, Bill's henchman were yawning and twitching in their seats. At the break most left, one passing close to Alan to whisper, "Better watch out cuz I'm gonna break both of your legs one of these days."

Part of the reason Billy was so bent out of shape was his problem with the city. Point Arena was working on its General Plan which involved some of the same issues and a number of the same players as the river project. Billy monopolized the second WAG meeting with complaints about "certain letters," written to the City Council in opposition to his gravel plant. Whenever there was a lull in the discussion, he waved a fistful of them at Debra. "Letters! Some of them are from members of WAG!" Debra maneuvered him onto the topic of habitat typing. John Hooper, who had the floor, said, "We'll need to be on Hay property…" and before he could get any farther, Billy was on his feet.

"No. No, no, no! If the truth is not going to be told then I can't cooperate. There have been letters!"

Alan said, "Billy, you've been going on about those letters all night. Waving them around. Poring over them. I bet you take 'em with you to the toilet. Read 'em over and over and over. You're gonna get hemorrhoids from those letters."

"I want assurance that there will be no more letters," Billy's voice rose two octaves.

"But those letters are about the City of Point Arena not WAG. This meeting is not a forum for City problems."

Debra called that night "memorable." The full taped transcript of the meeting ran to twenty-seven single-spaced typewritten pages. Debra, eliminating some of the diatribes, most of the cussing, and all of the scatological references, managed to transcribe the minutes in seventeen pages. Before the next meeting, she drafted a list of Ground Rules, and made everyone sign them.

Give the same priority to solving the concerns of others, including the public's concerns, as you will your own:

1. Make a commitment to listen carefully; ask questions to understand others and make statements that explain or educate.
2. Make a commitment to search for opportunities: we'll need creative solutions to make the process work.
3. State needs, problems, opportunities, not positions. Work on positive approaches to concerns raised.
4. Commit to achieving consent (consensus?) on the plan.
5. Commit to be an advocate for the agreed upon plan.
6. Attempt to protect each other and the process politically with your constituencies and the general public.
7. Weapons of war and any previous disagreements are to be left at the door on the way into our meeting.
8. Anyone may leave the process and the above ground rules, but only after telling the group why and allowing the WAG the chance to solve the problem.
9. All communications with the news media concerning these discussions will be by agreement of the group. Everyone will be mindful

of the impacts their public and private statements will have on the perceptions of the effort.

10. No WAG member will attribute suggestions, comments or ideas of another member to the news media or non-participants.
11. WAG members are encouraged to seek the best advice from people who are not in the room.
12. All of the members accept the responsibility to keep their friends, associates and constituents informed of the progress of the discussions.
13. Check rumors with facilitation team prior to acting.

"Who will be using this river in ten or fifteen years?"

"What kind of river are we going to get? Man designed and controlled?"

"The watershed is one of our most valuable assets — restore its health and diversity. Fish are an indicator."

"I'm worried that WAG will get in my way for logging at the headwaters."

"Will this study come back to haunt me?"

"It took eight years to get your program on the Mattole River off the ground. In eight years there won't be any fish left in the Garcia."

Small things, details. Every worry, every need, every consideration had to be probed, pierced and weighed. Meeting after meeting probing and weighing set off swirls and eddies which, in turn, brought up further considerations, and further conflicts, strife, tugs-of-war, clashes, skirmishes: "We need to concentrate on the estuary…."

"I am disappointed that we're dealing with only the lower seven miles."

WAG monthly meetings dragged on into the night so that returning to Berkeley afterwards would have been a real torture, so she slept over at our house. Alan always made breakfast for her. I ate, quiet as a mouse, reading my morning paper and listening to them rehash the previous night's doings.

"I thought Billy was going to blow a head gasket."

"Then Hooper stood up and said, 'The Mendocino County Water Agency is a fine institute!' He sounded like a southern gentleman defending a lady's honor, didn't he?"

"Do you think he'll get rid of Dennis?"

"Probably. The RCD thinks the whole project will be a bust if it loses without all the major players. If Bill threatens to quit…"

"But he will. He does. He threatens to quit whenever he's not getting his way… to hold us all over a barrel."

Billy had risen on his hind legs and accused the Water Agency of bias. Alan asked what he meant by that, provoking Billy to shout, "FrOG! The Water Agency representatives here are influenced by FrOG!"

Meeting after meeting Billy banged away at Jackson, attacking the validity of his reports.

"This Water Agency guy here says no gravel comes down the river. Let's see the studies…. We haven't seen any cross sections, not a single one…"

And later: "At the last Board of Supervisors meeting Jackson said he wanted me to put gravel back in the river!"

As exasperating as Bill was, there were times it was hard not to commiserate. Toward the end of one meeting a consulting fisheries biologist said that along the lower mainstream he had found a couple of small projects that could be undertaken by a few volunteers. "I have a couple of sites — one downstream of the Ishizaki Bar. Another is on Bed Rock above the trench where you restored a hole. If this log and root wad can be turned and cabled to the bank it would provide better protection than its current location…"

"Can we stop right there?" Bill's tenor voice sometimes sounds as though he's on the verge of tears. "Can we just stop right there? I took a lot of time and a lot of money to do that excavation. The Department of Fish and Game made me leave that log in that position. Who do I listen to? The Department of Fish and Game, the county Water Agency, or who?"

Full meetings, committee meetings. Amassing facts and figures: documents, field studies, interviews, statistics. Calculations. The process chugged on, always uphill. The threat of derailment present to the very end.

R&J Timber attorney, "Let the hydrologist on your land and it comes back to kick you. Why get involved in the project?"

Hooper, property owner, "With the $100,000 grant money from the Coastal Conservancy and the $70,000 from EPA, maybe we can interest some foundations."

Hay, “How much money has been spent already?”

Baxman Gravel, “I don’t like grants. Success depends on volunteer commitment.”

Craig Bell, fishing guide, “What about the finding regarding the introduction of exotic species?

Hay, “Does he mean cows?”

General laughter. Billy made a little joke, breaking the tension for an agreeable moment.

One year and three months after the WAG held its first meeting, the Garcia River Watershed Enhancement Plan was completed, a thorough and useful report. On the cover — a photograph of five fishermen holding a string of salmon; inside — history, methodology, findings, enhancement recommendations, monitoring needs, maintenance requirements, maps, graphs, figure, and five appendices. Improvement of salmonid habitat, stream restoration, and estuary enhancement and protection — the report stated all the goals, goals developed and agreed upon by members of the WAG “using a consensus approach.” *A consensus approach* — sounds so simple, so tidy.

REFERENCE NOTES

1. GRV Enterprises. To supplement the scanty information about the historic state of the river, Jack Monschske, the Watershed Management consultant, and Nick King, as GRV Enterprises, interviewed sixteen local residents.

Chapter Sixteen

WILD, WILD WEST: BILLY

Bill Hay was born and raised in Point Arena, but the old-timers don't consider him to be one of them. He wasn't particularly popular in high school, and I've heard his family got a jump start on their financial prosperity by rustling livestock. Whether or not this is true, Bill Hay is now a wealthy man, used to having his own way.

He owns a vast amount of property. Well-stocked ranch land, scattered tracts of real estate he is always trying develop for sale, Point Arena Waterworks, and Bed Rock, Inc. Gravel and Cement.

He also owns a fleet of gorgeous trucks that he keeps in sparkling condition. Alan drools over Bill's trucks. The Hay crew always wins a lot of the prizes given at the Annual Big Truck Show Down. Last year five of his drivers took home the gold — Paul Moore in the #91 Cement Bulk Trailer Truck, Bill's two sons in the #90 Transfer Truck and the #17 End-Up Dump Truck, and two other drivers in the #18 Service Trailer and the #88 Transfer trucks. Plus, in the "Convoy of Lights" Bed Rock took Best-of-Show.

In his early fifties, a short man, decidedly round in frame, Bill Hay is cocky, very cocky. Even the way he combs his hair is roosterish. Worse than anybody I've ever met, he hates to hear No. People speculate about why. Some say it's because he was a spoiled only child. Others insist it's because his parents were too hard on him. Whatever the reason, the man is like a rat terrier. When he grabs hold of a thing, he won't turn loose, not for anything. His fatal flaw, though, is he'd rather shred his opponent than end up with the prize, a characteristic which is playing hell with his business interests.

March 8, 1985. It is between 6 and 6:30 in the morning. The whole family is still in bed, sleeping the righteous sleep of the self-sufficient when, BAM! Doors yield to the violence of a gang of armed men, heavily armed, men. They burst into the house, violate the privacy of the bedrooms, shove a gun into each sleeping face. Karen Jewel, dark, plump, freckle-cheeked mother of the family begins to shriek. She thinks the communists have fallen upon them. But no. The terrible intruders have been dispatched by their own side, the good guys, the heroes. They represent the law.

Facing into the muzzles of loaded firearms, the Hays, all four of them — Bill, Karen, fourteen-year-old Bob, seventeen-year-old Dick — feel confused, terrified. At least one of them needs, but isn't allowed, to use the bathroom.

When they have the place "secured," the SWAT team departs, running in the second string: California Bureau of Narcotics Enforcement agents, Mendocino County Sheriff's deputies, Sonoma County Sheriff's Narcotics officers, Santa Rosa Police Narcotic investigators, U.S. Customs officials, and one Labrador retriever.

What the hell is going on here? Don't these guys realize they have stormed the home of a law-and-order man? A born-and-raised in Point Arena businessman fully equipped with a fleet of perfect trucks? Has the world gone bonkers? Special BNE agent Smith shows Bill the lawfully judge-signed warrant authorizing a search for, "Marijuana, marijuana debris, marijuana residue, and paraphernalia related to the use and sale of marijuana, consisting in part of and including, but not limited to, pipes, sifters, scales and other weighing devices, baggies, bale wire, plastic sheets, and; cocaine, cocaine residue and paraphernalia related to the use and sale of cocaine, consisting in part of and including, but not limited to, scales and other weighing devices, paper bindles, measuring devices, diluents and cutting agents, plastic bags, wooden storage boxes, and other containers commonly associated with the storage of cocaine, consisting in part of and including, but not limited to, U.S. currency, buyer lists, seller lists, inventory lists, recordation of sales… etc., etc., etc."

After the Hays have been "identified," as agent Smith later put it — though who these four people in their pajamas could have been if not the Hays is hard to imagine — the family is "allowed to move about while the search progressed." During this phase of the adventure Karen, looking anxiously out the window, sees a representative of the law simulating intercourse with the life-sized plaster deer in her front yard. She feels the urge to vomit. Her sense of security, or rather her lack of it, is not improved by the fact that her husband, separated from the rest of them now, is in a room alone with these brutes, who are doing who-knows-what to him. Not only must each family member suffer anxiety about his or her own safety, but each is also bedeviled by fears for the others.

Bill is interrogated. "Mr. Hay, you'd just as well open up. We don't suspect you of concealing contraband on these premises; we know for a fact that is the case. It will be better for you to tell us about it."

Harried and tormented, Bill nevertheless keeps on insisting he has no idea what Smith is talking about. Finally Smith lets him return to the bosom of his family, but pretty soon they drag him off again. Over and over.

"Don't lie to me, Hay! We know all about it. We've found them. We've found the drugs. You'd better tell us all you know."

For a good eight hours the ranch swarms with strangers who grub and scour the prim, white ranch with its plaster deer on the lawn, its painted lions at the gate. Possessions are strewn and scattered. It is going to cost the Hays seven hundred fifty dollars to get someone to clean up the mess later on. Every vehicle, every piece of equipment is moved. Every shed, storage room and barn is searched. Yet the big frisk turns up nothing, absolutely nothing.

"Sorry, Smith. We can't find anything — no narcotics or evidence of narcotics. Nada." (Not even any baggies or baling wire?)

Now it's Special Agent Smith who is anxious. What the hell is going on? He has it on the authority of a damned good informer, an informer who has always been right. In the past thirty-six months this guy has led authorities to seven successful drug busts. Fifteen arrests, for god's sake. And this informer, this reliable informer, has positively identified the Hay Ranch as the place where he saw 2′x2′x4′ bales of marijuana stacked ten feet high, and fifteen or so 2′x2½′x3½′ wooden crates full of cocaine packaged in plastic bags a half kilo to the bag. Everything was marked:

CUSCO 1

MACHU PICCHU

and stowed in an underground room beneath the floor of a white and blue barn type structure guarded by armed Latinos with more armed Latinos lined up along the access road. He described the property: Big spread, white house with blue trim, fruit trees before and behind, an air strip with a wind sock, a truck with a bull's head decal on door. It was only five days ago he had said all this.

He hadn't known where he was, had thought he was in Sonoma County, as a matter of fact. A couple of days later, on March 6, the authorities had taken him for a drive. As soon as they got to the H Bar H Ranch, the informer said, "This is it. This is the place."

"Are you sure?"

"Si."

Now a disappointed Smith looks around. No wind sock, but what the hell. No fruit trees in front of the house either, which, by the way, is trimmed in green rather than blue, but this guy, the informant — a very reliable informant — identified the place easily, without any coaxing or prior info. Sitting in a car parked on the highway, the authorities confronted him with various discrepancies in his details, but he was quick to point out as many points of recognition.

Well, hell, decides Smith, I'd better bring the informant in here now. Maybe he can show us where to look.

It took a while to locate the guy, lease a plane, and fly from the Bay Area. At 1400 hours the new arrivals taxi down the Hays' air strip. The informant is conducted straight to the ranch's central complex whereupon he shakes his head. "This is the wrong ranch."

"But what the hell, man! Two days ago you said it was the right ranch."

"Out there on the highway it looked right. But now I'm in here, it don't."

"Goddamn it all to hell."

"Lo siento."

They had served a warrant on the wrong ranch and tomorrow Smith is going to have to face the judge. Now he has to face Hay. Walking back to the big white house, Smith reasons, "The man's a reasonable human being. He'll understand how these things can happen." Manfully, Smith explains to the family what has happened. The reasonable human being blows his head gasket.

"I've been a peaceable, law-abiding citizen all my life. An upstanding citizen. I'm not used to being treated so, so…" When he is agitated Bill's tenor voice has an unfortunate tendency to get higher and higher until its timbre is tightened to a stridulous squeal.

"You have, in no way, been threatened or abused, Mr. Hay…"

"I want you to call the paper, the radio. Tell everybody we are absolutely innocent. Call our friends and family. Explain your mistake."

The calls duly made, Smith takes Bill on a tour of the place to survey the damage. Bill is fairly calm until he sees pieces of his heavy equipment moved out of the barn and left in the driveway.

"Left out! Look at this!"

"The search team, they don't know anything about these kinds of vehicles. They were scared to try to put them back, scared they couldn't do it safely."

Bill is somewhat mollified. "No. It's not easy to maneuver these babies." He settles for getting the search team to put half a dozen sacks of cement back onto the pallets where they had been. As he and Smith walk back to the house, Bill says, "I think I could show you the right ranch, the one you should have been searching. It corresponds to your description, right down to the bull's head on the back of the truck. I could tell you about a lot of criminal activity in this area. There's a barn not a mile and a half from where you're standing that's full of marijuana, and has been for years. Law enforcement knows about it, too, but local authorities won't do shit. Too busy hassling decent citizens. You fly me around and I'll show you places where narcotics traffic really is going on. I could point out any number of places."

Bill became so cooperative, so disposed to being an ally, that Jerome G. Smith was surprised — or claimed to be — when the Hay family sued him, the county, the state — sued everybody in sight. Civil rights damages and personal damages. The family had been deprived of their rights, were victims of wrongful conduct, had suffered injury and damage. The episode, according to Bill's doctor, caused an alteration in his personality, an alteration "characterized by tearfulness and a tendency to withdraw and a severe persistent depression. The memory will be erased only by senility or a prefrontal lobotomy."

The Hay family demanded nine-million dollars in damages and five million in punitive damages. That was on October 21, 1985. In February of 1988 the jury unanimously agreed on a million for each of the four family members for civil rights damages, and for personal damages voted eleven to one to award an additional million and a half to Bill, a million and a half to Karen, and a half million to each son — general opinion was that it was the deer buggery that clenched it. After the jury heard about that ugly little incident, they were out for blood. "It evoked," the defense complained, "an emotional bias."

However, you can't, as my mother used to say, get blood from a turnip. The county is perpetually broke and an appeal reduced the settlement to: William - $190,000; Karen - $175,000; Robert - $70,000; Richard - $70,000.

I can't imagine what this experience was like for a man like Bill Hay. He had never been a mild and modest sort of guy, but the drug bust seemed to unhinge him. His black hair went white in a matter of weeks.

Some people insist the tip was correct and the bust good, but came too late. I don't believe it. I've read all the court material, eight folders, a two-foot-high stack of papers, and I think the Hays were just as shocked and affronted as they claimed to be. To be fair to Bill's accusers, I try on the notion of his guilt, and have to admit that much of what he said and did on that fateful day would have looked the same whether he was playing it straight or bluffing. It takes an effort, but I can eventually manage to wrap my imagination around an unlikely tableau in which the confidential informer arrives by plane, proceeds straight to where he had seen the cache only to find it gone, says, "Oops, too late," leaving the BNE to get out of there with as much grace as possible. This scenario isn't completely persuasive, but I grant that it is conceivable. However one aspect of it is not conceivable, and if the court record didn't convince me the Hays were innocent as babes in the woods in this matter, this aspect alone would. The confidential informer originally saw armed guards surrounding the cocaine stash and other armed guards stationed along the access road. As I say, with effort I can imagine a guilty Bill trying to outtalk his accusers, but my imagination balks when it reaches those congeries of Latin men and their automatic assault rifles. The image of pretty, apple-cheeked Karen returning home from the grocery store, casually easing her purple Cadillac between lines of armed Latinos — it simply won't do. To imagine such a scene not only raises my eyebrows in an access of incredulity, but forces little snorts of uncontrollable laughter through my nose. No, this bust was definitely a thoroughgoing mistake.

REFERENCE NOTES

Though a dramatized account, all information comes directly from the court records of Case #52164, Hay vs. The County of Mendocino, et al., with one exception: The sentence on page 2, "She feels the urge to vomit" is pure fiction. Because Karen Hay did not provide the court with a precise description of how she felt when she saw the policeman humping the plaster deer, I was forced to extrapolate.

Chapter Seventeen

PRIVATE PROPERTY, PUBLIC TRUST

Like the settlers themselves, we steadfastly believe in the social fiction that lines on a map and signatures on a deed legitimately divide the earth. Of all the persistent qualities in American history, the values attached to property retain the most power.

Patricia Limerick, *The Legacy Of Conquest*

Blue Water Hole

Another Sunday restoration adventure. We find the bulk of our little work party at Bookends attempting a forced wake-up with double espresso. Last January and February a larger work party planted more than five hundred trees — red alders, primarily, with big leaf maple, ash, and bay mixed in — along the banks of Blue Water Hole Creek. Today six of us are returning to take off the browse protectors and pull up the steel stakes. Damage anywhere within a watershed affects the entire watershed, so FrOG contacted the new owner of hundreds of acres on this woefully, wretchedly wounded tributary of the Garcia to see if he wanted help. He could hire a stream restoration specialist to do the work, but FrOG will do it for free, using money from a private foundation grant to pay for trees and materials.

We drive up Mountain View Road to the barn where Eric signs in — the rancher likes to know who is on his property and when. We park at the gate and walk down an unsurfaced road, which is, winter after winter, collapsing piecemeal into the creek.

No rain for the past several days, yet water pours from the cutbank on our right. It scoots down a ditch, dozing across the road at intervals to eat out nasty little gullies. At the worst of them, Chuck stops with his pocket clinometer to measure the steepness of the gradient, while the rest of us use the shovel and a mattock we brought along for our tree work, to excavate waterbars.

"This road needs gravel and lots and lots and lots and lots more waterbars," Eric tells me. "Almost all the sediment fouling our waterways comes from roads. Logging, even clearcutting, doesn't muddy up streams and rivers as bad as roads do.

"What's this road's worst problem?" I ask him.

"Its existence!"

The official Handbook For Forest And Ranch Roads says the most important step for planning a road is "determining whether or not the road is actually needed." This particular road may have been needed in the ranch's former life, but not anymore. Now it is merely a botch in constant need of patching.

Leslie says, "It's insloped. Doesn't that make the drainage problem worse?"

"But if it was outsloped...Wooooo. Can you imagine how scary it would be to drive? Especially when it was muddy. You'd be watching that hill, wondering when you were gonna slide off."

Where the road levels, a stream flows across it because the culvert is plugged, buried, in fact, so thoroughly we can't even locate it. Pipes to the stream feed a showerhead mounted above an open platform, a bath for the hunters, who are in for a good season — or so I deduce from all the visible pig damage.

Rains this year were heavier than they have been in a long time, and when we get to our work site, we see that the new trees which were planted right in the stream bed have been swept away, their steel stakes bent double. We collect the stakes then roam up the creek removing the small net caps intended to keep birds from getting trapped in the browse protector tubes. We had planned to remove the browse protectors from around the newly planted trees, but the trees look far too young and succulent to be left exposed, so we'll wait until later in the season.

Slipping, sliding, scrabbling, we cover one arm of the creek, digging out stakes and taking off caps. Although a portion of the planting was wasted, the percentage of loss isn't high. Leslie, consummate planter, is pleased. Each sapling is her baby, especially the maples. She's definitely partial to the maples.

The erosion situation is grim.

"How did this beautiful place get to be such an eyesore?"

"Stornetta Brothers, who owned it for most of this century, decided at some point to convert it to grazing land. Turn forest into pasture," Eric says. "The county issues a permit, a conversion permit. I think it's pretty easy to get it. And then because you're taking your land out of timber production forever, you don't have to submit any kind of harvest plan. You just rip everything out. They came down here and cut down every tree, pulled up every bush. Wanted to convert it to a different kind of resource, an animal growing resource. Instead they converted it to a wasteland."

In the late afternoon, all finished, we rest. A nice pattern: work your butt off, then lie down in the grass. Not a particularly warm day, but warm enough in the sun by the old corral to shed our jackets. I want to talk poetry, but everyone else wants to talk policy. A long-standing conflict in which I am always outnumbered. I agree with my activist friends and husband, I am not as wholeheartedly involved as they. I approve of what they are doing, but I get bored with the subject. I enjoy the actual work, but when it comes to conversation, I long for flintier subjects. Thus I hover on the periphery. I am a FrOG sympathizer, but not a bona fide card-carrying FrOG.

Leslie has been recently appointed to Point Arena's new Planning Commission, and she tells us about the new owner of the old PG&E land adjacent to Alan's and my property. "When he heard the city wasn't going to let him change his zoning from agricultural to commercial, he began to complain, '*It's a taking! It's a taking!*' A taking...that's the new rallying cry. If they hear, No, to any plan they've cooked up for turning a profit, they blow the bugle: It's a taking!"

"Nor shall private property be taken for public use, without just compensation. That's what the Constitution says."

"Yes, but if you buy land in hopes of developing it in one particular way, then find out you can't — that isn't 'private property taken for public use.' You can still do something with it. Something different, something else. Just because one plan didn't pan out doesn't mean you forfeit your whole investment."

"Whenever a property owner puts a Humboldt crossing or a barbed wire fence across the river so boaters can't get by," Leslie insists, "*that's* a taking."

"Or puts up a No Trespassing sign. This is my land and you can't cross it to get to the beach..."

"Or drains Mono Lake. That's an honest-to-god taking."

"But L.A. does own the water rights..."

Down the valley, a large raptor circles high above the creek. We watch, trying to identify it from this distance. After a lengthy silence Leslie says, "We'll have to grab the battle cry, '*A Taking*,' for our side."

"What's our side?" I ask. If I can't talk poetry, I'll settle for being contrary. So they chide me. "Our side's everybody who likes the beach but can't afford oceanfront property."

"Everybody who wants to canoe or fish a whole river."

"Everybody who doesn't want to see a particular ecosystem get obliterated. Because it is a taking when somebody kills the last salmon, cuts down the last redwood, drains the...whatever."

"Just because you have the cash to buy a piece of land doesn't mean you have the right to take something that belongs to all of us."

"That golden eagle circling down there belongs to all of us even if it nests on so-and-so's private land. That's why so-and-so has no right to destroy its nest."

A pause for breath, then, "That bird is definitely not a golden eagle."

❦

The sparsely populated Garcia watershed, a patchwork of private lands, encompasses no public land whatsoever. Most property owners are individuals and families, but three commercial timber companies own sections of the watershed's 73,275 acres. Louisiana-Pacific owns 11,400 acres, Georgia-Pacific, 2,200 acres, and Coastal Forest Lands, LTD (formerly R&J Timber), owns 24,000 acres, a good third of the entire watershed. All three companies are under order to prepare and submit a panoramic document called a Sustained Yield Plan. Two years ago the California Board of Forestry ruled that, in Mendocino County, each owner of over 2,500 acres of timberland — soon to be upped to 50,000 — must concoct a sweeping, synoptic description of its entire county holding and an account what it intends to do with it.

Alan explained it to me: "The Z'Berg-Njedly Forest Practice Act wasn't doing its job. It was supposed to protect fish, wildlife, soils, and other resources, including the standing inventory of trees, but twenty years later industry is still practicing liquidation logging."

Liquidation logging? Isn't that enviro-rhetoric? Gadfly terminology?

Alan: "Well, you go figure it. Before Europeans got here, Mendocino averaged over 100,000 board feet per acre. The amount is down to 10,000 now. And the Garcia is at the bottom of the average. Talk to the geologist at

CDF. He says, 'What they've done to this watershed makes me ashamed to be a human being.'"

Why did Z'Berg-Njedly fall so short of its goals?

"It was a quantitative thing. Cumulative impacts. The law says do this and that but then says measurement isn't necessary. Depletion went right on. Mendocino County got upset about its dwindling forests, and asked the state to let us make our own forest rules. The state said, No, but Mendocino wouldn't shut up and go away. Finally, in 1994, the California Board of Forestry came up with this Sustained Yield Plan, this SYP rule just for us, just for our county."

So how did the timber companies take the news of the SYP rule?

Although only the southernmost bit of Georgia-Pacific's entire 198,000 acre holding reaches into the Garcia watershed, ninety-nine percent of it is in Mendocino County. So G-P set to work on a multi-species habitat conservation plan/sustained yield plan.

"Within the context of these plans," says a G-P forester, "listed and non-listed species will be addressed and planning will be driven so as to ensure these species will remain as viable populations across the ownership. To address these species, Georgia-Pacific will consult with the U.S. Fish and Wildlife Service, California Department of Fish and Game, and the National Marine Fisheries Service. In addition, Georgia-Pacific intends to work with the U.S. Environmental Protection Agency and the north Coast Regional Water Quality Control Board to address the need of TMDLs in those 303(d) listed watershed within its ownership."

The economic and policy consultant to Coastal Forestlands, LTD announced his company is preparing a SYP on its timberland properties. "In conducting forestry planning efforts, CFL recognizes the importance of the health of the Garcia River ecosystem and its fisheries to long-term forestland stewardship. In its SYP, CFL has assessed the cumulative impact with each watershed planing unit. CFL has always cooperated with landowners, residents and public officials to promote responsible stewardship of the forest, watershed, fisheries, and wildlife in balance with appropriate and sustainable resource use, employment and private economic activity."

And Louisiana-Pacific, after proposing and evaluating for a few months and 1,500 SYP pages, announced it was selling all of its holdings, everything.

For years Alan has been battling these companies about water quality, and he is skeptical about the accuracy of their reports. "One day a company forester took a Regional Water Quality staff member for a site inspection. They were driving along a haul road that suddenly ramped itself over a huge landslide. 'What's this?' asked the woman from Water Quality. Her mouth just gaped open. She was looking at a huge mass wasting event that wasn't even mentioned in the SYP! The companies think they can leave out a lot since their area is too vast for ground-truthing."

SYPs, voluminous amounts of non-perfect information, can easily be organized, or disorganized, in such a way so as to provide something to hide in rather than something to edify.

For decades timber harvesting has gone where the public could not see it. Since all the out-of-the-way trees are gone now, industry's work is getting to be more conspicuous. The sight of cleared ground and slaughtered timber upsets people around here. The conflict, according to at least one timber owner, revolves around the question of what we want from our land? "Do we need it to produce timber or do we want it to be used for something different from that? And then you get to the issue — and one of the reasons it's such a divisive issue is it gets down to basic property rights issues. Historically in our society, if you do own the land you do basically have the rights — you have the first say over what you do on it. And we apply that principle on almost everything except timberland. Now when you come to timberland we, as a society, are starting to tell the forest owners that you have to produce wildlife and you have to do many other things. And you have to maintain your forests in a way that is pretty to look at."

Timberland owners have bought their property, paid their taxes and believe they have a right to harvest their crop. Economically, California needs these private timber owners and sees them as the most efficient way of satisfying the demand for wood. All related legislation is aimed at preserving private timberland, while encouraging better management in order to keep the land in the tree-producing business. Thus, the timber industry argues, it's just plain perverse to get in the way of our timber harvests.

Dorothy Halliday says the same thing, and she considers herself a conservationist, a steward of the land. "It is hard," she says, "to separate who we are from where we live."[1] She and Joe have never cut their timber. They preserved their big trees against future need, but now, Dorothy complains, the restrictions are so tough and timber harvest plans so expensive the Halliday timber has turned into money in the bank they can never withdraw. This seems unfair and a threat to American liberty. "The loss of property rights cannot be born by the land of the free."

"Our family should surely have a right to keep the land, build a house, cut the timber — as needed — without too much of a hassle — and pass it on to another of our line. We have earned that right and no one should be able to deny it."

Dorothy's family tree has a sprig from every one of the earliest transplants: Shepperds, Hamiltons, Olivers, Fairbanks. Her father's people arrived in the 1850s; her mother's were hard on their heels. Seven generations so far have lived here. Dorothy grew up on her family's ranch on Brush Creek. Now her home is her husband's family ranch on Windy Hollow Road. From the time the land was first patented in 1879 until 1912 when the Hallidays bought it, Dorothy has counted seventy-nine separate transactions on it. She gleaned this surprising information from an old abstract. What were all those transactions about? She guesses most of them were mortgages and trades with people owning adjacent properties. "They liked to square up their parcels. You know, trade a triangle here for a rectangle there."[2]

Some nineteenth-century land changed hands to pay debts or in gambling bets. The pages of the county's oldest records testify to lands shuffled like cards and promiscuously dealt out. Property was repeatedly bought, sold, traded and wagered. Westering pioneers brought with them a fervor for land — for the land's beauty, but more, for its bounty. They were after opportunity, and opportunity meant unrestricted access to resources. The West was where you went to avoid regulation. Use up one place, move on to another. But there is no longer any place to move on to. Point Arena represents one of the last ditch stands. If you can't evade regulation here, you may not be able to evade regulation at all — not and remain part of the USA. This is why my community is so lunatic. In Point Arena modern reality pitches into the well-entrenched, romantic conviction that if you are not free — that is to say, not thoroughly and absolutely unlimited by any human agency whatsoever — you are a slave.

Vigorously opposed elements work to control Point Arena. On one side, a shortsighted capitalism declares itself direct descendent of what was gained by the American Revolution: individual freedom and sacred rights of private property. The other side, too, invokes the blessing of its revolutionary forbears. "Today the most numerous heirs of the farmers of Lexington and Concord are the little groups scattered all over the country whose names begin with 'Save':

Save Our Land, Save Our Valley, Save Our Mountains, Save Our Streams, Save Our Farmland."[3]

Everybody claims inalienable rights. A colleague of mine at the library told me the last time she visited her daughter, a ranger at Glacier National Park, she found herself surrounded by a great buckskin-clad crowd of men toting muskets. A club called "Mountain Men" on their annual outing, they were in high dudgeon to learn they weren't allowed to wash their clothes in the lake. She understood their disappointment, and so do I. It would be lovely to return, even temporarily, to a past when the continent was wild and its inhabitants lived off the land, fishing, hunting, gathering berries, drinking from clear streams, cooking over an open fire, shitting wherever the peristalsis suggested. But there are too many of us now. If we all wash our clothes in the lake, pretty soon we'll have a glacier-rimmed bubble bath.

Desire for elbowroom and the aesthetic splendor of untrammeled wilderness is a romantic notion that has far outlived the date on its box. Except for isolated pockets here and there, wilderness simply doesn't exist anymore. It is a romantic ideal. But the sanctity of property rights is every bit as romantic a concept as the mystique of the woods. With a population vast and growing, how are we to decide which property rights to protect? Those of the woman who wants to raise pigs, or those of her neighbor who can't sell his house because of swinish odors. Do we give priority to the hillside owner who needs to strip the vegetation from around his house site for fire protection, or to the family below him who will be buried in mud come the first rain? Is the factory which needs to dispose of its manufacturing waste more important than the adjacent neighborhood which insists on unpolluted wells? And what about propertyless citizens. Have they no right to such things as clean air? Even if we decree that individual property rights are never-ever under any circumstance to be breached, how are we to resolve competing rights?

Freedom and opportunity: sacred principles — but construed differently, they are sacred principles in conflict with each other. How to reconcile public interest with the rights of the individual has always been the great dilemma of American democracy. The sovereign power of the people vs. the sovereign rights of the person. Private property vs. equality and social justice. All of us are keenly sensitive to infringements on our freedom, but what, anymore, constitutes a threat to liberty, and what a preservation of liberty? Things just aren't as simple as they used to be.

Dorothy wags her head, "Private property is not a dirty word." Leslie stamps her foot, "Public trust is not a communist slogan." Two romantic notions emerged from a single point, moved away from each other until, reaching the limits of their expectations, began to head back to where they started. Continuity in one track of U.S. history turns out to be on a collision course with continuity in another track of U.S. history.

We are a nation of romantics — romantics of different stripes, perhaps, but romantics nonetheless. And we are going to have to face the facts of modern life: For better or worse, untrammeled wilderness is a thing of the past. For better or worse, regulation is an ineluctable aspect of private ownership.

Buckridge Bar

The Annual FrOG Regatta. Or, the Annual FrOG Flotilla. Neither is exactly right. I call it the Annual FrOG Ricotta.

Peter Reimuller launched the event some years ago. He wanted to acquaint locals with their river, believing that when people see what they have, they are more likely to take an active role in protecting it.

The annual FrOG float is well publicized, and everyone is invited to participate. Around nine on a Sunday morning in winter, when the river is full, everyone assembles at the Eureka Hill bridge. Peter Dobbins always runs the river a day or two before to be sure all is safe for a gaggle of novices. In 1995 thirty-one people, of all ages and persuasions, loaded themselves into eighteen crafts, a wide variety of them — kayaks, canoes, inflatable rafts — including a canary-yellow kiwi, with a ten-year-old boy at its helm, and a three-seater ocean kayak with an alert Irish setter amidships. We were a motley but jolly troupe.

The day was Sunday, April 2, a sparkling day — not always the case in early spring — and we were having a hilarious time. We were all strung out along the river with Peter Reimuller in the rear, "to bring in the bodies." Peter Dobbins, his canoe stocked with first aid equipment, miles of rope, a come-along, and a chain saw, was well in advance of the rest of us, scouting for obstacles and hazards.

As we approached Buckridge Bar, site of the historic Garcia Mill with its extravagant flume, now the home of Bill Hay's Bed Rock gravel plant, I heard a gunshot. Fear constricted my throat. Another shot. Alan and I were third in line. Raven was between us and Peter, and he, Raven, saw the bullets hit — the first splatted into the left bank, the second splashed into the water about twenty feet in front of Peter's bow. Alan and I came round the curve in time to see the next two shots, which struck the right bank not more than fifteen feet from Peter. Up the hill next to the Bed Rock building I could see a young man holding his gun with two hands, like a cop in the movies. It was little Eddy Christiansen. I did not recognize him, but Alan and Raven did. Peter stopped paddling as soon as the first shot sounded, and as we came up beside him, Eddy turned his back on the river and began to shoot in the opposite direction. Someone else was with him. Was it his mother? Other boats reached us and everybody was shouting at Eddy who continued to blast away. It was all I could do to keep Alan from beaching our canoe and going up the hill to confront the foolish fellow. At worst Alan would have gotten shot; at best he would have been accused of trespassing.

We continued on down the river to a sunny gravel bar where we stopped for lunch. After I crawled out from under the basic fear of being gunned down, my biggest concern was that the children would be scared to death. I needn't have worried. Our adult crowd was shaken to varying degrees, but the kids were thrilled. "Why was that boy shooting at Peter?" They clamored around asking excited questions.

"Bill Hay doesn't want us on the river."

"But why."

"Bill hates to see FrOGgies on the water, because he hates FrOGgies."

Though he has never done anything this audacious, Billy has gone to some fairly extreme lengths to close river access to everybody but his own people. Once he went so far as to install locks on gates into Georgia-Pacific land. When the G-P forester came to do an inspection, he couldn't get in.

The war with Bed Rock has been long and tiresome. Since 1986, neighboring property owners and recreational river users, boldly led by FrOG, have been appearing at County Planning Commission hearings and County Board of Supervisors meetings to challenge Billy's permit applications. When his opponents win, they complain that Billy cheats. Taking by stealth what he cannot get legally, he creeps in when no one is looking to scoop up more gravel than his permit allows. Billy harasses trespassers, and boaters are frequently surprised by obstructions in the river in front of his gravel plant. Cables and wires, and now bullets.

If a river lover, or anyone else with an ax to grind (Billy has raised the ire of the other local gravel businesses) reports his infractions to the authorities, Billy gets even in less-than-honorable ways. He accuses people of being drug dealers and marijuana growers. He hires thugs to threaten and menace. Once a couple of tourists walking near Buckridge Bar, inadvertently trespassing, were violently accosted by a Bed Rock "security man," wildly shouting that he was going to blow their brains out. After he fired at them, he forced them face down onto the gravel, and terrified them for a while before allowing them to leave. Another employee, Eddy's stepfather, admitted he had been "...encouraged to beat up Alan Levine, hospitalize him — that was very strongly encouraged by Billy. But Alan wouldn't fight. That guy would run from me, would go in a building, would not fight. I was told to beat the hell out of John Hooper, I was supposed to beat the hell out of anyone who got in Billy's way." Billy himself once assaulted Peter Reimuller. Billy had a gun in his hand when he saw Peter and Nick King walking near the river. Furious, he came barreling toward Peter who didn't know if he was about to be shot or walloped. Bill dropped the weapon and roundhoused Peter such a blow it knocked him to the ground. When the sheriff arrived, he told Peter, "If you charge Mr. Hay with assault, he's going to charge you with trespass, then I got to take you both in," so Peter didn't pursue the matter. He was already scared of Billy since, on two occasions, someone unseen had blown out the front windows of his house with some sort of gun. He couldn't prove Billy was behind it, but knew he was.

Bill hates to see FrOGgies on the water because he hates FrOGgies, but there's more to it than that. According to the Public Trust Doctrine, no one claiming an interest on a "navigable" river has the right to continue a use that interferes with public access. In determining which waterways are navigable, the courts use a straightforward approach: If a small boat can travel it — even if travel involves some portage — the waterway is navigable. It was easy to prove the Garcia to be "navigable in fact"; people have been using it for as long as people have been here, ten or twelve thousand years.

American case law, by way of English common law, traces all the way back to the Roman codes. When a conflict of interest without an already prescribed remedy arises in our nation, the court bases its decision on the constitution, but often the court is obliged to excavate beneath the constitution. Such judicial interpretations and applications then become the precedents for further interpretations, and so on. The Public Trust Doctrine, originally designed to protect the rights of the public to use waterways for navigation, commerce, fisheries, more recently has been updated by the authority of several California

Supreme Court rulings to include recreation and preservation of open space and ecological units.

The State of California, as the sovereign representative of the people, owns and controls, much like an individual property owner, various interests in all its waterways. In England the ancient Public Trust Doctrine included certain royal responsibilities. In monarch-deficient California, these responsibilities devolve to the State Lands Commission, which protects public rights — the right of all of us, not just those of us with enough money to buy big hunks of land — to use a watercourse even where the watercourse's bed is privately owned.

Although the powers-that-be decided, yes, the Garcia is navigable, the further step of getting the Garcia declared "sovereign land" would help improve the health of the river, since businesses involved in resource extraction on "sovereign land" have to pay special fees to the state for extra permits and leases. However, proving land to be "sovereign" is an involved matter that seems to me to need a Time Machine. To establish the Garcia as "sovereign land," one must determine exactly what the river was doing — its erosion, accretion, meandering — back in 1850 when California was admitted to the union and thereby succeeded to the title of all sovereign lands held up until then by the U.S. of A. A complicated endeavor FrOG member Judy Kohl, wife of the famous educator, is working on. All this makes Bill Hay feel picked on. He complains about it often and loudly.

"Trying to keep people off the river was probably purely pragmatic at first," said a Flotilla kayaker, as he accepted a sandwich from Peter R. who always packs a passel of extra food. "But you're saying the navigability thing is a done deal. So why is he still hassling you guys? What's he got to gain?"

"Looks like he's just getting in his own way now," said the kayaker's girlfriend. "Looks like he'd rather beat you guys than make money."

"Yeah," said a little boy, "if I wanted to make money, I'd play the good guy, even if I had to fake it." Wee Machiavellis, these kids of ex-hippies.

We refused to let the shooting incident spoil our fun. We spent the next couple of hours reabsorbing the adrenaline overdose. What we couldn't absorb we applied to hard paddling, loud jokes, and the constructive consumption of chocolate-covered Waverly Wafers.

When the trip was over and everyone was out of the water and headed home, we passengers of the first four boats went looking for a sheriff. The very young new deputy turned out to be the one on duty that day. As he took our statements, his hands shook, and when Peter R. made a joke about open season on environmentalists, the poor fellow's big brown eyes showed panic. It took him a second or two to decide Peter was joking. Depositing a nervous laugh, the young deputy vowed with all his heart to arrest Eddy immediately and drove away looking positively miserable. Billy Hay, as everyone knew, was the deputy's landlord.

Eddy was tried nearly a year later. To the end, he and his mother swore Eddy was only doing a little target practice. The jury thought otherwise and convicted him of negligent discharge of a weapon, a felony offense.

Before the trial Eddy's stepfather, describing his job as a "thug for Billy Hay," defected. "I just got sick of the bullshit, my ex-woman, the whole works, and I left. I told him I won't say nothing to no one, just leave me alone, but I just don't want part of it anymore, it's sick. That won't do with those people, you're either for 'em or you're totally against them…" Billy gave the man such a hard time for quitting, the ex-thug went public with his story which included information about the shot gun attack on Peter Reimuller's house, vandalism of John Hooper's dome, an earlier river shooting, bugging and vandalism of the mayor's office, "importing" voters to influence the 1994 city elections, as well as various other spyings and strong-arm tactics.

Despite the ex-thug's testimony, the DA's office refused to prosecute, citing insufficient evidence and the difficulty of proving patterns of threat and harassment. The weekend after a transcript of the taped testimony appeared in a local newspaper, somebody shot the ex-thug's dog.

REFERENCE NOTES

1. Dorothy Halliday, *Over the Dam.*

2. Conversation with Dorothy.

3. Wendell Berry, *The Unsettling Of America.*

In General: I have gleaned so much information from Dorothy Halliday that I have lost track of precisely where some of her words came from. Her memoir, Over the Dam, taped interviews for Yesterday's News and for the school's Gifted and Talented classes, newspaper pieces she has written, and personal conversations - all sources, many repeating the same information, are mixed together in my notes.

Chapter Eighteen

RIVER SEASONS: FALL

Throughout the first summer we lived here, my love for the place was laced with anxiety. I was intimidated by the landscape, by the weather. A harsh northwest wind never let up. It whipped the waters of the ocean. It bent the trees and pruned the shrubs. The heath-like vegetation near the shore looked like Arctic tundra.

The ocean current is ten degrees colder along the coast than it is fifty miles out to sea. Winds moving over the face of these chilly waters snatch up a salty fog, a fog made exceedingly dense by its admixture of salt particles. Summer fog comes and goes, and my first summer here, it mostly came. Day after day it galloped across our broad palomino-colored pastures.

I was never warm except when we sought heat inland on the Ridge, where the climate is markedly different from down on the coastal flats. I was cold and I was plagued by a vague uneasiness. The whole setting was simply too passionate, too dramatic. And that was before I got a taste of the wild winter! Yet I never stopped wanting to live here. I was in love. The Mendocino Coast was the province of my dreams, so I adjusted; and, as I did, the most angst-provoking aspects of the place became its most seductive.

Though late, summer eventually arrived. Late in August or early September, scorching inland temperatures dropped enough to check the flow of sea air racing across the face of the land on its way to the low pressure of the superheated interior. The cooler it became inland, the less blow and fog here, so the coast warmed up a bit.

Year-round temperatures fluctuate little — in fact Point Arena's temperatures are among the most constant in the state, warmest and coolest months differing by less than 10°. Perhaps this is why people say we have only two seasons — wet winter, dry summer. But those people are wrong; we have all four seasons. Two of them are subtle, though, their changes discreet.

Fall is one of the subtle seasons. It emerges from summer with no fanfare at all, modulating in a hazy beauty of air and light. Deciduous trees quietly, modestly drop their colorless leaves, and, following the year's first rain, mushrooms push up through the litter: big red fly agaric, small gecko-colored psilocybins, mahogany boletes, white puff balls.

> 10/11 Chilly morning. Field fencing is decorated with drops of water and pure, shining cobwebs. Up from the hollows, all up and down the road, patches of ground fog drift, spread, disappear. The sun sits like a gold egg in the low clouds, then rises above them — fence posts, telephone poles begin to smoke.

Every morning, year round, as soon as I wake up, I jog to the river and back. By mid-fall it is dark when I set out. Windy Hollow Road is little more than a broken yellow line. Gradually, as light seeps into the sky, I trot through a picture show of silhouettes: the masts and rigging of power poles and telephone poles; slumping grape-stake fence strung along the top with an ineffective afterthought of barbed wire; skeletons of scrubby willows; the black clots of bull pines on the hills.

Back home our steel gate stands open — this is not the season of ranging livestock. The gravel driveway dips slightly as it crosses a little stream headed for Hathaway Creek, tributary to the Garcia. This morning I can't see the creek's water through the willows, but I remember a morning last winter when the tiny stream was so swollen it backed up at the culvert and threatened to breach and wash away our drive. Stooping to pick up my morning paper, I wonder if we ought to trim back some willows before this season's rains get heavy. Maybe the dense vegetation drags at the stream's flow.

Past the culvert the willow-walled stream angles away from the drive, leaving a piece of tan grass meadow, dry, dark bracken fern, and dark frail hemlock skeletons — everything dried up and appearing held-together by tangled skeins of dewy spider web.

A few feet farther, the driveway starts to climb, a smooth gravel surface scooped with more and more erosion scars until it comes to resemble a miniature Grand Coulee. To my left, as I trudge uphill, the stream runs through a ravine crowded with red alder. Frayed brown alder leaves lie in the still-green undergrowth. A few, dark and raggedy, dangle from the limbs. Among them I see two things I overlooked all summer: in one tree a robin's nest, in another, a paper wasp nest as big as a sheep's head. Gray alder bark glows slightly in the morning light. Over the years I've watched the blue-gray skins lose their white blotches while the limbs gradually acquired goatees of Spanish moss. On the slope where they grow, my alders have begun to cock this way and that, forsaking, by degrees, the uprightness of their youth.

To my right is the hill from which the driveway was cut. On top, one tall bull pine looms over an assortment of shrubs and creepers: orange bush monkey-flower, hemlock, water cress, creeping charlie mint, wild blackberry, miners' lettuce, ferns, and I-don't-know-what-all. Pieces of this hill— Point Arena is on the Pacific Plate, composed not of Franciscan mélange, but worse, of "suspect terrain of uncertain origin" — fall regularly onto the drive and Alan has to scoop them away with the tractor. Once he spent a sweaty hour wrestling a great clod — several leafless, unspecified species of vegetation still clinging to it — into the tractor bucket. Three days later he was able to identify at least one of those plants as poison oak.

Well above the stream now, the driveway turns north and leaves the ravine altogether. Looking across the top of the sliced hill, I have a long view across a pasture to pastures on the opposite side of Windy Hollow, past them and on to the hills of the Ridge. Beyond the Ridge lies Ukiah, then the rest of the United States, and the rising sun. To my left is a stand of the ubiquitous bull pines which, season to season, never change, except to grow taller, until they finally fall over. They grow quickly, die young, contributing their vegetable mass to the humus supply. Beyond them, out of sight, is the pond. I walk a few yards — there's the calves' pasture. A few yards more — up on the hill, stands our house. This morning something in the shading of the roof looks irregular. Are some of the shingles loose? I'll have to check today when we climb up to clean the chimney.

Fall arrives bearing the gift of surplus time, a small cornucopia of idle hours. Tourists have gone home. Fishing season has closed. Orchards and summer vegetable gardens are through producing. Marijuana crops are harvested and ready for market. Coast residents flush, are ready for vacation.

Though our household neither serves tourists nor produces marijuana, we take it easy in the fall just like everybody else. Hay planting still looms, but, as disking is impossible with the ground still so dry, I can do nothing about it until after the ground is wet, so I set aside a Saturday to hike up Pardaloe Creek to the highest point in the watershed. No rain for many months. Creeks and streams not dried up entirely are mere trickles, so, since I plan to walk right up the creek bed, now is the time to go. Of the eight property owners along Pardaloe Creek, I know of three who denied access to the Watershed Advisory Group study team. My walk is innocent of information-gathering motives, so they might give me permission to cross their respective properties, but because none of the three live on, or anywhere near the creek, they are bound to be hard to track down. I decide to save myself the trouble and simply walk up the creek. I understand I need neither a by-your-leave nor mother-may-I from anyone if I merely stay below the mean high flow line, but Alan says, to be safe, I ought to keep my feet wet.

Pardaloe Creek is the easternmost tributary of the Garcia. To get there I drive from Point Arena south on the Highway 1 until I get to Fish Rock Road, named for a long-gone shipping point. The cove in the lee of two tall rock islands was large enough for five or six vessels to lie at anchor, fairly well protected from northwest weather. On a cliff at the north end of a long, sandy beach bisected by the stream draining Fish Rock gulch, a loading chute projected over fifteen feet of rock-strewn water. The shore settlement, vanished now without a trace, was small — two or three houses, a blacksmith shop, a school, a saloon, a store, post office with a warehouse. For a while a potter worked at Fish Rock making and selling bean pots, butter crocks and bricks. Behind the store was a barn with a carriage shed and stalls for five horses, the four carriage horses, and the owner's buggy mare. Also within the barnyard stood a bunkhouse and a cookhouse for tanbarkers.

The first woodsmen came for lumber, primarily redwood lumber, but they found tan oak growing alongside the redwoods, and tan-oak bark was valued highly at the time for its tannic acid, necessary for tanning hides for leather. The tree, *Notholithocarpus densiflorus*, looks like a cross between a chinquapin and an oak. A broadleaf evergreen, seventy to ninety feet tall, with a diameter of from one to three feet — it grows within the redwood belt. Its range extends farther north and south than the redwoods, but where it parts company with the giants, it gets stubby. I guess it needs sequoia inspiration for stature.

The dark gray trunk is hard — *litho* means stone — and cut by seams and cross-checks into smooth square plates. Closely spaced branches stretch skyward in a lush crown of oval leathery leaves, glossy light green on top, a dull blue-green underneath. The tan oak's large acorns were a staple in the diet of local natives who ground them into flour. During the first twenty years of this century almost all the mature tan oak was cut for its bark. The rest of the tree was left where it fell, even though it could have been used for fine furniture. Since it was so close-grained it weighed, dry, forty-two and a half pounds per cubic foot.

Over the course of time the cost of hauling the tan bark out of the forest became higher than the cost of importing other types of tanning materials, and the tan barking business came to an end; but, at the beginning tan oak industry was profitable, so when word of this new, abundant source of bark reached the outside world, a whole fresh set of woods workers surged into the Garcia watershed. Tan bark operations were entirely separate from logging operations; tan barking was done by different men in different camps. Because logging ruined standing tan bark, it was peeled each year before logging began. The work was done primarily by Italian newcomers from Lombardy, a region of Italy so far north that many immigrants were not actually Italian at all but Italian-speaking Swiss or Austrians.

> "My father came here in 1892 and the reason mostly Italian people came to this country, to this area, was for the tan bark, and to homestead property, naturally. They would homestead 160 acres and they would start tan barking and then they would work on the 160 acres — in those days they had it all picket-fenced. They would work making pickets, to fence all their stuff off. And, of course, they planted their vineyards and their chestnut trees. But the primary reason they come to this country is — they passed up all the good ground over there in the Anderson Valley — because the only way they could make a dollar was in the tan bark."[1]

Above Fish Rock, Signal Ridge blossomed into an Italian colony of twelve or fifteen families. Settlers rode horses up from Yorkville. Some walked all the way from Swiss Colony at Cloverdale, traveling for two or three days straight over the roadless mountains. Pulled by tan bark and by sweet homesteading deals, prospective settlers were, at the same time, pushed by a severely depressed economy back home.

> "The reason they left over there was, hell, they were all starving, all of Europe was the same. So they come to the country over here. When my mother came here she said, 'Hell yes, I'll go marry him,' because she thought that — I can still remember her saying it — she said, 'I thought the streets over here was paved with gold.' Boy, they had hell when they first got here. You can imagine coming out of a city over there, and come walking up in here to a little cabin. I remember mother — she had my father's mother with her, an old lady, in her 60s. Over there I guess they never had any buzzards, and when them big old buzzards were flying around — they'd maybe killed a deer, or something, and left some bones around — the

buzzards would be flying around the house. Both of them women were scared to death. They figured the birds were coming to get them. That's what mother used to say. She's go out there with the broom and shake a broom at them."[2]

In another early account, a woman finds herself so disheartened by the redwoods she can barely tolerate her new home. The giant trees, she claimed, screened her house from the sun, made life gloomy and lonely. If she could return to Signal Ridge today she wouldn't face the same problem. The big bad redwoods are all but gone.

Yet the Ridge remains a forest. I turn left off Highway 1 onto Fish Rock Road. Right past the county dump, the road's paved surface turns to gravel, and it begins to climb until it is running along the top of Signal Ridge. I am driving through an alley of trees. To my left lies the Garcia watershed, to my right, the Gualala watershed. Two kindred rivers. With headwaters emanating from virtually the same ground, their tributaries — some of them tangled like strands of hair from separate heads together on one pillow — tumble west. From the ridge top down tree-covered slopes, Gualala tribs sideslip south and Garcia tribs sideslip north. Trees, trees everywhere. I can see more bald spots in the hillsides than I would have seen a century ago, but this is still a thickly forested area. The legitimate hue and cry about overharvest of timber can be misleading: Not trees, per se, but merchantable timber has been wiped out. An abundance of trees stand, shoulder to shoulder, but they are either of species without commercial value, or they are too young, lacking the girth to make milling profitable, "pecker poles," they call them.

Everything grows wonderfully well on Signal Ridge. Nineteenth-century homesteaders planted chestnuts, and fruit: cherries, loquats, apples, pears, figs, plums, peaches, quinces and the indispensable grapes, table grapes and wine grapes of every variety. As soon as their orchards and vineyards were producing, the growers began to carry surplus down to the coast, traveling twenty-five miles on a dirt trail to get to Point Arena, the big city! There they found other Italians and Italian-speaking Swiss, farming and dairying on the fertile bench lands, a community of strangers, but ones speaking the tongue native to the Signal Ridgers. So they linked up with these lowlanders, often staying in their homes rather than in one of Point Arena's several hotels. The Signal Ridge settlers traded produce from their hotter drier neighborhood for things growing on the coast, soon establishing an effective, reliable barter system.

"We had the grapes, we would send them down a ton of grapes or a fifty gallon barrel of wine, and instead of giving us money they would give us potatoes, they would give us seed oats, they would give us hay, they would give us whatever. I remember the Stornettas down there had a creamery, they used to give us cheese, they used to give us butter. They would have maybe fifty pounds of butter. They would put it down in barrels in salt water and the water was salty, they would put the fresh butter down in there, and it would keep in an old cellar, it would keep half the summer in salt water. And the same thing with eggs, we used to put eggs down in that water glass, whole big crock of eggs, they would stay that way for six months, you know, in this water glass they called it. It was a kind of a liquid that you could buy. So that's what they done, mostly in all water. And actually we never really sold grapes to the wineries until, oh when, about, after the war when we really started selling to the wineries."[3]

Fifteen or sixteen miles inland I reach the traverse hogback known as Zeni Ridge, and soon the Zeni Ranch comes into view. George Zeni sleeps today in the very room he was born in. In 1892 his father came over from the old country, homesteaded his 160 acres according to the rules, and after five years wrote his mother asking her to bring him an Italian bride. She went right to work. In 1900 George's father married his mother, a woman he'd never before laid eyes on. She was nineteen; he was thirty-three. They raised twelve children, and throughout their fifty-five years together, according to George, "things got better and better and better all along the way."

His father acquired a team of mules for packing tan bark out of the woods. He made five dollars a month extra because of those mules. Pack trains hauled tan bark to the closest spot accessible to wagons, a "dump" it was called. A train consisted of a horse carrying the packer followed by four, six or even eight mules, each carrying around three-hundred pounds. Tan barkers had to chisel pack trials out of a relentlessly rugged landscape — the woods hereabout still bear traces of their Herculean feat.

From the dump, wagons drawn by four and six-horse teams took the tan bark down to the most convenient shipping point, which for the Signal Ridge area was Fish Rock Landing. This meant more roads, so while woods workers peeled and hauled bark, another set of men chopped at the earth with pick and shovel. Conditions being what they were, tan barking left behind some idiosyncratic roads.

Trees were cut, the bark peeled. Peelers worked in pairs, each equipped with a three-foot-long pole ax, its handle marked a foot from the end to measure the bark, to measure off four-foot strips. The men girdled the trees and peeled off bark which rolled up into what they called a "curl."

Tan bark slipped off readily only when the sap was flowing so tan barking could be done only in spring — mid-April to late June, exact dates depending on the weather. During the off-season, Signal Ridge settlers supplemented their incomes pruning vineyards for a dollar a day. They walked forty-five miles down the mountain to the Asti Swiss Colony, where they stayed for two months. "They worked two months and they came back with sixty-five dollars apiece and they didn't know how in the hell to spend it. There was no place to spend it, anyway."[4]

Where Fish Rock Road crosses Pardaloe Creek, I pull over and park on the right at the bottom of a short road leading up to a cluster of houses built around a meadow. Other than this trim tract, the upper creek is a semi-unpopulated forest composed of conifers laced with hardwoods, brush fields and meadows.

I change shoes, put on my day pack, lock the truck, and skitter down loose rock to the creek bed. Pardaloe Peak stands some forty-four miles from the Garcia's mouth, but how far it is from where I start my trek, I don't know, so I give myself permission to turn around whenever I feel like it — certainly in time to be back on the road before dark.

Today the sky is clear blue, no trace of cloud. A honey of a day. The upper creek is enough inland to evade the marine influence. Fog is rare; not much wind. Average temperatures are significantly higher than near the coast. The creek runs through solid bedrock, but has accumulated ample gravel and large slippery cobble to stumble and totter me. The going isn't effortless, but I've known worse.

Early in the century — some people guess, though they can't know for sure, it was in 1906 — access to Pardaloe Creek from the ocean was blocked by a great landslide. Steelhead in there at the time became landlocked. Late in the sixties the California Department of Fish and Game dynamited the impasse, and the salmonids began to come back to spawn. The steelhead first, and then in 1994 someone found a coho carcass. Today I see some small fish swimming in the clear water. Are they steelhead fingerlings? Stickleback? Sculpin?

Lizards sun themselves on rocks in the company of frogs I don't notice til they plosh into the creek to get away from me. The width of the bed fluctuates — fifteen feet, six feet, thirty feet — with enough water running down it to keep my feet wet. Twice, in narrow spots, I have to climb eight-foot log piles.

The creek side is printed at the broad spots with deer tracks, pig tracks, cow tracks, but nary a sign of human tread. A leaf floats to the ground like a paper boat on a pond. At one point I am pattered by a crisp brown shower, as though the tree, provoked by my passing, spouted its leaves all at once. Though I can't say why, I am oddly, thoroughly happy.

After slogging along for about an hour, I come to a hole deeper than any I've yet waded. I can't go through without wetting the crotch of my shorts. Nor can I go around. The left bank rises straight up, and the right is impassable, invaded by a thick leaning tree. Ought I chance leaving the creek? From maps I knew this to be property forbidden to the WAG, but I figure if I scamper up there then back down here fast enough, it'll be more like a sneeze than a trespass. So I scramble up the embankment. Dirt and pebbles — mini-cascades of Franciscan mélange — give way with every step. At the top, slightly above the creek, I am walking through soft, dry dust pressed with a new set of tracks, those of a D4 Cat. The going here is a heck of a lot easier than down in the creek bed, and the scenery is just as good. I keep telling my law-abiding self, Get back into that creek! but mile after mile passes with me still on top. I never lose sight of the creek, but occasionally the descent to it is so precipitous I won't be able to get down there if I come face to face with a menacing, irate, gun-toting border guard. I spend the rest of the day pondering a strategy for when I get caught, but suffer scoldings only from the blue jays.

As my path goes gently but steadily up, the creek beside me becomes less and less of a creek and more and more of a trickle too narrow for two feet to stride through side by side — impossible to walk in even if I am forced to. Now and then the bed goes completely dry and I say, Well, that's that for Pardaloe Creek. But pretty soon water reappears, usually in the form of green mosquito pools.

Eventually, my rudimentary road crosses to the north side of the creek where it is instantly transformed into a good, new gravel road which I follow to its end. The creek, or more precisely, the creek bed is out of sight. Pardaloe Peak, 2470' high, the highest point in the watershed, is a few hundred feet more up a glacier of brown oak leaves. I gaze upward. I take an apple out of my day pack. Crisp as glass. Eating it, I turn around and begin to retrace my steps.

When George Zeni was a kid, his family had about thirty acres of grapes they plowed with horses. Directly he got home from school, George and his sisters were expected to cultivate two rows of vines apicce. They had to hoe all around the vines, take the suckers off, pull up ferns before they could have dinner.

At wine making time the kids stomped the grapes. The farm had a mechanical crusher for the initial grape crushing, but when fermentation set in, the barefoot children climbed into the barrel to crush down the pomace in order to keep it from souring on top. For a couple of weeks until the wine was completely fermented, they had to press the top under again and again. Then the liquid was drawn off into tanks. "It was all crude. Everything was natural. Never put anything into it. Whatever it was, it was."[5]

His family didn't grow grapes to make money. They grew grapes because they drank wine. Arriving in the USA, Italian immigrants, for whom wine was virtually synonymous with food, found themselves amid a people, though not universally sober, paying homage to the virtues of abstemiousness. In Point Arena, newly-arrived little Joe Scaramella and his brother learned from their American teacher that no alcohol was permitted at school, ever. Being as a swallow of wine was the only way to wash down a lunch, the schoolboys were forced to duck into the bushes every day at noon.[6]

When their vineyards were young and not yet producing vast quantities, the wine makers themselves consumed most of what they made. They kept a portion for barter with Point Arena Italians, and they sold a portion to Gualala tie makers who walked up to Signal Ridge to pack their week's supply of wine — eight or ten gallons — all the way back down to the coast.[7]

Although they grew several varieties of grapes, they mixed them all together in the barrels, separated only as red and white. They ran some of it through a still to make brandy. Eventually George's father established a bonded winery — just in time for Prohibition. The powers-that-be revoked his license, but, according to George, Prohibition affected grape growing and wine making hardly at all.

> "We had the grapes and we made the wine. The only thing is that you had to go underground so to speak, you couldn't do it legally.

> The Italians still drank their wine and we made and they drank it. In fact, it probably helped us out. Personally I think, like if you read this article that this Hinds wrote, he said the same thing: that production went up double during prohibition…
>
> Well, my father got caught. He had three thousand gallons of wine over here and they pulled all the plugs out of the barrels and let the wine run clear down on the road and they found his still and they took an ax and chopped all his still up and they took him over to jail in Ukiah. But, hell, he had six or seven kids so they just kept him overnight and they charged him five hundred bucks. Alright, they charged him five hundred dollars. Now how in the hell was he going to pay that five hundred dollars back? The minute he got home he went and got another still and fired it up to get the money to pay them. It's just that simple, you know. They never slowed nothing down. Hell it wasn't two days everything was fired back up again...Do you know why Greenwood Ridge up there was called Vinegar Ridge? You probably don't know that it was called Vinegar Ridge. All those Dagos up there made wine but when the revenuers came along they said, 'Well, we're not making wine we're making vinegar.' The Prohibition guys would come. 'Oh hell, all we've got is vinegar.' And they would show them a barrel of vinegar there. But in the meantime they had l,ooo gallons of wine buried somewhere. That's why they call it Vinegar Ridge."[8]

After Prohibition George's father returned to openhanded wine making, but could no longer turn a profit. Large wineries were putting the small wine makers out of business. According to George, the big wineries contrived to get batches of small vintners' wine condemned. Condemned wine could be sold only for vinegar, so the big wineries turned around and bought it for a pittance. "There was a bunch of connivers there, you know. They paid you twelve cents a gallon but you know they never made no vinegar... they sold it for wine. They lied to you. They are a bunch of crooks."[9]

The Italian grape growers of Signal Ridge, well-schooled by now in outsmarting the big guys, managed to hide thousands of gallons of wine, sometimes hauling it to Point Arena or Gualala. In the forties, when it was legal to do so, the Zenis opened a little bar at their ranch. A bar license allowed them to sell wine, but not wine they themselves made, so they hauled their grapes to another small local winery. Every ton of grapes yielded 140 or 150 gallons of wine. The winery gave Zeni 100 gallons and kept the rest in payment. To be on the square, the Zenis bought a bottling license for $10, and fudged its authority a bit by drawing the wine directly from the barrel into jars which they sold behind the bar. This arrangement went on for only four or five years before new regulations axed it. Time to go underground again. "You had to be scrounging all the time because you always had to try to keep a step ahead of them."

George Zeni was born in 1923. Seventy-four years later he is as full of vitality and plans for the future as he was in his youth when he ran barefoot over the hills all day with his brothers and sisters. After his first wife died, he married Shirley McMillan, whose parents were, for fifty years, the popular owners of McMillan's Store, now the Point Arena General Store.

One of George's sons helps him run his 160 acre ranch where he grows grapes, Christmas trees, chestnuts. When he needs extra cash, he sells some timber. George likes to talk about his green thumb. "I can take anything and put it in the ground and stomp on it and water it and, hell, it'll grow. Cuss it a little bit. Now a lot of people say, 'Oh, I can't make that grow.' Well, hell, that's no problem. I can make anything grow. In fact, Shirley can tell you that."

"He sure can, he can make anything grow. He has a green thumb."

"I do all the pruning; I do all the cultivating. My boy helps me sulfur a little bit. You know you got to sulfur about twice for mildew. And I succor. Shirley helps me dig around and hoe. Yeah, she's a hell of a hoer. She just hoes up a storm…when it's time to play around with the grapes in June, you have to do a lot of hoeing and this and that, then the Christmas trees come on, so my son generally goes pruning Christmas trees. He prunes Christmas trees mostly."

The Zenis hire Mexicans to help George prune the vineyards, and when the time comes to harvest the grapes, family members and friends from all around drive up for the weekend. They feast on polenta and stew and wine, then commence picking grapes, gathering them all in two or three days. The whole affair is a big party.

REFERENCE NOTES

1. George Zeni, *Yesterday's News,* interview, gza01.ppl.

2. George Zeni, *Yesterday's News,* interview gza05.ppl.

3. George Zeni, *Yesterday's News,* interview gza04.sup.

4. George Zeni, *Yesterday's News,* interview gza1.ind.

5. George Zeni, *Yesterday's News,* interview.

6. Joe Scaramella quoted in Bruce Levene, *Mendocino County Remembered.*

7. George Zeni, *Yesterday's News,* interview gza03.ind.

8. George Zeni, *Yesterday's News,* interview gza09.pro.

9. George Zeni, *Yesterday's News,* interview.

Chapter Nineteen

RIVER SEASONS: WINTER

Hampered, but not defeated, by drizzle and fog, the intrepid census takers slogged through the mud, peered through the murk. The Garcia River estuary is a bird motel. Scores of migratory birds, joining an already sizable and diverse feathered endemic population, overwinter here. At Christmas time the Mendocino Coast Audubon Society counts the whole crowd. Around the mouth and along the lower two miles of the river the 1996 Annual Christmas Bird Count observed: several species of loons, grebes, shearwaters, cormorants, two brown pelicans, a great blue heron, tundra swans, a black swan, three species of geese, a few green-winged teal, four hundred fifty mallards, a few gadwalls, dozens of American wigeons, a dozen ring-necked ducks, some scoters, a couple of goldeneyes, numerous buffleheads, two species of mergansers, a northern harrier, a Cooper's hawk, a red-shouldered hawk, a red-tailed hawk, kestrels, a merlin, a peregrine falcon, California quails, Virginia rails, a sora, many American coots, some black-bellied plovers, killdeers, turnstones, surfbirds, two dozen each dunlin and red phalarope, one hundred seventy-five mew gulls, a dozen ring-billed gulls, nearly two hundred California gulls, ninety herring gulls, one Thayer's gull, one glaucous gull, western gulls, glaucous-winged gulls, many rock doves, one mourning dove, a belted kingfisher, a downy woodpecker, two kinds of flickers, numerous black phoebes, a Stellar's jay, ravens, a couple of chestnut-backed chickadees, two kinds of wren, three golden-crowned kinglets, a dozen ruby-crowned kinglets, a smattering of robins and wrentits, a dozen American pipits, two hundred fifty European starlings, a Hutton's vireo, more than sixty warblers of three different species, more than a hundred sparrows of four different species, two species of junco, numerous red-winged blackbirds and Brewer's blackbirds, over three dozen western meadowlarks, one house finch, fifty house sparrows, seventy-one pine siskins and one — for the first time ever — great-tailed grackle. All birds were seen within a few hours on one foggy and rainy day. Without even trying I can think of other birds — owls, for example, or snowy egrets and turkey vultures — I see at the estuary regularly. Birds missing on the bleak December 30 of the "count," were probably present the day before and/or the day following.

The swans steal the estuary show. After nesting on the tundra of northern Alaska and Canada, they wing in to settle on a soggy Stornetta Brothers' field. Each year, on one day and without warning, they arrive en masse — a white blessing. When I see them, I know winter has begun.

Tundra swans, *Olor columbianus*, used to be called whistling swans. One hundred to three hundred overwinter on the Garcia every year. This past winter saw one hundred seventy-five of the big beauties. Adults are snow-white with black legs, black feet, black bills with a bright yellow spot below each eye. Young birds are a grayer shade of white. They, some only three months old when they arrive, have been on the move for half their lives. In March the flock flies away. One day they are here, then they are gone. I never see them leaving.

Garcia estuary extends a little more than a mile and three-quarters from the confluence of Hathaway Creek to where the river enters the ocean. You can see the estuary from Highway 1, just south of where the road crosses the river. The road, the river, and Hathaway Creek form a misshapen triangle (the road leg is as sinuous as the river leg). The triangle is filled in by the Stornetta Brothers' fertile field beyond which lies the estuary. Fairly small as estuaries go, this one includes eighty acres of open water and mud flats, plus another one hundred fifty acres of upland-type vegetation.

When the estuary was first surveyed in 1870, the river's mouth was exactly where it is today, hard against the high, erosion-resistant bluffs of the point. But the river channel has, over the years, swung farther and farther north. Most Northern California rivers close up in summer when the flow of water is low, allowing sand to choke the flow out to the ocean. But the Garcia, like many of its human advocates, enjoys an ever open mouth. At the beach, a big grass-covered dune, serves as a six hundred fifty foot buffer between the river's last meander and the surf. Recently, though, the dune has dwindled to a low sand bar only two hundred fifty feet wide. If the sand bar were ever breached by waves, tides, or flood, the river would gain a different outlet, a much broader one situated away from the bluffs. The new outlet would slow the current, and silt deposits would close the Garcia in the summer, making it impossible for spawning fish to return, destroying the estuary's fish nursery, wreaking havoc with the bird, mammal and reptile communities, as well as dealing an economic blow to the Stornetta Brothers whose crops would be drowned.

When the Watershed Advisory Group first studied the river it proposed beefing up the old sand bar and armoring it with vegetation to make it impenetrable. However, in the long run, well-enough got left alone. Someone sensible pointed out that the outlet is probably never going to plug up, and even if it does and another mouth opens, ocean waves will tend to push it back up against the bluffs.

Since the original 1870 survey, the estuary has gotten wider and the river has changed shape. As late as 1965 the river made a sharp bend at Pot Hole — a hole beloved of swimmers — then ran straight as an arrow to the bluffs and Miner Hole, most celebrated fishing hole on the entire watercourse. The river's channel has lost so much of its bend, though, that Pot Hole has been left high and dry, and the scouring forces, which used to keep Miner Hole big and deep, have lost their kick so that Miner Hole has filled up with silt.

To oblige the anadromous fish and their intrepid stalkers, the WAG wanted to fix Miner Hole by realigning the fourteen feet of the upper estuary channel to restore the lost meander. This was supposed to encourage the river, flowing along the bluffs, to scour the bed near Miner Hole. The cost of such a project turned out to be beyond the group's means, but before WAG got back to its proverbial drawing board, two successive winters dumped so much water into the river it began reforming its bends naturally. All may come right in the estuary without human interference.

Winter is rain, and rain is winter. In the Garcia's upper watershed the annual precipitation is over sixty inches. At Point Arena it is around forty inches. Almost all of it comes down within three or four consecutive months. My first winter here I wrote in my journal:

> 12/15 It doesn't ever get very cold — the mean winter temperature ranges from 44° to 48° — but it rains and rains and rains. And rains. Water pours down the inside wall of my chicken coop, the goats' grain grows mold. Nothing in the house ever dries. From every door knob hangs a dripping garment. Puddles form between rooms. We are well into our second hurricane in 48 hours…

The marine influence that makes our climate temperate makes it intemperate, as well, bringing forth the storms that ravage trees and demolish wharves. Compliments of the sea, we get temperatures which fluctuate little, yet all hell is guaranteed to break loose several times a year.

My first storm experiences were grandiose enough, but unbeknownst to me, that particular winter was exceptionally mild. Then came the amazing storm of January 1983. Wind ripped our gates off their hinges. It snatched shingles from a roof I had laid only a few weeks before and hurled them into the bull pine forest where it was busy knocking down trees — the copse directly behind our new house was the scene of wholesale slaughter. At Arena Cove, a pumped-up sea took away the wharf entirely.

Some winters are worse than others, but none passes without big storms. We lose power so often we stay prepared with a nice variety of lanterns, oil lamps and candles. We heat with wood, cook with gas, and tell time with battery-powered clocks. We even use a hand-operated coffee grinder my grandmother used to keep in her breakfast nook solely for decoration. The hardest loss for me is running water. Because we pump from a well, when the electricity goes, indoor plumbing goes. We maintain a good supply of plastic bottles filled with water, but it is surprisingly hard to remember not to flush a toilet, especially for kids. In every blackout, even ones commencing at 2 AM, I immediately made a circuit of the bathrooms to tape toilet handles to their tanks.

In sixteen years I've lived through such a great number of storms my memory no longer distinguishes one from another, but, along with the '83 titan, one other storm stands out. February of '86, it was. Egad! What a storm. Sitting in bed I could feel the wall at my back flex as the wind punched the south face of the house. Rain burst against my window like gravel slung from a catapult. One terrific gust actually popped the pane from its glazing. A friend, Alan Sharp, had eaten dinner with me. He should have just stayed all night, but he didn't. Driving his car back to Sea Ranch, he told me later, felt like steering a small sail boat in a high sea.

The gale persisted all night and into the morning. At breakfast I saw the baby cow's gate blow open. I tried to close it, but the wind was so fierce I couldn't. The kids and I were chilly, but if I lighted a fire, smoke blew back down the chimney filling the house. Two days of this. Trees toppled; roofs flew off. Power was off for days and days

To the south, the Russian River was sixteen feet above flood level, and, just beyond Fort Ross, a piece of Highway 1 disappeared in a slide. North, the rising Navarro closed Highway 128. We were stuck between them. Practically in our back yard, the Garcia spread out and covered both estuary and highway. Before the storm demonstrated its full potential, my husband had gone to Elk to rehearse music with a friend. Now he couldn't get home. Monday, at low tide, I drove down to check the state of the road. Rounding the curve above the estuary I saw a vast body of water where Garcia flats ought to be. All the fields, the road, everything from Miner Hole to the bridge was transformed into a lagoon. By my calculations, I wouldn't be seeing Alan again until Easter.

The flats flood when the river rises in conjunction with the tide. Against such an eventuality, locals check tide schedules before traveling north for even a few hours. One day I went to work in Caspar without the least concern for getting cut off from home because it had long since stopped raining. What I didn't realize was the rain had not stopped in the headwaters. It had, in fact, kept coming down in torrents. In the middle of my project a call came from home to warn me the river was rising fast. Leaving a big mess at the Black Bear Press, I raced the flood. I reached the Garcia bridge just as the Cal Trans man got out of his truck to set out the ROAD CLOSED sign. The pavement was submerged, but not deeply yet, so he let me go on. Leaving a wake, I rolled through the rising water, the last car to pass for several days.

"Man harnesses the wind and the water, but alas! they kick over the traces and the harness does not amount to much."[1] Anna Reed, mother, activist, journalist, editor. Anna Madora Morrison, she was, just twenty-one years old in 1871 when she first visited Point Arena. Most of the members of her big family were suffering from malaria, so it fell to Anna, the oldest child, to support them. Nineteenth-century America's mania for lectures gave her the means: a self-styled rustic reverberation of the Lyceum movement. She traveled around Northern California, delivering lectures then passing the hat. Denizens of the backwoods, with a yen for feasting their ears on the likes of George Catlin, Horace Mann, or Ralph Waldo Emerson, happily settled for pretty, quick-witted Anna Morrison.

> "Her lecture, 'Woman, Her Rights and Proper Sphere of Action,' was an able one...Miss Morrison is sincere and earnest in her convictions and sustains them with great ability. She must be heard to be appreciated. To those who have not seen her we can only describe her as a beautiful young lady, with cheeks like the petals of a rose, with a sparkling, loving dark brown eye, beaming with intelligence, and rich dark brown hair. Her enunciation is clear, distinct and melodious, her language elegant and forcible, her smile winning and fascinating, her disposition most amiable, and her whole life characterized by a noble devotion and true morality...." 'Juanita' [a.k.a. John C. McPherson]
> *The Mendocino Democrat,* 12/15/1871

On December 13, 1871, Anna's itinerary brought her to Point Arena in the middle of an intense winter storm.

> Wednesday, Dec. 13. Reached Point Arena. Lectured, collection $12.25/...Garcia Mills, $21.50... Saturday, Dec. 16. Here we are at Gualala, close by the sea. Collection $7.75.

On December 19 she celebrated her twenty-second birthday in Point Arena. Before she and her little brother who traveled with her could leave for Greenwood and her next lecture engagement, the swollen river gobbled up its bridge. "The Garcia bridge has...succumbed, and so, water bound we are for some days yet to come. Slides innumerable are everywhere, the very face of things changed by the force of the pitiless storm." Anna chucked her itinerary.

From her diary she appears not to have found her stormy captivity a great hardship. She and her brother put up at Lyman's Hotel, a large boarding house, still standing today, blue and Victorianly picturesque, at the corner of Main Street and Eureka Hill Road. Lyman's was full of young people. Every evening they pushed back the chairs and called in the fiddler.

Of course, Anna had no idea how long she would have to stay. Day after day she checked on the river only to find herself still marooned. One morning, though, the mail got through— "broke the blockade of the storm," as Anna put it. The postmaster, LeGrand Morse, son of Luco's long ago agent, Dr. Julius Morse, needed a large market basket to carry the Morrisons' mail.

At last, seven weeks after they arrived, they were able to resume their journey.

> February 11. Caspar, Mendocino County. Here it is almost the middle of February, and not one line of a Journal recorded. Well, I am not entirely to blame, as I have had no opportunity of securing a Journal in the out-of-the-world places where I have been. For two months I have been storm bound on the coast. Have visited Gualala, Point Arena, Garcia Mills, Cuffey's Cove, Navarro Ridge, Little River, Mendocino City and Caspar, where I am at present. Came here today through the glorious sunshine. The breeze is sweet and bracing. I hope the weather is now settled, for the prolonged storms have caused me much inconvenience. But the two months have not been wasted. I have made friendships that can end only in death - I trust not even then...every event of these days is engraved upon the pages of memory in letters that burn and glow with sweet intensity.

> Oh! this winter by the sea! It can never be forgotten. Its memory is valued at a price no gold can ever buy. And may it live in my heart till my hair is white as snow.[2]

Anna Morrison's diaries are filled with tales of rejected suitors. The following August, after a whirlwind courtship, she married a forty-three year old man who came to one of her lectures. John Reed had made his fortune in the California Gold Rush. Three months before he met Anna, he sold his two mines, and was well-fixed when the newlyweds moved to Ukiah. Over the next twenty years John Reed lost most of his money. He died in 1900, a poor man, leaving Anna with five children and fiscal problems like those of her young days. After a short-lived farming venture, she returned to her old vocation, this time committing her earnest convictions to paper. She worked for one newspaper, then another, before accumulating enough capital to buy Carl Purdy's house in 1904 and found her own magazine, *The Northern Crown.*

She never gave up lecturing and was a popular speaker at social meetings and celebrations. In 1892 she was the first woman ever asked to give the annual address at the California State Fair. Forever favored with offices and honors, a community-minded career woman, surrounded by a large, demanding family, Anna Morrison Reed continued to ruminate on her sojourn to the Coast.

> "Thirty years ago, on one thirteenth day of December, we first saw the stormy coast of Point Arena. There for seven long weeks we were stormed in. There the gay party of young people at Lyman's Hotel, laughed and sang, and danced the hours away, to the music of J.T. Mills' violin..."[3]

REFERENCE NOTES

1. Editorial, *The Northern Crown*, March 1907, in *Anna Morrison Reed: 1849-1921*, edited by John E. Keller, page 143.

2. Anna Morrison Reed's Diaries, in *Anna Morrison Reed: 1849-1921*, edited by John E. Keller.

3. Editorial, *The Northern Crown*, March 1907, in *Anna Morrison Reed: 1849-1921*, edited by John E. Keller.

Chapter Twenty

RIVER SEASONS: SPRING

Alders and willows in bud. First of the California finches, bright yellow, bounding down the hill ahead of me. The advent of spring. No dramatic transfiguring. Winter doesn't halt; it simply winds down. Just when we start thinking rain has been falling since the beginning of time, one clear day comes. Then another and another. Things turn green, but slowly, slowly. I never notice the process has begun until every field is Easter green and the sleek mahogany-colored willow branches are spotted with fuzzy white catkins.

One morning when the sun was particularly bright and warm Peter called. During the previous weeks the Garcia River had gone through a series of floods, and Peter was itching to see what the drastically high waters had done to the stream channel. Within the hour three of us were launching two canoes beside the Eureka Hill Bridge.

The river was alive now and kicking. Paddling was going to be easy. The water would impel us along; all we needed to do was steer. Because we expected to run into obstructions— crapola in the water, Peter calls it — we packed, along with our usual gear, my folding saw.

The deep-green water was vigorous. We hadn't been on the river since early December and, glad to be there again, we were in high spirits, joking and singing silly songs while Peter aimed his camera to record high-water marks, changes in the stream's course and banks. A powerful magician, the flood, intermittently turning our old friend Garcia into a stranger.

Ahead of Alan and me, Peter maneuvered his canoe to river-right where the main channel used to run. But today river-right looked like a tangle of strainers, so Alan chose to pass to the left of a skinny, new island of alders. Beneath us now, beneath the water, lay a gravel bar, and as we neared the end of the skinny island, where our route would merge with Peter's, the water got shallower and shallower.

In a second we were going to have to make a sharp right and then a sharp left. "Now," Alan called, "Pull right." From his seat he couldn't see how shallow things were up under the bow. I gave the paddle my all but couldn't get it in deeply enough for a good bite. Try as I might, I couldn't move us to the right.

"Pull! Right! Hard!" His voice lost its nonchalance.

We simply weren't going to evade the mess on our left. As soon as we entered the deep, fast-moving channel, we broached against a big, downed alder. Our right gunwale dipped dangerously. Thrown off balance by the impact, I couldn't heave my body to the downriver side fast enough to level things off. The canoe rolled over. As I went under the water I still could hear Alan frantically shouting, "High side! High side!"

I came up face to face with the uppermost branches of the tree. Alan was to my left, slightly upstream. I had no idea where the canoe was. I tried to pull myself up onto the trunk, but powerful current and yielding branches kept me neck-deep in the water. In fact with every passing second I was sinking deeper, my flotation vest as effective as a chiffon scarf.

Alan was only five feet from me, yet I could scarcely hear his voice in the loud rush of the river. "Climb onto the tree," he yelled, but he, too, was still in the water. I bobbed up with just enough time to shout, "Don't worry about me. Get yourself out," before being dragged down again. Selfless love, or did I judge his best interests to be my best interests? Who knows. I know only for some reason I needed to assure him I was doing just fine.

When I first tumbled in and felt a force of water stronger than any I had experienced ever before, I thought: Oh shit. This is it. This is drowning. But then, heartened by my stalwart struggle — though I had ample evidence it was getting me nowhere — I began to think: I've gotten us out of tight spots before. I'll get us out of this one. Finally, though, utterly submerged and no longer surfacing even occasionally, I relaxed into the not-entirely-useful conviction that as long as I could see daylight I was safe. So, eyes wide open, I kept my face turned upward. Above me the cloudy green water rippled in the sun. The tree's budding limbs shivered in the pulsing current. I'll never forget how that tree looked.

Alan swears I was underwater when finally he got himself out, but could this be true? I had glommed onto the muzzy notion that the reason I was underwater was that he was walking on my tree and his weight was pushing it down. Once or twice I tried to tell him to get off the tree so I could catch my breath. To attract his attention I wanted to wave my hand, but couldn't persuade myself to turn loose of the branch with even one of my hands —

I was scarcely managing to hang on with both of them. I was determined not to let go lest the river sweep me under the strainer where I would be trapped beyond retrieval. So, hands gloved in fingerless bicycle gloves, I clutched my limber little branch.

I became aware of a big hand grabbing the waistband at the back of my pants. Having gotten out of the water, Alan made his way to the downstream side of me. From the fixed point of my arms, my whole body drifted downstream, riding like a pennant in the wind. He took hold of my ankle and forced me to let go of the limb. As my torso floated toward him, he hauled me out by my britches. That's how he says it happened, but how can it be true when I could swear I never gave up my fix on the sustaining sunlight?

With Alan's help, I made it to the substantial trunk of a tree behind the alder. Sitting, I inched my way across to the left bank. Half way I spotted the green bottom of our overturned canoe just as it broke loose and headed downstream. Peter miraculously appeared and, seeing our canoe on the move, turned around to chase it.

Now Alan began to fret about whether to rescue his hat. He could see it hanging on a snag and wanted my permission to go back into the water to get it. I told him he was out of his cotton pickin' mind. We hobbled across the broad gravel bar. We couldn't stop talking, going over the event. We wanted to stop our verbiage, but, compelled to relate the details of the accident again and again, we simply couldn't stop talking about it.

Peter recovered our canoe for us. He had first to paddle upstream to find out what the devil had gone wrong. Then he had to chase the canoe and, single-handedly, capture it, dump the water out, and tow it back upstream. Amazing feats of canoe prowess. The current and Peter's waning energy stopped him before he made it all the way to us, so Alan and I stumped and sidled along a steep embankment to a spot across the river and slightly upstream from the rock where our canoe was tied. Peter ferried me over to it. Poor Alan, though, had to dive in and swim. As his blue-clad torso swept past us, Peter tossed him the rescue line and we hauled him aboard.

We still faced a couple more hours of paddling.

Two weeks later we approached the Garcia again. Again we put in at the bridge. Although I pestered for several days to take this trip, I was more than a little nervous.

The river had receded enough that the downed alder was almost entirely exposed, and the subsidiary channel Alan and I had so unhappily chosen, was high and dry, solid gravel. We eddied out and walked around, investigating. None of us could decide exactly where I would have gone had I let go. Peter thought it was well I had hung on. Alan, gazing at the multilimbed strainer, shook his head. "I just don't know…"

We hoped to find some of our gear. I say "our" out of generosity to the One Who Saved My Life. But, truth to tell, I lost nothing. I had, as Alan had taught me, carabined everything to a thwart or to a seat. Nor had I dropped my paddle. When we went under, I hung onto it, and when I bobbed up for the first time, I quickly wedged it into the arms of the waiting tree.

Much of Alan's gear had been properly hooked onto something. His dry bag with our nice dry clothes, his day pack with his lunch, the extra paddle, the bailing bucket, the rescue line — all were where they should have been when Peter righted our canoe. But his paddle had disappeared along with a few important things he had carelessly stowed. Our car keys, for example. Alan was paddling with them in his pocket. And his new Gor-Tex jacket, casually tucked under a rope. His hat had been on his head where it belonged, so I won't fault him for that loss.

Today we found nothing but the jacket. And a sorry sight it was too, with pounds and pounds of silt packed between Gor-Tex shell and inner lining. Alan looked awfully sad. He held up the soiled and weighty mass, and Peter said, "Oh, nice. A jacket anchor."

I was skittish. Whenever the canoe rocked, even slightly, I grabbed the gunwales. And I kept trying to get Alan to steer straight down the middle of the river, even when the channel was clearly somewhere else. More than once I turned loudly apprehensive. "A strainer," I warned. Alan's tone was uncharacteristically mild when he said, "Well, yes, I guess that is a strainer. Or it would be one if it was down here near the water. But it's way up the bank, so we don't need to worry about it."

The sky was overcast. After lunch the wind picked up, making us bloody cold. Not a fine day for the river, but a necessary trip.

Chapter Twenty-one

RIVER SEASONS: SUMMER

Early. Seven or seven-thirty a.m. We parked at Voorhees Grove, laced up our walking shoes, and began to poke around the brush looking for the trail. We didn't know what we were doing, were directed by instructions, sketchy instructions from various and contradictory sources.

My son Preston, his friend Suzanne, and I were bound, on this gray August day, for the Point Arena Hot Springs, seven or eight miles up the Garcia River. We located a thread of trail and began to single-file through the brush, but within a couple of hundred yards, the trail had disappeared entirely. Peering across the shallow summer river, we thought we could see a path on the other side, so we took off our socks and shoes, and waded across, sat down, put the socks and shoes back on, and set out again.

Two days earlier, Preston and Suzanne had arrived in California from a year in Austria with oodles of things to tell me, so when the trail disappeared again, we blamed our absorbing conversation for distracting us onto a false fork. We backtracked. No forks. Should we recross the river? Much discussion — Suzanne and Preston rarely made any sort of decision without exhaustive review of theses and antitheses. At length it was decided: back across. Down we sat upon three boulders, and, once more, we stripped off all footwear. Back on the other side we followed a bit of trail until it petered out. P and S drew themselves up for another mooting, but I said, "Screw it," and slogged across the water fully shod. We were never going to complete a round-trip journey to the hot springs today if we didn't keep moving. Most people stay the night after the long trek up there, but we couldn't, as we were flying to Hawai'i the next morning.

The trail was gone for long stretches. It wasn't merely invisible, it was nonexistent. As soon as we were able to admit the truth of this inconvenient fact, the choice to plod right up the middle of the river was an easy one to make. The riverbed was too rocky to walk barefoot, so before long even the last holdout, Suzanne, surrendered to wet shoes. My shoes, an ancient pair of

Nikes, were so full of holes the sand and gravel churning over the tops and into them, were able to exit conveniently through the sides and toes.

Midmorning the sun broke through the thick ceiling. Soon, glad to be together, we turned warm and cheerful. At a certain point where the going was easy and the scenery fine, we smelled fresh coffee. A hallucination? Round the bend we came upon a man and two children camping in a stand of young redwoods. Their breakfast stirred Suzanne to take a sandwich from her day pack.

Preston said, "Mother, in Suzanne's family they eat when they're hungry. Nobody taught them how important it is to wait til mealtime." His tone was philosophical, perhaps a bit wistful, no hint of reproach, but I got the message.

"Are you hungry," I asked.

"Yes." Pause. "Are you?"

"Yes." Pause. "Why don't you eat something?" I asked him.

He sighed, consulted his watch, and left his lunch untouched. He and I both tried not to look at Suzanne taking big noisy bites now out of an apple as she walked along.

The nature of the trail made progress so slow we couldn't judge with any confidence how far we had come. I had heard tales of hopeful bathers returning home without so much as a glimpse of the hot springs. My private opinion was that they had turned around too soon, yet it was entirely possible they, without a guiding landmark, had passed them by. However, as we approached the springs, I saw — or rather smelled — that it would be impossible to pass them without noticing.

The smell of sulfur was accompanied by a change in the river. Rocks became boulders. Banks rose and closed in, canyon-like. Then the river's shallow flow deepened into a broad swimming hole. Above it we found two concrete tubs three feet square and four and a half feet deep, but one of them was broken so it held no more than three feet of the steaming mineral water that flowed into them.

⚜

> The Point Arena mineral springs, situated about twelve miles east of this place were bonded by the firm of Tindall, Kimball & Welles some weeks ago to give those gentlemen an opportunity of surveying the land and making the necessary investigations prior to purchasing

> the property. Last week Mr. Tindall went over the ground and ran the lines, and, after a thorough inspection of the premises, reports that he is more than pleased with the intended purchase. The springs are surrounded by high mountains and are now difficult to reach, but Mr. Tindall assures us that a good road can be made on an easy grade. The springs are a valuable piece of property that if Mr. Tindall's report is accepted by the other members of the firm, Point Arena will soon boast of a pleasure resort second to none in the State. The water of these mineral springs differ in temperature ranging from 106 degrees to ice cold and flows in large quantities. Just what properties the water contains we are unable to say at this time, but we do know that many a sufferer of disease and sickness has received wonderful benefits from it. Notwithstanding that there are no accommodations there at present and that visitors are compelled to walk or ride on horseback over the mountains, scores of people have camped at the springs this summer and enjoyed the benefits of the invigorating waters. The gentlemen who contemplate buying the property are wide awake business men, and that they will make the springs attractive and fashionable is a certainty. *Point Arena Record*, September 1, 1893

Mr. Tindall was mistaken about the road. The hot springs was never easy to reach. Nor did these particular wide-awake businessmen buy the property. But within two years Frank Kelly of Caspar bought the springs and launched the big venture.

> The Point Arena Hot Springs, recently purchased by Dr. McCornack and Frank Kelly, are now in readiness for patrons. Mr. Kelly spent the winter there and built five cottages 12 by 13 feet, intended to accommodate twenty-four persons. These cottages are comfortable, being lined and papered and each one heated by a stove.
>
> Two baths have also been put in, making with the original 'hole in the ground,' three bathing places. The water is carried in pipes but twelve feet from the reservoir to the bath tubs, so that it loses neither strength nor heat in the transmission.
>
> Most of the grading down an abundance of water is always flowing. The temperature is 112 degrees, and for the cure of rheumatism and other complaints is equal to any in the state. *Point Arena Record*, June 13, 1896

Soon a three-story hotel was added to the cottages on the hill. The resort had everything — bar, billiard table, duck-pin bowling alley, croquet lawn, a horseshoe quadrangle, and a dining room that served elegant and toothsome meals. In the evenings the dining room became a hall for singing, dancing and general merrymaking, when the staff pushed all the tables and chairs against the walls and opened the lid of the upright piano. From the hotel building a wooden ramp led down to several enclosed redwood bathhouses, where guests could soak in the hot mineral water.

Old photographs of the place show soaring redwoods, rustic structures, smiling guests — most of them dressed to the teeth. Women wore long, high-necked dresses, and large elaborate hats. The men wore straw hats, bowlers, or caps with their stiff collars, jackets, and ties.

> The guests wandered through the forest walks, down to the rustic bridges, arbors and pavilions at the baths, sat upon the rocks along the beautiful banks of the Garcia river, swung in the hammocks, danced in the hall and put in a glorious day.[1]

The two concrete tubs, all that is left of the grand resort, were collection tubs for the hot water before it was piped into the bath houses. Preston and Suzanne refused to get into them without putting on their bathing suits so I, reluctantly, did the same.

"Bet if I weren't here, you guys would soak naked," I said, meaning: If you weren't here I would shed these threads in two shakes of feather boa. They looked at me wide-eyed. Under no circumstances whatsoever, they told me, would they consider taking off their clothes in public. I looked around. The place seemed thoroughly private to me, but under no circumstance whatsoever would I argue with those two.

For years before the bonding, the buying, and the building, the Point Arena Hot Springs was a popular camping spot. Bathers came to it by foot or horse. After the resort was built, stage coach or horse and buggy brought in the guests. The wearisome twelve-mile trip from Point Arena did not keep people away, though. The resort was touted as therapeutic, fashionable and fun. Visitors came by the score, local residents as well as visitors who traveled to Point Arena by boat. They landed at the wharf one day, spent the night at one of the town's three hotels, then pushed on next day to the hot springs.

> All parties wishing to visit the Point Arena Hot Spring should see Frank Beebe at his place. Horses can be secured and packing done

> at all hours. Meals served if desired. Hay and grain kept on hand. Terms very reasonable. *Point Arena Record*, September 25, 1896

Around the time of World War I, the resort's popularity went into a decline. Joe Scaramella, thinks automobiles ruined the business. Ironically, the first car he ever saw was one driven by a wealthy visitor headed for the hot springs. From that day on, horseless carriages made their way up the coast more frequently. "As people got into the habit of driving, they chose less and less often to visit places inaccessible by car," said Mr. Scaramella.[2] The Point Arena Hot Springs was definitely inaccessible by car.

Eventually the resort closed. Many locals remember hiking in to the springs to camp or hunt or fish when they were kids. In the '20s, they say the property was still intact — pillows on the beds, balls on the billiard table, glass panes in all the windows. Even as late as the late '40s, beds remained in the cabins, and, inside the hotel, the cash register and the piano stood in their original places. But over the years things were subtracted piecemeal. Souvenir hunters, thieves (is there a difference?), vandals and self-appointed custodians of public safety — all participated in the ruin.

Today a timber company, Coastal Forest Lands, owns the property. Afraid someone would get hurt, loggers knocked down the few crumbling bathhouses still clinging to existence in the '60s. But, as in the days before the resort was built, people come. They walk in or ride their horses. They camp, hunt, soak in the hot springs, swim in the cold river.

> Situated in the gorge of the river, with a dense forest of redwood surrounding, it is an ideal place to pass the hot summer months of the interior, or the cold foggy ones of the coast. Aurelius Carpenter, *A History Of Mendocino And Lake Counties*, 1914.

The site was thick with huge redwoods. After the price of lumber went sky high following World War II, logging took, within one decade, all but a few of the mature redwoods. Because of their location on a steep talus slope, a grove of six old-growth trees fifty-odd yards upstream of the hot springs were spared by the timber company. In the fall of 1993 a hiker noticed they were marked for harvest. He called Alan, and Alan called Coastal Forest Lands' forester and its attorney, Bryan Gaynor. Alan and Bryan had worked together on the WAG, drafting the Garcia Watershed Management Plan. The plan had propounded, among other things, the necessity of preserving riparian cover: "High temperatures in the main stem may be a limiting factor for coho salmon…which may be at high risk of extinction in the Garcia."

"Those six trees, their size, age, and location — some are within 20 feet of the river — make them ideal streamside canopy," Alan said. "Besides, the slope isn't stable. You all can't get those trees out of there safely." Bryan agreed and assured him the trees would be left standing.

Next July, Alan and I received a loud message on our answering machine. "They're gone! All six. I thought you said they were going to leave them." Eric Dahlhoff was either close to tears or furious, or both.

So much for CFL's good neighbor policy. We knew Bryan Gaynor's telephone promise was in no way legally binding, but we had expected him to do what he said he would do, or refrain from doing what he said he wouldn't do.

News spread fast among the FrOGs. Soon one and all were hopping mad.

> "The Point Arena Hot Springs are protected by law and deserve special consideration as a national and historic resource of the highest importance. We implore Coastal Forest Lands to stop cutting timber within sight of the springs…."[3]

Eric was perplexed though. When he saw them, the giant trees still lay on the ground where they were cut. After felling them, why had no one taken them away? The answer arrived several weeks after the question. I came home from working at the library one afternoon to find an intriguing message on the answering machine. A gritty, resolute female voice said, "This is Samantha Burkey. I'm a private investigator in Ukiah, and I need to talk to Alan Levine. Would he please call me at 468-1044 before five o'clock. It's very important."

Well, well, well, I thought, a plot thickens. I didn't know which plot was thickening — plots around here are numerous — so I waited on baited tenterhooks until Alan got home, which he did at 4:55, just barely in time to catch Ms. Burkey. She said she had found records indicating that he, Alan, had made much noise about a timber harvest plan above the Point Arena Hot Springs which had ended in the death of one Jose Rodriquez. The young man's family in Mexico had retained a Ukiah lawyer to investigate. Ms. Burkey worked for the lawyer and she wanted Alan to give her a run down on the six trees. Logging is dangerous work — according to the 1993 Bureau of Labor Statistics, of every 100,000 loggers working, 133 are going to die on the job, making it, after commercial fishing, the second riskiest way to make a living in the state — but Rodriquez's family seemed to sense something bizarre about the fatal accident.

Safety regulations exist, but loggers don't really like to see them enforced. Because the huge old growth trees are gone, loggers have to work faster to make the same amount of money from the smaller trees. Also, the easy ground has been picked clean forcing loggers to work steep terrain. They know what's at stake and want to be left alone to work fast enough to make good money. Safety regulations get in the way.

The logger most imperiled, the true bronco buster of the woods, is the faller or chopper. Riding treacherous terrain, wielding a three-foot, 13,000 rpm, 7 hp engine, multi-toothed chain, he kicks down big, unpredictable towers of wood. The faller gets paid for his risks, making $150 to $300 a day. An exceptionally skilled faller might even make as much as $500 in a day.

The others on the logging team are the bucker, who trims the branches and cuts the tree into logs. Logs roll and, sometimes, they roll right over the bucker himself. The landingman takes the logs off the yarder. He is in double jeopardy from both wood and equipment. On the bottom rung of the logging ladder is the choker-setter, who puts the cable around logs and hooks them onto the yarder.

Jose Rodriguez had been a choker-setter for three years. After hearing of his death, Sherlock FrOGies poured over last spring's newspapers to find what they had overlooked at the time: "A Ukiah logger was killed Monday in a freak rock slide that buried him under hundreds of square yards of dirt and rock in the Mendocino County hills south of Boonville….Jose Rodriguez, 23, died shortly after noon while working in steep terrain."[4]

Jose Rodriguez had been an employee of Matthews Skyline Logging which was working a contract job for Coastal Forest Lands at the hot springs. FrOG contacted Coastal Forest Lands, the California Department of Forestry, Fire Protection, the California Department of Fish and Game, and the State Water Quality Control Board. Their policy is never to leave anyone out.

They found out the California Department of Forestry had already begun an investigation by requesting the Division of Mines and Geology to review the landslide to see if it was caused by logging-related activities, and to determine if the hazard ought to have been addressed sooner — no engineering geologist had participated in the preharvest inspection since the plan had asked for no new roads.

Engineer's Geologic Review of Fatal Landslide on THP 1-93-024 MEN. Inspection date: April 28, 1994

Geologic Conditions: Area underlain by the Coastal Belt of the Franciscan Complex in the Garcia River watershed. The bedrock observed in the vicinity of the fatal landslide is a well inducted sandstone that is hard and strong. This relatively high strength is what allows for the high steep slopes....The brittle bedrock is broken by several fracture trends, including one that is parallel to the slope. Davenport (1984) mapped dormant debris slides on either side of the spur ridge that failed. He also mapped the steeply inclined side slopes along the Garcia River as debris slide slopes.

Observations: The fatal landslide was a rockfall that failed from the nose of a steeply inclined spur ridge. The landslide source is estimated to be 30 feet wide at the crown, which is roughly 300 feet above the Garcia River, increasing to 60 feet at its widest location. It is about 100 feet long (down the slope). Talus and slide debris settled out between the base of the source area and the river. No equipment operations had occurred in the immediate vicinity of this landslide. The slide's location on the nose of a ridge would have precluded either side cast soil or concentrated runoff that could have been generated upslope from affecting the stability of the slope.

The geometry of the spur ridge includes very steep (100 percent and greater) segments separated by ground inclined at 50 to 65 percent. The crown of failure occurred at a break in slope between a 120 percent below and a 65 percent slope above. Although the entire rock fall was from the convex nose of the ridge and did not extend into the topographic draws on either side of the ridge, accumulated talus in the draws indicates that similar failures occurred in the past from the sides of the spur ridges in the area...

The majority of the failed material consists of angular clasts of the underlying Franciscan bedrock. The failure occurred above a steeply inclined fracture plane that paralleled the ground surface.

The material above the controlling fracture surface was moist, as observed in the margins of the slide source area. Rainfall earlier in the week prior to the landslide may have resulted in some increase in driving forces through seepage pressures, while reducing frictional

> forces resisting failure. The hillslope had undergone many episodes of perched water, so this was not in itself the controlling factor.
>
> One 28 inch dbh pine tree was felled across the top of the ridge about 50 to 60 feet above the crown of the rockfall. The forester estimated that the tree was felled about one week prior to the landslide. It is possible that energy from the tree hitting the ground may have weakened the unstable mass, but the timing of the failure several days after the tree was felled indicates that this was not a major factor it triggering the landslide.
>
> The landslide occurred during a work break in the cable yarding activities. The logs that were left on the site where Mr. Rodriguez was killed shows that yarding this area had just begun…
>
> The maps included with the THP identify several unstable areas on the slopes above the Garcia River. These unstable areas are debris slides and rockfalls similar to that which killed Mr. Rodriquez. Some of these older landslide scars are much larger than the one that filed in April."
>
> **Conclusion:** The rockfall landslide failed from a naturally unstable slope. Yarding activities apparently did not have a major role in reducing the stability of the slope. It was probably not possible to identify that the slope was ready to fail.

Yet if "it was probably not possible to identify that the slope was ready to fail" how is it the FrOGs, who are neither geologists nor engineers, were able to warn Coastal Forest Lands, way back in the fall of 1993, that taking out those trees would be dangerous.

CFL insists that the accident was a freak, that Jose Rodriquez was simply in the wrong place at the wrong time. His family thinks otherwise. After gathering various bits of information, the Ukiah lawyer filed a wrongful death suit.

The slide originated one-hundred-fifty feet or so above the working men. It originated in an area of scrub oak where no cutting was done, but above that was an area where cutting had been done. Moreover, the skyline cable yarder itself is a heavy rig and its action of hauling heavy logs up the slope might have weakened a hillside of unstable Franciscan mélange. According to the geologist's report, when the area was mapped in 1984, landslide danger was documented.

The accident happened at lunch break. "The sun rose gloriously over these majestic trees that environ this charming spot, and ere the noon hour was reached..."[5] The yarder lowered the crew's lunch boxes eight or nine hundred feet into the canyon. As Jose Rodriguez was taking the lunch boxes off the hook, a few rocks trickled down the slope, then, bam! The whole hillside collapsed at once. The four other loggers hightailed it out of there, but Rodriquez tried to protect himself by hunkering down behind the felled timber. He was buried under hundreds of square yards of dirt and rock. The other men tried to dig him out. They were shaken. Poor Rodriquez. A good boy. A happy boy. He had been happy all the time.

REFERENCE NOTES

1. *Point Arena Record*, July, 1901.

2. *Independent Coast Observer*, February 21, 1992.

3. Friends of the Garcia, letter to the editor, *Independent Coast Observer*, August 5, 1994.

4. *The Press Democrat*, April 12, 1994.

5. *Point Arena Record*, July, 1901.

Chapter Twenty-two

RESTORATION

I've seen the Garcia River flowing at 37,000 cubic feet per second. That's a river I want to stay out of, a murky, treacherous river. In other seasons I've walked right up the middle of the riverbed without getting my shoelaces wet. At four cubic feet per second the Garcia is scarcely a river at all, just a trickle in a gravely wash.

Geography creates rivers. From high ground flows a river. The cast of the terrain gives the Garcia 73,275 acres to drain, 114 square miles. From highest point to mouth, the river measures approximately 44 miles, but add the length of all the tributaries to the length of the mainstem and you end up with 105 miles of river. In its upper tributaries, the Garcia's gradient is steep — small volumes of swiftly moving water. As the river approaches sea level, the gradient levels. The lagging flow becomes downright sluggish at the river's alluvial valley.

Once it has tapped its mountains, a river has a life of its own. It forms an organic solidarity with everything in its range. Rivers are powerful and precious things, especially in the West. The Garcia River chases through a thin strip of Pacific littoral, from San Francisco north, beyond the rain shadows which keep the rest of the West dry. For all its verdure, though, the Garcia watershed is part of the arid West. It receives not one drop of water from the sky for more than half the year — the half which includes the growing season. A single year of below average rainfall emphasizes the area's fundamental lack of water: faucets run brackish, ponds get shallow, grasses wither. A couple of years of drought brings the community to its knees: wells go dry, lakes and streams evaporate, dishwater has to be diverted to irrigation, toilet flushing becomes a luxury.

A languid trickle, or a gymnastic torrent, or any intermediate variation — the Garcia River changes form as the water supply fluctuates. And as it flows, however it flows, the river gives and the river takes away.

River lingo. Some terms are oddly poetic: runnel, mill race, freshet, thalweg. The first time I heard somebody say "thalweg," I thought she was using an acronym. But, as it turns out, thalweg is a real word, referring to the lowest place in the cross section of a river channel.

The new river word I am introduced to today is deadman, a verb: deadman, deadmaned, deadmaning. "We deadmaned in all this woody debris," Craig Bell tells the assembly rallied for streamside restoration at Stogie Stornetta's ranch. The Garcia is feeding on Stogie's pasture, gobbling up his generous slice of bottomland. During last winter's floods Craig assisted Stogie with some emergency remedies, bioengineering techniques discovered, or rather, rediscovered recently by one Evan Engber of Humboldt County. Craig worked wonders with one particular remedy — an ancient Chinese practice that Engber, working to restore his own riverside property, encountered in a sixteenth-century German manuscript. Large grids woven of willow limbs are partially buried in the river bank where they sprout, taking root and securing both themselves and the soil to the spot. Craig and his Mendocino Watershed Service crew planted a number of these woven mats last year.

Elsewhere they used another technique. They cabled dead wood — a great tangle of branches and downed trees large and small — together then secured the mass to the bank by means of more cables laid in three trenches dug from river to pasture. They attached the pasture ends of the three cables to large trees lying in a fourth trench excavated across the ends of the cable trenches, then filled in all trenches, burying the giant trunk and the cables. "We deadmaned all this woody debris to the bank here," Craig now tells us, "and it worked pretty good. See. Not much erosion."

Stogie nods, "Yup."

After the Watershed Advisory Group completed its enhancement plan, the Resource Conservation District established the Mendocino Watershed Service to do the work. When Craig Bell, a local sports-fishing guide, was hired as MWS director, he applied for money President Clinton was currently offering to offset job loss in counties hit by reduced timber harvesting in national forests. Craig's proposal to train locals in the art and science of stream restoration landed $450,000 for the City of Point Arena. Craig oversaw the training of forty people, some of whom MWS now employs on the Garcia. Since landowners were not obliged to pay for MWS restoration work, Craig was obliged to write more and more grant proposals — cruel work for an outdoorsman.

The community's active interest in restoring the Garcia has managed, in a fairly short time, to heal some of the river's nastiest wounds. This year the Garcia saw a few salmon return to spawn — not hordes of salmon, but more than it had hosted in a long time. And the steelhead population was downright bountiful. Up and down the river happy fishermen stood in their waders. The previous winter had brought heavy rain filling the Garcia to flood stage more than once.

The extra water did more for the fish than human intervention. However, since not all floods are promptly followed by bumper crops of fish, we assume our efforts are making a mark, and so, on a glorious mid-February Sunday morning, we turn out in a crowd to plant willows at Stogie's. The planting involves nothing more elaborate than jabbing fresh-cut willow branches of different sizes into the stream bank. "Not elaborate, maybe, but effective," says Craig, pointing out that most of what he planted in the same fashion last year is beginning to bud.

We carry armload upon armload of willow down to the river. Craig shows us exactly where he wants us to plant them, horizontal to the flowing water and in close-set rows. When he begins to tell us about Evan Engber's woven mat method of streamside stabilization, he describes it as, "...a very old method, ancient, devised in China centuries ago."

"Uh, oh," said a teenage boy, a high-school athlete whose father is one of Craig's fishing clients. "'Ancient methods' are guaranteed to break your back." Sure enough, hauling limbs and climbing muddy cut-banks is followed by swinging hand sledges and manipulating heavy iron bars.

Along with the countless willow sticks Craig cut from trees at Oz, he has brought fourteen pots of Sitka spruces. "Before today," he announces, "the southern extent of the Sitka spruce's range was Big River, thirty-six miles from here." Craig is keen for the spruces to move into the Garcia watershed and thrive. He envisions, ten or twenty years hence, rich riparian growth along this piece of river. He describes it as though he can actually see it.

As Craig speaks, Stogie nods and smiles. He is grateful for any help he can get. His ranch, the portion of Rafael Garcia's Rancho Del Norte bought in 1855 by John Hamilton, has begun diminishing with every passing winter season.

Saturday, March 2. Upriver slightly from Stogie Stornetta's property, Vernon Kendall has an even worse erosion problem. Vern's river front field, prime agricultural land, is a good seven acres smaller than it was a couple of years ago. As we walk across the diminishing pasture, we admire its thick crop of clover, and grass, with a smattering of vetch. Six of Vern's black-face Suffolks are obviously enjoying it — his deteriorating fences have allowed promiscuous traipsing among fields. A wall of unused fence posts, some of them decades old, are stacked near a barn full of rusting and inactive machinery. His fields are littered with sheep carcasses in varying stages of decomposition. Driving in, we passed a freshly killed lamb with a small turkey vulture feasting on one of its red haunches.

Vern's wife died recently, and he himself is in very poor health. He has, in fact, just returned from the hospital and cannot come outside to greet us, much less help us.

The Kendall place lies on the side of a gentle hill. A green apron of land fans out from the house and barns, a three-sided vista which slopes to the curve of the river. The curve, once a bulging loop, is getting steadily flatter as the river eats the land.

Vern's property has few trees but the verge of the river supports a skimpy stretch of willows and alders. Vern tried to check shrinkage of his pasture by chopping down the alders, cabling them to their stumps, then heaving them over the embankment. This was the worst thing he could have done, short of going out with a shovel and spoon-feeding his soil to the river. The trees were the only protection the embankment had. With them gone, the brink slipped away more quickly than ever. Vern has been asking for help, drastic help, for some time. Craig is keen to plant a batch of woven willow mats, but to do so he will need to peel back the bank, and moving that much riparian dirt requires a permit from the Army Corps of Engineers, and Craig is having trouble getting one.

"They're treating this thing like a request for the construction of a forty-acre shopping center," he complains. While his more substantial remedies wait, he can do nothing but plant trees, and that's why we're here. California Fish and Game gave Craig two thousand baby alders, leftovers from another project. "No warning. They just telephoned and said, 'Hey Craig, if you want two thousand free trees, come right now and get 'em!'" Craig hadn't much time to rally a work party, but he managed to get Peter Dobbins, Alan and me, and one other fellow who has never worked before on a river but wants to see what it's like. All four of us have other commitments for the afternoon, so we try to complete the morning's task quickly. Stick the shovel into the damp ground — a slice is all you need. Then poke in the little tree, taking care not to J-root it. Afterwards, kick the slice closed with your toe and do another.

A beautiful day. The sun is spread like butter across the luscious pasture, a slice of land I've passed many times while paddling down the river. A face-to-face view of the eroding bank looks like a sweetmeat — alternating gravel and soil layers are layers of nougat and fondant.

While we plant, Peter mutters, "We aren't just giving this guy something else to cut down, are we?" Unlike Craig, Peter doesn't feel protective towards Vern Kendall, a man obviously at the end of his life. "He's no longer competent to manage this land. Old age, ill health...whatever. None of it gives him the right to fuck things up this badly."

Across from the eroding bank, the Unnamed Tributary of AT&T fame enters the river. Directly upstream is the Manchester Ranchería, some of its houses visible from the Kendall home. Vern has always had a good relationship with the ranchería people, numbering some of the older men among his friends. He hasn't much use, though, for the younger Pomo generation — hasn't too much use for the younger generation of any culture, I'll warrant.

Vern Kendall was born in 1912 on the old Sheppard Ranch. His great-grandfather, a Nova Scotian, came here sometime between 1850 and 1855 by way of Vermont. Unlike most immigrants to the West at that time, Ichobad Kendall wasn't interested in gold. Nor was he interested in timber. He was a rancher, and he brought cattle with him, picking them up as he crossed the continent.

Before buying his place on the river, Vern and his wife, Clara, ran the Halliday Ranch — the Harris Ranch it was still called then even though the Hallidays now owned it. But the Kendalls wanted a place of their own. The opportunity to buy this one came along just at the season when the Halliday cows were beginning to freshen. It was a terrible time for the Kendalls to leave, but some fast talking by Joe Halliday's mother maneuvered Joe into the dairy business, allowing the Kendalls to go their own way.

Vern and Clara worked hard to make themselves a nice place. They milked a few cows, tended a garden — "You grew your vegetables or you didn't have any," says Vern — smoked meat. Vern has been in agriculture his whole life. As a kid he milked twenty cows at his father's dairy. After the morning milking, he carted the milk in a spring wagon pulled by a team of horses to the creamery, where he dumped it and washed the cans. From there he went to school. At night he came home to milk again. This was before he got to the sixth grade. He went to junior high and high school in the San Joaquin Valley where he worked eight or ten hours a day — for a dollar a day and board — bucking hay, doing irrigation work, or running a hay press which bound a dozen shocks of hay at a time and took a dozen men to operate.

Vern Kendall's is the same story the other old-timers tell: work your butt off on someone else's farm until you have enough money to acquire one of your own, a farm that drinks up your energy and your cash and gives back precious little, so to keep your farm you end up getting a second job. So while working his own acres, Vern worked for twelve years at the saw mill above Alder Creek.

Chapter Twenty-three

WILD, WILD WEST: STOGIE

To all appearances, Stogie Stornetta is simply an old-fashioned, mellow, elderly farmer. A familiar type around here. Before the Sunday when I helped with streamside restoration at his place, I had never met him. It was odd I hadn't, though, because he was a close neighbor whose personal history had influenced the direction of my own life. My decision to live in Point Arena was a side effect of choices he made. In 1979, or so rumor has it, he was romancing the pretty blonde divorcee who owned eighty acres I was soon to buy. Stogie had, in fact, created the driveway to our house. The pretty blonde divorcee was a young and classy woman, so the first thing I thought when I met Stogie — albeit fifteen years after the alleged romance — was, "What the heck did she see in this graceless old fart with barnyard and stable all over his boots?" I was thoroughly mystified. Stogie seemed congenial enough — I liked him just fine — but I would never have allowed him anywhere near my bed. The rumor mill had more to offer. It claimed the pretty divorcee had packed up and left town with indecorous haste because of Stogie's liaison with yet *another* woman, a liaison far muckier than Stogie's old boots.

Craggy face, low-slung butt, bandy legs, Stogie was an unlikely Lothario, yet he and girlfriend #2 — a widow who owned the bowling alley — were arrested and charged with plotting to murder Stogie's wife! When the news broke, no one believed a word of it. Everybody liked Stogie. They'd known him all their lives. His family had been here since 1870. The whole thing must be a mistake…or something more sinister. Hadn't he and the McDermott woman tried to unseat the 5th district county supervisor?

Carol McDermott was a singularly unpopular newcomer. She moved here with her third husband who had died soon thereafter when his throat was slashed in an automobile accident near Alder Creek. I never met Carol, but I saw photographs of her. She was a sixteen years younger than Stogie, but you couldn't tell it by looking. Her neck was thick. She wore big round eye glasses and bouffant hair-do. Very respectable looking, like a Midwestern nurse.

The most flamboyant character in the story was Richard Nail, a Fresno man with a long record of car thefts. He was the late Mr. McDermott's stepbrother. One dark night in December of 1979 he approached the sheriff claiming Carol and Stogie were offering him $20,000 to kill poor old Gloria, Stogie's lawfully wedded wife. "Carol told me she had a boyfriend that was quite wealthy and they wanted to get rid of his wife." Nail looked like a character from a swashbuckling novel. Thirty-ish, lean, long dark hair, and a dark slouch hat cocked over one eye. He wore the hat and a bulletproof vest every day in court. His second day on the stand, he added a pair of dark glasses.

Nail told the sheriff he hadn't refused Carol and Stogie's offer because he was afraid of them, but he never entertained the slightest intention of actually doing what they wanted, so he stalled. He told them he needed to construct a remote control device to "kill the electronics in Gloria's car" causing her to smash up. If the wreck failed to kill her, Nail was to leap into the breach and cut the woman's throat. It was a beautiful plan, guaranteed to work, but he needed a scanner to tell him where the police were. While he was putting together the remote control device, Carol was supposed to get him a scanner.

His first meeting was with Carol alone. She took him home to the house next to the bowling alley where she served him a piece of pie, telling him as he ate, "The woman you're going to kill made this." That night he slept in Carol's travel trailer, and the next morning she showed him prospective oil drilling sites on Stogie's property. "I'm going to be a rich woman," she said.

"What if Henry doesn't go along with the program?" Nail asked.

"Well, we'll just have to get rid of Henry."

When Nail came to Carol's place the second time, Henry — Stogie — was with her. He had bought a scanner for Nail, who showed the pair his "device," a bogus contraption fashioned from four flashlight batteries taped together with an assortment of wires sticking out. His employers hurried him off to tail Gloria. Nail followed her as far as Jenner, then went his own way. When Gloria returned home, safe and sound, Carol phoned Nail. Why had nothing happened? Nail explained that the electronics of Gloria's car were so powerful they overrode his device.

For the next several days they dithered back and forth on the telephone. Nail promised to try again after Christmas. Carol suggested he get Gloria on her way to Ukiah. Planning to overtake and warn her, he followed Mrs. S up Mountain View Road but lost her before they got to Booneville.

Carol's New Years Eve call was an ultimatum: *get the job done*, so Nail had to confess he couldn't manage the business alone. He was going to need an assistant. Carol sighed and said get one but be quick about it. That's when he went to the sheriff, a friend in Sonoma County. It was late at night, but upon hearing the story, the friend took him straight to his boss, who, by pure, perverse coincidence was Carol McDermott's former brother-in-law. The three men sat around his kitchen table talking until the boss believed the bizarre tale enough to contact the Mendocino County authorities.

Next day Nail drove to the coast in the company of Max, an undercover Mendocino sheriff. Max went queasy when he came face to face with Stogie; he'd met this guy before in the line of duty. But Stogie must not have recognized him because he accepted Max as the heroin addict he pretended to be. Carol did too. She handed him six hundred dollars and a key to the Stornetta home. Henry gave him a plan of the house folded inside a second payment of a thousand dollars.

"We got to get this over with," Stogie said. He was all raw nerves. "We can't keep it up like this." He told Max and Nail he would arrange for them to get into his garage. They were to fake a burglary, then kidnap Gloria. Max, equipped with a body transmitter, was taping every word of this meeting.

On Thursday Stogie dropped the two men off near his house, then went to the bowling alley where he spent most evenings. He planned to call his wife at precisely eight p.m. and ask her to bring him something. The killers were to be waiting for her in the garage, but when Max and Nail reached the ranch, they strode up to the front door and knocked. Poor homespun Gloria. She'd been Stogie's wife for thirty-three years. When the two men told her why they were there, she fell into hysterics and was in no condition to answer the telephone when Stogie rang. Max had no choice but to take the call himself. "Your wife is dead," he said.

The lovers were arrested that night in the bowling alley. They were charged with conspiracy to commit murder and with soliciting to commit murder.

"It's false, a lie and I can prove it," Stogie shouted. As the event unfolded, he sometimes seemed more concerned about the disgrace of marital infidelity than he was about the felony charges.

"I like to bowl," he said over and over again. "That's as far as it ever went! I'm home with my wife by 6:30 every night."

The trial was moved to Placer County. Stogie continued to protest his innocence until July when he pleaded guilty to lesser charges in return for testifying against Carol, who pleaded guilty to solicitation to commit murder after the charge of conspiracy was dropped. She was sentenced to eighteen months in jail. After she served her sentence, she stayed on in Placer County.

Stogie was fined and sentenced to a year in jail to be followed by a five-year probation.

Nail, ever clad in his bulletproof vest, demanded that the D.A. pay all his expenses — he had been living in hiding throughout the legal rigmarole — plus a hundred dollars a day for his testimony. His demands were never met.

When Stogie got out of jail, Gloria took him back. "He's changed one hundred percent from what he was. He is very attentive toward me and his surroundings and his home and his family," she said at his parole hearing in May of '81. She never balked at giving him a second chance, but then she'd never believed the charges in the first place. "He told me it was all true, but I don't believe it."

REFERENCE NOTES

Though a dramatized account, all information in "Wild, Wild West: Stogie" was taken from court records and depositions in Case 7077-C.

Chapter Twenty-four

AT HOME

Mid-May. I was impatient to get the vegetable garden started. Sunny weather, no wind. Perfect for getting bean and squash seeds to sprout. All winter and early spring it had rained, much big rain — floods, all that sort of thing. In the west corner of the garden, the low corner, a slash pile, ready to be burned, was a castle of woody debris surrounded by a moat.

Every time I told Alan I wanted to plant my vegetables he said, "Gotta wait. Ground's too wet. Gotta wait."

Alan went to Santa Rosa for two days. He would do various tasks and chores on Tuesday, stay overnight, then drive next afternoon to the airport to collect Carey and the baby, who were coming for a visit.

Wednesday morning, instead of fretting over my unplanted garden, I decided do something about it. If I couldn't rototill, I would, instead, fertilize the garden with manure and composted hay from the goat shed. Straight after breakfast I drove the tractor into the goat yard and, with much help from the two goats, shoveled the bucket full — then added a heap more just for good measure. I raised the bucket and eased the big orange Kubota over to the garden. At the fence I hopped down, unhooked the field fencing — the tractor doesn't fit through the gate. I drove slowly to avoid spilling my overfull load. The tractor bounced across the weedy ground I had never tilled or planted, but as it drove onto soil routinely turned over, the tractor bounced no more. Smooth. Precisely like driving onto an acre of Crisco. The wheels sank in and stuck. I hastily shifted into low range, gear one, put the tractor into four wheel drive, then slowly eased back on the clutch. The wheels spun in place.

"Oh, shit." I jumped down. The bottom half of the big back tires were invisible in the mud. I dug out around them, packed in some burlap bags, threw on a few shovels full of my load, got back in the driver's seat, checked: 4WD/Lo/First, revved up the rpms, eased back on the clutch. Careful, careful, slow, slow. The wheels flung burlap bags, manure and hay out behind them. When I dismounted I saw that now I was in all the way up to the axle.

Over the telephone Laurie told me Nick and Marty were gone, but maybe

Chester could help. Chester's twelve, but he aspires to be a dirt farmer, so I said, "Why not?" Chester was able to give me a pointer or two which might have helped at the onset, but not now. When I tried what he suggested, the wheels went round and round in the fertile black mud.

I called Nick at the ambulance headquarters. To my great relief he said, "Piece of cake. Just use the loader to dig yourself out. Dump the bucket and keep tipping it til it won't go any farther, til it's as upside-down as it'll go. Then lower it until you lift the front wheels off the ground. You're in reverse now, so you slowly back up while rotating the bucket back the other way, the shoveling direction. It gives you a backwards push. You'll dig yourself right out."

Yes! I had forgotten that technique; Alan had shown me before, but I had forgotten. I understood just what to do, but I couldn't bear to waste all my hard manure and hay shoveling work by dumping the load all in a heap many yards away from the plot I wanted to garden, so before extricating the tractor, I unloaded the bucket by hand, shoveling the load into a wheelbarrow and rolling it over to the where I intended to plant. This took some time, but I was no longer worried.

When the manure was all spread, I fired up the tractor motor and pressed the bucket into the ground. Up came those front wheels. Yes! No... The bucket itself began to sink. Pretty fast we were down under again. This wasn't going to work.

I called Marty. Now I was in tears. Marty drove his tractor over, bringing with him a city employee, Dan. I was enormously grateful. These guys were gonna fix things. Marty lashed the two machines together and began to tug me backwards while I worked at driving the same direction. Bang! The tow chain broke, scaring the daylights out of me. Take two, chain two. But my tractor simply wouldn't budge, and when Marty's tractor began to sink, he decided to abort the rescue operation.

Before going, Marty counseled me to leave the thing where it was until the ground dried. He was afraid I was going to do the Kubota some damage. Yet the idea of Alan coming home late tonight to find his precious tractor in this state was too awful to consider. I had but one other resource: Don Sorensen. I called him and said, "I don't care how big your bill is, I'll pay whatever it takes to get you to come up here with your backhoe." Couldn't it wait? he wanted to know. "Oh, Don," I wailed, "Alan's gonna kill me, literally slaughter me where I stand, if he comes home to this mess."

"How long do we have?" And I calculated Zero Hour to be sometime between 9 and 10 pm.

"Well," Don said, and he sounded like he was laughing, "I guess I have time to go get me some lunch first."

It seemed an eternity, but finally, amidst dust and a great roar, the backhoe, a truly gargantuan piece of equipment, came crawling up the hill, followed by Virginia Sorensen in her husband's pick-up truck.

In the blink of an eye I could see the backhoe not fitting between the fence posts, but I was wrong. Without an inch to spare on either side, Don maneuvered the machine into the garden. He climbed down to survey the situation and said, "You're stuck in the mud." His round face, ruddy from the sun, was perfectly solemn yet he still seemed to be laughing.

From the time they got here until they were gone, I never left off chattering, thanking them for the help, apologizing for my idiocy. Don told me at least a dozen times, and Virginia half again as many, that this could have happened to anyone. "Low place here," Don said. After a time the spot where the tractor was mired did begin to look a bit low.

Don is a backhoe artist. He dances it like a ballerina. A short man with powerful arms and hands, fingers as big around as Hormel sausages, Don, when melded with the towering six tons of metal, is as graceful as a cat. In mere minutes, without a fumble or a wasted move, he had popped my little pip-squeak tractor out of its grave. I thanked him again and again. I called him a knight in shining armor, and meant it. I was earnestly and immensely grateful. His blue eyes laughed.

When she managed to get a word in, Virginia remarked that there sure was a lot of water over here by the fence post. Oh, dear. The water line runs beside the fence post.... I ran to shut off the valve at the well, and told the Sorensens to go on about their business. I would take care of this new misadventure. But, no, the backhoe had broken the pipe, and Don insisted on fixing it.

The pipe broke in a spot where it runs above the ground on the way to the cows' watering trough. "That's good luck, isn't it?" I said, "That it runs above ground? Makes it easier to fix, doesn't it?" And Virginia mumbled something about if the pipe wasn't above ground, it maybe wouldn't have broken. In our workshop I located a piece of 1½" pvc pipe and the hacksaw. We had two couplings of just the right size. We were low on pvc adhesive, but what we had looked like enough.

"Sandpaper," said Don.

"What grit?" I wanted to know. We always have loads and loads of sandpaper. "What grit?"

Don looked at me but said nothing.

"Coarse or fine?"

Don, mouth still closed, raised his eyebrows, and following a moment's pause, Virginia said, "I don't think it matters."

Toting supplies, we trooped back to the broken water line, where Don measured, cut, glued. "Oh, thank you, thank you…." I went through all that again, and when we were done tried to send them on their way, saying that I would turn the water back on in… how long will it take that glue to set? But, no, again. Don would wait to make sure the pipe was not going to leak. Virginia looked at her watch. She had a beauty shop appointment at 3:00. Still plenty of time.

When I turned the water on, the newly patched pipe stayed dry as a bone, while all around our feet a vast lake welled up. No one said a word — we just commenced digging for the underground pipe. I made a vague gesture toward convincing them to leave the problem with me, but by now I knew Don was in for the whole toot and scramble.

Now a desperate scrounging began. Alan had a fair amount of scrap pvc lying around, but most of it was thin flimsy stuff Don refused to use. I collected all the adequate lengths I could find while Don ransacked the workshop for couplings. Virginia was dispatched to retrieve pvc pipe from the Sorensen pickup. Digging and bailing out the hole, Don and I worked with what materials we had for as long as we could but the water line, which angles, goes down, then angles again, was broken in several places, and we finally had to face the fact that someone was going to have to make a trip to the hardware store. Our little band was forced to separate — Virginia went to her appointment, Don took the backhoe home, I drove to Manchester with a precise plumbing list: so many elbows, so many couplings, a can of Wet Weld Blue pvc cement.

Don and I spent the remainder of the afternoon as deeply mired in muck as the tractor had been. Measuring, sawing, gluing, combined with digging and continual bailing of water that collected at the bottom of our hole.

Near the end, Don glued a coupling to our last piece of pipe only to discover the pipe had a crack down one side. I had wondered what it would take to douse the blue sparks of laughter flashing forth from his eyes. I now had to cannibalize my pvc/chicken wire strawberry frames to come up with a good hunk of the right stuff.

Underground we had compiled a strange piece of plumbing — a promiscuous arrangement of elbows and angles and arms and turns — white pipe daubed with purple and blue. But when I turned on the water (after, of course, being obliged to crouch in the bottom of the well house with the black widow spiders for 3 minutes holding the reset button of the underachieving pressure pump), I turned the blue Sorensen eyes back on, as well. Everything proved fit as a fiddle, tight as a drum. We took turns shoveling the dirt back into the hole. A strange piece of plumbing was buried there but it worked. Even then Don stayed on, helping me hose off the tractor, from which brick sized clods of mud plopped beneath the water's press.

Before I collapsed into a bath tub, I wrapped a marinating London broil and took it, with a loaf of bread, over to Marty and his family by way of gratitude. On the way I bought a bottle of Cognac for Don.

Don Sorensen refused to accept anything from me — not pay nor reward of any kind. He would take nothing I could think to offer. He wouldn't even promise to let me treat him and Virginia to dinner some night in the future. Nothing.

The chivalrous tractor rescue was not Don Sorensen's first act of gallantry on my behalf.

> 2/1/82: It took Don Sorensen eight hours to pull out nine or ten trees and level the site. I called him the Knight on the Golden Backhoe. He works very hard. When I say it took him 8 hours, I mean 8 hours straight without one single break.
>
> Alan and I worked ourselves to the ground, too - especially Alan, cutting up the trees with his chain saw, while I stacked wood. We worked all day and barely made a dent in the mess. Those trees, bull pine, some of them 60 or 70 feet tall. We'll get some firewood out of the day's job, but we'll have to have a bonfire as well.
>
> The site looks good, though. Very good. I think we've picked a pretty spot. I took some photographs of the clearing and leveling work, some of Alan with his chain saw, of Don lifting mammoth trunks to free Alan's chain saw when it got pinched. I took some of

the pictures from the ground and some from the roof of the mobile home. Don obliged me by waiting to push some of the trees over until I got my camera ready.

2/3/82 My left thumbnail is turquoise, and Alan's back is so sore that I have to tie his shoes for him.

2/7/82 Today while Don was digging out the foundation for us, his wife came by on her horse to watch for a while. When I saw her through the window I thought, Oh, gracious, she's going to want to buy a dozen of my eggs, and I don't have enough. But then it occurred to me: Who's going to transport a carton of eggs, Virginia on her horse or Don on his backhoe? and I stopped worrying.

Don helped us from the beginning. Even before we moved here someone gave us his name and, by phone, we hired him to unearth the septic system for the county inspector to check.

We arrived in an Audi Fox and an old school bus. As soon as we had unpacked our belongings, I was steamed up to start building a house. For one thing, I was not overfond of the mobile home. For another, I needed a job.

Peter Dobbins, an experienced house builder, showed us how to prepare the site. After we chalked lines on the ground, Don dug trenches for a perimeter foundation, and we constructed the foundation forms. But we had to postpone pouring the cement because of the weather. Finally, in the middle of March, we decided the time was right. We worked hard. A complete novice carpenter, I was slow at hammering in nails, so Peter and Alan gave me the job of cutting rebar and wiring it together. My hands, soon covered with innumerable tiny scratches, ached for days afterwards. My legs hurt, too, like saddle-sore, from climbing over the foundation forms.

The cement trucks were scheduled for Tuesday, but it rained Monday night so we were obliged to postpone the pour for another two days. After two days the ground was still too wet for the cement trucks, so the business got postponed again. I was hopping with impatience.

Finally the big day arrived, but the pour did not go as planned.

3/22/1982 When at 9:07 am, almost 100 yards shy of the house site, the first cement truck got stuck in the mud, I was very anxious. The stuff has to be out of the mixer within a certain amount of time or it hardens where it is. I was very anxious, especially after Hugh, who had come to watch, said, "I see you're going to have a bunker in your front yard." He figured the driver would have to dump the load right there where he was mired.

Over the phone Gualala Aggregates told me the second truck was on its way, and, being four wheel drive, would pull the other truck out. I hung up and came out the front door just in time to see the second truck begin to sink into the ground. It had not gotten as far, even, as its predecessor. Two 53 ton trucks, full of cement, stuck, up to their axles in my front yard.

Peter had brought two friends, George and Michael, to help with the pour. Anna had strolled over to watch, bringing Hugh Brady and a blacksmith named Lloyd, who was in town to shoe her horses. When the quagmire disaster began to unfold, Hugh, seeing what was about to happen, hightailed it home. But George, Michael, Lloyd and Anna pitched in to help. We were going to have to empty those trucks where they stood.

First thing Anna and I did was go looking for Don Sorensen. We bumped into him (almost literally, so frantically was I driving) at the corner of Windy Hollow and Riverside. When I told him there were two cement trucks stuck in front of my mobile home, he had to control himself to keep from laughing. He followed us up the hill, viewed the problem then hurried home to fetch his backhoe. He managed as well, by some undisclosed means, to enlist a PG&E backhoe. Don and the other backhoe driver succeeded in dislodging one of the cement trucks, and while it poured its load into the foundation forms, the rest of us tackled the other truck. Fill a backhoe bucket, fill a galvanized pail, fill a wheelbarrow full — an uninterrupted procession trudging back and forth between foundation and mired truck until the revolving mixer was scraped clean.

Things moved lickety-split. I shoveled gray glop and operated a giant vibrator which, while (allegedly) dislodging air bubbles lurking in the wet cement, threw cement into my face, most particularly into my eyes. I had never worked so hard in my life.

At four o'clock we realized we had too much cement, so Peter and I raced out to the animal house and built a frame for a 14′ x 14′ slab, piecing together odd lengths of rebar to reinforce it. I spread the cement by walking around in it in my high rubber boots.

After the circus was over, I paid Michael and George, as agreed, and convinced Lloyd, who had offered his services as a volunteer, to take a salary as well. Anna would accept no money but said yes to letting Alan replace the lost sapphire in her favorite ring.

Don, who most certainly had saved the day and knew it — "Who else could have gotten the PG&E backhoe?" he asked. "Pretty good, huh?" — would take nothing. He was adamant. He told me I mustn't pay the PG&E man either, but recommended I give him a new bottle of good whiskey.

When everyone had gone except Anna, Alan, Peter, and George, we scratched our initials in the wet cement, then collapsed with beers, laughing uproariously at things that weren't funny.

Before we poured the foundation, we had to decide where, precisely, to put the house. After much discussion we picked a spot and laid out the whole thing with stakes and string. Two goats and two dogs followed us around, watching with the silent, grave interest of graduate students. Alan backed off with the tape measure. Peter, siting through the short, inverted telescope of the dumpy level, choreographed: "Stop. Step to the left four inches. Back to the right an inch."

By late afternoon a thirty-nine foot by sixty-two foot rectangle lay marked off directly in front of the mobile home. By the next morning I decided the spot was all wrong. Peter would have to bring his dumpy level back over.

That was the first week in January. For the next three weeks stakes were pulled and pounded and pulled again. The house-to-be was waltzed around the already established septic system, until Alan mutinied. He absolutely was not going to go through the long process again. It was time to build.

The task of constructing a 2700 square foot house seemed daunting. I asked Peter if it was actually possible to start with stacks of lumber, boxes of nails, and end up with a house. He thought about it before he answered.

"No," he said, "it's not possible to build a house. But it is possible to build a foundation. And it is possible erect a frame. And it is possible to run electrical wires and plumbing pipes. And it is possible to lay a roof, to put in windows and doors...."

We broke ground in February of 1982, and in July of 1983 we moved into an almost finished house, a handsome house, a sturdy dwelling, somewhat overbuilt, secured thoroughly enough with Simpson strong ties to withstand a nine-point earthquake.

Peter was the only one of us with building experience. Many of the tools we used belonged to Peter, and when he had such things to cart, he came over in his truck. But his house and land were just south of ours, and often he rode to work through the two adjoining pastures on his motorcycle or on his Arabian mare, unnerving thoroughly my goats.

If Peter was the most experienced carpenter amongst us, I was, unarguably, the least experienced. At first I bent one out of every three nails I tried to sink. Every male in the county condescended, at one time or another, to show me how to swing a hammer. "Don't choke up on it so much." If I heard this once, I heard it a zillion times. Peter, however, quickly gave up trying to teach me to hammer straight, and taught me instead various methods for extracting weewaw nails. He also taught me to measure and cut with a circular saw, demonstrating how to flip 50 feet of extension cord to unhook it from whatever it's gotten caught on rather than walk all the way back to lose it.

By June the downstairs was framed. Of all the stages the house went through, I liked the skeleton stage best. We had laid the downstairs floor before framing, and now we lay the same 2x6 t&g fir on top of the downstairs walls, making the upstairs floor the downstairs ceiling. After we framed the upstairs, we did the t&g fir thing again, working on a slanted surface twenty to thirty feet above the ground. The morning when we started, I was terrified. The first board was the toughest because there was nothing but the rafters to stand on. Even the second and third board provided precious little standing room. About a third of the way up, I finally lost my urge to crawl on hands and knees. By afternoon, while we waited for Alan to cut and hand up the next board, Peter and I sang and pluckily executed soft shoe routines on the roof.

The laying of the composition roofing shingles has to be done just so. The pattern is tricky and Peter showed us precisely how it must be done. The first quandary, though, was getting the heavy roofing material up onto the roof. Alan's bright idea was to use a hay elevator, a conveyor belt used to load hay into a barn. Billy Hay loaned us his, and it worked, though not flawlessly. Every third load, on its way up, mischievously flopped over the side making an awful mess when it hit the ground. Once a load began to slip we, groaning, could do nothing but watch a slow-motion train wreck impossible to interrupt. Eventually we moved the immense load from ground to the roof.

The first layer of shingles runs along the bottom edge. The guys — Peter, Alan, Chris, and my son, Preston, fresh from boarding school and uncertain about whether or not he wanted to go to college (after six months as a carpenter's helper, he was dispatching applications to every college he'd ever heard of) — came up with a scheme for applying this rather dangerous first run. They would tie a rope around my waist and, holding securely in their collective grasp, would lower me to the steeply pitched roof's edge.

"It makes perfect sense," they said. "You're the lightest, the easiest one to hang onto if you fall."

So, safety line secured, I crabbed my way down the slope to work under the watchful eye and firm grip of Peter, Chris, Alan, and Preston — each had one hand around the rope — sitting side by side on the roof's peak. In my mind's eye I see them guzzling cans of beer and Pepsi. They insist they were not. Maybe I misremember in the matter of the cold drinks, but I am most certain they were lolling, expending no energy beyond what it took to flap their jaws as they issued instructions to me and prattled about what an important job holding the rope was.

Working on the roof, I could see for miles and miles in all directions. One afternoon, hacking at a shingle with my dull utility knife, I heard the snap of a camera shutter. Preston had my Pentax aimed right at me. Behind me rose a spectacular rainbow, both ends touching the ground. His picture: mamma — straggly hair, torn jeans, carpenter's belt like saddle bags on a pack mule — kneeling perfectly centered within the curve of the polychrome arch.

I wish I could say that over time I became an A-number-one carpenter, but I can't. I never could hammer worth a damn. From bending one in every three nails, I did manage to improve to bending only one in five or six, but I always needed many blows to do the job; I never approached driving in a nail with the three blows boasted by hot carpenters. I began the project with a decided fear of the circular saw, and, although by the end I was able to use it well enough, I never heard the tool's screech without visualizing what my thigh would look like if I slipped. I always wanted more hands than I had when I put in the blocking, and I blocked the entire house using a C-clamp to hold each block in place between the studs while I nailed it in. My drilling skills remained firmly iffy; many holes took off at a wonky angles. And then there was the matter of that monster drill, the Hole Hog, we brought out in the face of major screw ups. I tried using it twice. Both times the Hole Hog whipped around me in a violent spiral while the drill's embedded bit stuck, unmoving, in the wood.

My lack of capability notwithstanding, building a house made me feel capable. To start with nothing and end up with something as consequential as a house, a home, gave me the feeling I was equal to anything.

Chapter Twenty-five

MANCHESTER

One mile north of the Garcia River, bellied up to Brush Creek, is Manchester, the little hamlet inextricably bound by both history and geography to Point Arena. The two form a compound community, one simultaneously separated and united by the river.

Manchester sprang up in 1857 exactly where it is now, a mile and a half from the coast. Smeeton Chase described Manchester as, "six cottages, a store and post office, a weather beaten church on a hill." Mr. Chase, journeying up the coast on horseback, wrote his description in 1911, but substitute "school" for "church", and his words adequately describe Manchester today.

From the 1890s until the late 1950s a thriving creamery operated in Manchester, making the little town the hub of local dairy farming. But for creamery employees, farmers, loggers, ranchería residents, going to "town" customarily meant going to Point Arena. In the days of wagon travel, going to town was a fairly long ride. But after the automobile and paved highway turned the trip into a ten-minute drive, Manchester might have gone the way of ghost hamlets such as Fish Rock if the river had not kept it on the map. The Garcia habitually floods, separating everybody north of it from the mail and supplies in Point Arena. This problem of the seasonal flooding keeps Manchester's store, post office and small elementary school in business.

Though Manchester and Point Arena have ever been closely identified, local lore speaks of a time when the two, like the nation as a whole, were not one-and-indivisible. During the Civil War — or so the story goes — Manchester favored the South, while Point Arena was four-square behind the Union. At the time Manchester had no post office. Manchester men, arriving in Point Arena for their mail, had to run a Yankee gauntlet. Tense parleys in front of the Point Arena post office ultimately led to brawls. Finally, Manchester is said to have applied for a post office of its own. Locals swear to this tale. Maybe it is true, and, again, maybe it isn't. The Manchester post office was established on December 1, 1871, a mite late for a Civil War connection. Besides, the fact is several Manchester men served in the U.S. militia during the War Between the States. In all probability a fist fight did take place at the Point Arena post office in 1863, but I doubt the lines of enmity were as sharply geographical as the story wants them to be.

With the creamery gone, Manchester amounts to half a dozen houses, a store and post office facing each other across Highway 1, and an elementary school. But, waiting in the wings, Manchester possesses something more, something precious: Manchester Beach, a paragon among landscapes. Manchester Beach, a distinctive five-mile sweep of shoreline reaching north from the mouth of the Garcia to a mile and a quarter past Alder Creek, has been since 1973 a thousand-acre state park. Between rich silage-flavored dairy land, and a roistering sea, Manchester State Beach has everything: breaking waves, sandy shore, wind-swept dunes, wildlife, salty grasslands, hazy lagoons.

I have seen a surfer in Manchester's waters once or twice, but the cold, rough surf, a joy to watch, never invites me in. The boisterous waves snatching my ankles do not suggest a swim.

At one end of the beach, the lighthouse stands sentinel on the tall bluffs of the point, a promontory which has run through a series of names since Juan Rodrigues Cabrillo in 1542 — no one can say what name the Pomos used — dubbed it Punta Arenas. The following year Bartolome Ferrer referred to it as Cabo de Fortunas. Two centuries later Captain George Vancouver was calling it Punta Barrio de Arena. The United States post office, established nearby in 1858 was named Punta Arenas Post Office. Disestablished and reestablished thirty years later, the name emerged as Point Arenas. Ultimately the final 's' was dropped: Point Arena. All variations of Punta Arenas can be translated as sandy point, but in 1907 W. W. Fairbanks, in an article he wrote for the Northern Crown, offered a different interpretation. Point Arena, he insisted, referred to the point of a ring or circle.

> Should one have any doubt as to the title being appropriate, he should climb to the summit of the mountain range on the east. With the great Pacific far below and every curve and angle of its coast line plainly visible, one discovers that to the north of this bold headland, the shore swings far to the east in the form of a semicircle of which Point Arena is the extreme southern point.

Because the globe is dotted with Sandy Points in multiple languages, I found the Fairbanks translation imaginative, more to my liking than "sandy point," but entirely wrong, of course. In Spanish enclosed exhibition areas came to be called *arenas* not because they were round, but because they were spread with sand. Besides — all consideration of the Spanish language aside — the point was named as seen from the deck of a ship, not from the summit of the mountain range.

If Mr. Fairbanks' translation is mistaken, his description certainly isn't. The shore is curved, a graceful crescent, slightly flattened, running north and south. Into this shallow bowl of beach the Pacific's southerly currents ladle tons and tons of driftwood, strewing the long expanse of sand with immense logs, burls, and stumps.

Manchester State Park's zoological population is a Who's Who of rare and endangered species. A sizable community of Point Arena mountain beavers burrows in the marine terrace at the edge of the coastal dune and coastal scrub area south of the AT&T property. The beavers keep company with western snowy plovers, bald eagles, American peregrine falcons, brown pelicans. Lotis blue butterflies flit among ten sensitive plant species, and, close by, red-legged frogs splash, along with tidewater gobys, and several anadromous fish. Offshore the endangered grey and humpback whales pass in season.

I walk Manchester beach several times a week. With three or four different points of access, I get a variety of walks. Going in at Alder Creek on the north end, I follow the San Andreas Fault to the shore, then walk south.

If I enter the park at its center, where the AT&T cable from Japan makes its continental landfall, I can get to the beach along a path winding through a mix of northern dune scrub and northern coastal scrub — dune sage, wild buckwheat, and bush lupine — then through a bit of wetland which includes the solemn little lagoon, Davis Lake; or, I can park closer to the great melee of waves and simply walk up a sandy rise.

What I most often do, though, is go to Manchester Beach by way of the southernmost access, a ten-minute hike through the dunes. These dunes shelter a small stand of beach pine, *Pinus contorta*; a rare subspecies of *P. contorta* grows no farther south than here. Up and over the last lofty dunes, I suddenly confront the ocean in all its noisy vigor. The wind smells of salt and living, thriving fishes. I can turn left toward the lighthouse for a fifteen or twenty-minute walk to the Garcia River mouth, or I can turn right and walk north for nearly five miles before I run out of beach.

Along the way the backdrop varies: dunes, wildflower-covered cliffs, tough gray-green grasses of the Brush Creek and Davis Lake wetland areas. I make my way around driftwood debris and strands of seaweed and kelp, strewn across the sand. In the churning surf I see sea lions, shiny black heads in a washing machine. Today a small elderly Pomo man stands at the water's edge casting his net at the waves.

Undulating black lines in the sky — flocks of birds going south— while on the ground, all up and down the beach, other birds march in fussy clusters, taking to the air when I get close. Out at sea in winter I can watch grey whales pass, swimming down to Baja California to breed; six months later I see them traveling to the Bering and Chukchi seas.

Off Arena Point at the south end of Manchester Beach, out beyond the surf, something disturbs the surface of the sea. Blue, green, gray, brown, or purple — the water changes color according to the sky — but always this one splurge of white where the swell breaks on Wash Rock. Hundreds of years ago the point reached all the way to Wash Rock, now a ten-acre reef standing in a hundred feet of water. With steeply vertical sides, the completely bare and flat top of the rock is visible only at low tide. The rock, or more accurately rocks, is an agglomeration of several sedimentary masses of varying hardness weathering at different rates. A lithic fretwork of perforations, penetrations, caves, spiracles, vents, portholes, blowholes, gaping holes, pinholes, loopholes is occupied by a rich miscellany of marine life feasting on nutrients delivered to them by upwelling and by currents stirred by the Garcia emptying below the point.

No plants grow on Wash Rock, but below the waterline the reef is a veritable garden of invertebrates, colonial forms interspersed with individual sessiles. Bryozoans' mats, sponges, sea squirts, barnacles, hydras cover the walls, while schools of blue and black rock fish and eels swim in and out of the recesses, over and around the cobble and boulders surrounding the reef's base. Dungeness crab, redtail, surfperch, California halibut, huge ling cod, and Yelloweye. But oddly, no sea urchins, or abalone, probably because there is no seaweed.

In the sandy ocean floor around Wash Rock lie the remains of the many ships which met their end on this reef. The most recent was the 1949 wreck of the *Pacific Enterprise*. The eleven-ton British freighter was headed south with fifty-nine people aboard. A thick salty fog obscured everything, even the light from the lighthouse. The vessel shuddered onto the reef, twenty miles from where the captain thought he was. He would have hit the point itself if a great sob from the fog horn hadn't warned him just in time. Upon hearing it, he urgently ordered a full turn to starboard. Evading the point, he brought his ship right onto Wash Rock.

An hour and a half later, alerted by the lighthouse keeper, a Coast Guard lifeboat came alongside the solidly stuck *Pacific Enterprise* to take the five passengers off. Fog began to lift. A fine September morning revealed huge rips in the freighter's hull. She had twenty-eight feet of water in her forward holds, but, inasmuch as she wasn't in immediate danger of sinking, Captain and crew stayed aboard.

When the rescue boats arrived, they could do nothing except stand by. For three days the ship hung onto the reef with the northwest swell battering her hull. Then she began to falter.

The Coast Guard ordered everyone off, so the captain came ashore, but he was too late for the party. The day after the crash he was to have celebrated his retirement. A party had been planned in Los Angeles, and a ceremony complete with a solid gold commemoratory watch. This was his final trip.

It took three weeks for the big ship to break up and sink. Scores of people came to watch. They swarmed the bluffs, giving the lighthouse keeper heart quakes lest they come to harm on the crumbly ledges. The keeper's little daughter sat on her porch selling her mother's peaches for a dime each to the sightseers.

The ship sunk in two sections, first the bow, then the next day the remainder. After the vessel had disappeared, cargo began to wash onto the beach: canned goods, and lumber, and one- hundred pound sacks of flour miraculously dry inside a thin crust. For a number of days, going to Manchester Beach was like going to the market. The most valuable part of the cargo, a shipment of lead, did not drift ashore, needless to say, so someone bought the salvage rights and sent divers to Wash Rock to bring it up.

The hundred-mile Mendocino Coast has been the scene of a remarkable number of marine disasters. In 1862, the *Elizabeth Buckley* did precisely what the *Pacific Enterprise* did, got stuck on Wash Rock in a heavy fog and with the same outcome. From 1850 to 1950, more than a hundred vessels — schooners, sloops, steamers, ships with sails, ships with motors — were lost between Gualala and Shelter Cove, and this tally omits damaged crafts which ultimately managed to limp to shore. Foggy, reef-bound, studded with rocky shoals, the Mendocino Coast was treacherous. Furthermore, it offered little protection from weather. Vessels lying at anchor in one of the dog-hole ports had little room to maneuver when hit by the frequent storms. Too often their moorings parted, and they ended up ashore.

One hundred years, one hundred miles, one hundred ships, and a full fifth of them, including John Hamilton's first ship the *Helen*, went down within spitting distance of *Punta Arenas*. When vessels reached the point, whether traveling north or south, they were obliged to change course to avoid going too far seaward. Persuaded by fog, storm, darkness, or general confusion, the officer in charge tended to alter course too soon and come dangerously close to shore.

The alarming number of ships going aground at *Punta Arenas* prompted the construction in 1870 of a lighthouse. The first lighthouse was a brick tower with elaborate wrought iron balconies, and a keeper's house big enough to house several families. It remained the tallest structure north of San Francisco until the 1906 earthquake cracked it in six places. Though not demolished it was damaged so badly it had to be pulled down along with the keeper's house. The undamaged lantern was set on a temporary frame while a new lighthouse, one engineered to withstand temblors, was built by a company specializing in industrial smokestacks — which is precisely what the Point Arena lighthouse looks like.

A one hundred fifteen foot tower of steel-reinforced concrete housed a first order Fresnel lens. The lens, made up of 666 hand-ground prisms, so effectively intensified and reflected light that the burn of its single lamp could be seen twenty miles out at sea. The lens required a lot of attention. Before electricity, the six-foot diameter, two-ton lens was turned by clockworks. To keep the light circling, a keeper had to wind it up every four hours. To do so he must, at regular intervals, crank a weight suspended in the center shaft up to the top of the tower. The fuel (oil first, then kerosene) and the wicks demanded constant care, as well as the lens. Consequently several keepers were always on duty at the lighthouse until the lamp was replaced in 1926 by two 1,000 watt lamps turned by a small electric motor.

The Fresnel lens is still in place at the top of the lighthouse, but the beacon, set now on the tower's balcony, is automated. Visible twenty-five miles out at sea, it is more practical and more powerful than the Fresnel, but not half as beautiful as the six feet of 666 prisms.

Although it was a great boon, the Point Arena lighthouse didn't completely eliminate marine disasters within its range. Five years after it was put into service, the steamer *Eastport* fetched up on Manchester Beach and was a total loss. All aboard were saved, though, which was not the case with the unfortunate *San Benito.* Loaded with coal, the *San Benito* ran aground at Manchester in 1896 at two a.m. amidst heavy seas. Through the inky darkness the crew's cries for help could barely be heard on shore above the percussion of the surf and the keening of the wind. All but two of the steam collier's life boats were lost. These two were lowered and loaded. One quickly capsized, drowning all six men aboard. Seventy-five yards from the safety of the shore, the *San Benito* sank within the brief space of twenty minutes time. Her smokestack is still visible at low tide.

> At 3 am Saturday July 31, 1909, in a dense fog the two masted steam schooner *Winnnebago*, south bound, heavily loaded, ran afoul of Wash Rock and was wrecked. Nothing but the prow mast and smoke stack were visible within thirty minutes of the time she first struck, and her steel hull was punctured by the reef.
>
> As soon as the vessel struck, she took a heavy list and her immense deckload of heavy lumber was carried away, then righting herself, the vessel drifted inshore settling at the stern and now lies within a few hundred feet of one of the most powerful lighthouses lights on the coast — a total loss.
>
> When it was seen the boat was settling, Captain Treanor ordered the boats cleared away and with his wife and four children and the crew of twenty-two seamen got into the tow boats and failing to make a landing on account of the high surf, darkness and fog, pulled out to open sea, and about three hours afterwards were picked up by the lifesaving crew near the harbor entrance. The crew all spoke highly of the pluck, courage, and coolness, and bravery shown by Mrs. Treanor who had her four little children to look after and who in the midst of the excitement and danger maintained her presence of mind and by words lent encouragement to those around her. Mrs. Treanor and the children with the members of the crew, left on Saturday evening's *Sea Foam*, the captain remaining over until next day before traveling overland to Los Angeles. *Point Arena Record*, August 13, 1909

⚜

Along with many accidents, the lighthouse witnessed another landing, a landing of a different sort, a deliberate one, a curious one. The event was lost to local lore, but the fifteen people who made the landing did not forget it.

It was their big adventure, the adventure of a lifetime, and they kept it alive, passing the tale down through the generations.

In 1995, without forewarning or fanfare, a small delegation of Japanese travelers arrived in Point Arena in a bus. A writer, an historian, a video crew, they were searching for the past. A sixty-eight year old man among them explained that in 1913 his great uncle was captain of a sampan which landed in Point Arena with fifteen men from Ehime prefecture of western Japan.

No one here knew anything about it. No one's parents or grandparents had ever mentioned it. Wise, perhaps, to blink away the strange incident, to keep mum, because the good folks of Point Arena had not behaved in an admirable manner.

From verbal descriptions and a faded drawing, the Japanese historian and the Japanese writer, working with descendants of the voyagers, identified the landing site just south of the lighthouse, a place where, year by year, the sea eats the bluffs, leaving grass-topped islands stranded in the water, small in width but tall. Some resemble little towers, sedimentary copies of the lighthouse stationed in the background. The bluffs are full of blow holes and sea caves which exhale a chill, dank miasma onto patches of cobbley beach. On a day in August the weary, hungry and sick would-be immigrants pulled their boat onto one of these tiny pocket beaches. They had been at sea for sixty days. Though weak, they managed to climb to the top of the tall bluff and walk through a hay field in search of food. They were well aware of the five-year-old exclusionary treaty which made their entry into the United States illegal. They knew they needed to lay low, but they were so terribly hungry and thirsty.

Fortunately for them, the first people they met were a Pomo family, who treated the strangers kindly, ministering to their needs before giving them extra food and water to take back to the hay field for those travelers too weak to walk. The next day the Japanese sailors couldn't find the Pomo family, and hunger drove some of them into town searching for the Chinese man, lone remnant of a larger Chinese population from logging's heyday, who owned a store. The ailing band of Asian strangers were wildly conspicuous and were immediately arrested.

After it was over, the journey itself, not the ordeal and disgrace of capture, was what the participants told and retold. Why they made the daring attempt in the first place has gotten screened by passing time. As best as can be pieced together, the trip was prompted by four men who had lived for a time in the U.S.A. After going home to Japan for a visit, they were prevented from returning by new legislation.

Ehime was a seafaring province: "Armed traders," insists the historian, "not pirates." It had its own local navy and all its residents were good sailors. The four men wanting to return to the U.S. talked eleven others into investing a year's income in a boat and sailing it to California. An existing photograph of the boat shows a graceful sampan, about thirty-five feet long, with a long raking sharp bow and three square sails.

They planned, upon reaching the continent, to divide into three groups, then travel overland to places where friends or relatives lived. Two of the groups were to go to Seattle and one to Watsonville, California. Instead, all together and in the company of a Federal Immigration Inspector, they went to Angel Island. Piled into their sampan, they were ignominiously towed by steamer. Despite their explanations to the contrary, the U.S. media decided a "deeper plot is believed… The Japanese like California and would be delighted if the state fell into their possession."[1] These unarmed provincials were denounced as the first strike of an invasion. No treatment of them could be too severe. They were kept locked up until they could be shipped back home. The sampan, *Tejin Maru*, was confiscated and sold at auction.

"The moon goes always to the west," Genji whispered.
"All aimless is my journey through the clouds.
It shames me that the unswerving moon should see me."[2]

The eleven 1995 Japanese visitors in the bus were followed two months later by an official delegation of descendants of the original travelers. This time the City was prepared for them. The honored guests arrived on the fiftieth anniversary of the bombing of Hiroshima, a coincidence significant of nothing, but it supplied Mayor Earlygrow with a sage theme for his welcome speech. On a Sunday in August, the same season of the 1913 arrival, at the weekly farmer's market, city officials of Point Arena greeted the city officials of Yawatahama City. Afterwards everyone retired to an elegant meal at Pangaea, Point Arena's four-star restaurant. In dark suits and neck ties, Yawatahama's mayor, its chairman of the Chamber of Commerce and its managing director, its City Council Head, its Director of Business and Travel, a Rotary Cub representative, and several representatives of the Lions Club of Yawatahama City sat down with Point Arena's mayor, City Council members, Lion's Club president, Rotary Club representative, and two Mendocino County Supervisors.

All dined on fresh local salmon, locally grown vegetables, and wine from a vineyard on Mountain View Road.

The Japanese stayed for a couple of days, sightseeing and meeting people. A year later, John Biaggi is still kicking himself. When the delegation visited his home, he didn't have a proper sort of tea to serve them. "I had to give them *Constant Comment!*" he told me with chagrin. He laughed, but I could tell he minded. After the delegation left, the city received a beautiful brass plaque set into the face of a four-foot by two-foot block of polished marble with a picture of the *Tejin Maru* incised in copper on top. Installed at Arena Cove for all to see, the plaque reads, first in Japanese, then in English,

> This monument is dedicated to the fifteen young men from Yawatahama, Japan who sailed 11,000 kilometers across the Pacific in a 15 meter wooden boat to realize their vision of coming to America, landing at Point Arena on August 13, 1913. Their dreams and courage continue to be a source of inspiration and a foundation of the friendship between the people of Yawatahama and Point Arena.

REFERENCE NOTES

1. *Point Arena Record,* August 15, 1913

2. Murasaki Shikibu, *The Tale of Genji*, translated by Edward G. Seidensticker, Alfred A. Knopf.

Chapter Twenty-six

TIME TRAVEL

I stand supplicant-like, patiently tapping at the door, but history which took place only yesterday is hard enough to penetrate. Hundred-year-old history is thoroughly obscured. I struggle to get a clear picture from other people's renditions. Memory — individual or collective — is shifty. Words, by even the most scrupulously honest talebearers, are equivocal.

Egged on by a mulish curiosity, though, I research. I try to be as reliable a reporter as one can be. Tracking facts, I go as far as possible. Even so, I can't run those facts any farther back than the horse's mouth: questionable rememberings conveyed in equivocal words.

Little has been written about Point Arena or the Garcia watershed. The primary sources are two big, fat histories of the county, written more than a century ago. Supplementing these books are a handful of oral histories committed to print, a few magazine and newspaper articles, several books on logging with minor references to the Garcia River, a couple of unpublished Ph.D. dissertations, a couple of spiral-bound scientific studies with a bit of history thrown into the preface, and the county records in the Ukiah courthouse.

I read and read and read. Sometimes what I read one day contradicts what I read the day before so I check things. Investigating the earliest history, I have made a troubling discovery. Nine times out of ten the footnote I consult refers me back to one of the two big, fat one-hundred-year-old history books.

The first of these two volumes, Lyman Palmer's 1880 *History of Mendocino County*, is chock-full of interesting things, but is it reliable? To compile his book Palmer, a county resident, moseyed over to the coast, talked to a couple of people, then wrote down what they said. Sometimes his informants say different things. He writes down both versions. And they, the informants, are all men, all U.S. citizens, all English-speaking. In short, Palmer's sampling is neither broad nor representative, and his information stands unverified by any outside source. Still, everyone who followed him — journalists, Ph.D. candidates, local descendants of the original cast of characters — read Palmer's book and retold it as gospel. Palmer's version of who did what and when has become unquestioned reality.

In 1914, building on Palmer, Aurelius Carpenter produced *History of Mendocino and Lake Counties*. His account, though able to fill in information for the ensuing years, was removed a step further from the earliest days of settlement (N.B. I say "settlement;" neither Palmer nor Carpenter has one word to say about the native population), and sometimes gets things wrong. In one place Carpenter says William Shoemake came to Arena Township in 1852, in another place he gives the date as 1856. And he makes rather a muddle of Raphael Garcia land grant, an affair which is muddle enough without help. For example Carpenter writes that Garcia's grant was "never seriously urged," and "was not considered at all by the settlers, and none [of the land] was ever purchase by them." Not true. According to handwritten deeds kept in Ukiah, at least six parties bought pieces of grant land from Jose Leandro Luco before the final decree was issued against the Mexican grant.

Palmer writes that Mart T. Smith told him when he arrived in Arena Township about thirty families were living there. "Nearly all jumped or squatted on the grant, knowing it was in litigation, and hoping it would end as it did, and thus give them a priority claim upon the tract on which they had settled." The exceptions, "as far was known, were Hamilton, Shepard and Shoemake," all of whom had purchased their land from Luco.

When Carpenter says the grant was "never seriously urged," he might have meant urged by Luco, since Palmer claims it was a "well-known secret that money was an important factor in the confirmation or rejection of those grants; and unfortunately for Luco, he had expended his means in riotous living and had nothing left with which to fight his claim."[1]

But in trying to piece together the past, what choice do we have but to turn to these early histories? Moreover, much of what Carpenter and Palmer relate, though sketchy and superficial, does bear up under whatever scrutiny can be brought to it; so, trusting, I proceed with what I hope is merely a partial picture and not total humbuggery.

Today I am tracking one Pilar Samiento. What happened to her? Carpenter and Palmer say Luco lost most of his land. Yet in Ukiah, entered by hand in the Book of Deeds #1, I found six land transactions with Jose Leandro Luco as the grantor. I recognize most of the names, but Page 149 gives Pilar Samiento as the grantee. In 1860 she paid Luco $1000 for a piece "…of Rancho Del Norte, commencing at a point in Punto Arena Creek, N.W. corner of land occupied by David Bebee following creek to Ocean, then south to S.W. corner of land of S.B. Campbell east to lands of one Stevenson; then south along Stevensen and Levy to point of…" here the writing becomes illegible.

I've searched, but there is no record of Pilar Samiento selling this parcel or any other property. I continue to ponder: What became of Pilar Samiento? The next time I go to Ukiah for a county Library Advisory Board meeting, I return to the Records Office. Staring at the microfilm, I see the answer. Ms. Samiento's address is San Francisco. Luco is in San Francisco when he unloads the property, and only later does he get it recorded in Mendocino County. After the Supreme Court declares the grant invalid, Pilar Samiento, unlike the other buyers, can't retain possession of her purchase under the Conness Act, because she has neither occupied it nor improved it.

One minor mystery solved, but solving it uncovers another. Running my eye down all the names in the index of the Book of Miscellaneous Transactions, I catch sight of Thomas Nugent in the grantee list. The year is 1874, and he seems to be buying a paper mill from someone named Pollard. Pollard is the party of the first part, Nugent the party of the second part and the land under transaction is the "North half of the NW quarter of Section 29 and the NE quarter of the NE quarter of Section 30 in Twp 13…with the paper mill." There was only one paper mill in the county at the time — the one he, Nugent, sold to Shoemake, et al, in the spring of 1871. Is it possible Nugent was able to buy back the business after it went belly up and sell it again? The mill stood idle for several years before going south, but for exactly how many years? I decide to check on the 1879 transaction, but the Records office woman is standing beside me pointing to her watch. The office is closing. It's five o'clock. I figured I had been there for twenty minutes when in fact I'd been there for two hours.

Moungovan is an easy historic character to stalk. He left a good clear trail. Everybody who knew him liked to talk about him.

> "…We used to camp out on the Garcia in the summer. One year when we were camping out there I found some goose eggs on the shore of the river. I knew Mrs. Moungovan had the geese so I took the eggs down and gave them to her. Tom used to josh me about it. He said why didn't I keep them and eat 'em."[2]

Tom's father, Michael, came from Ireland, his mother, Anna, from Germany. She had family in Gualala, so that's where they settled. In 1887 their third child, Thomas, was born. Michael worked in logging as a bull puncher. The family hoarded money until Michael had enough to buy land on the Garcia River, "the old Lee place," they called it. The "old" part amuses me since, from my remove, local U.S. history was brand new.

When Michael set out from Gualala to pay for his new property, he had on his person, as part of his payment, $2,000 in gold coin. His employer counseled him, with so much cash, to stay away from well-traveled roads; so, Michael took a "trail up the Gualala North Fork, over the Pete Cuneo Flat, to the South Fork of the Garcia" and on to the mainstem and the Lee Ranch. I thought this odyssey might be easily available to me so one Saturday I walked it. Pete Cuneo Flat turns out to be a flat area on Fish Rock road just east of the dump. After crossing Pete Cuneo Flat, I followed the Garcia South Fork to the Garcia mainstem. Where the tributary flowed into the mainstem, I recognized the camp site of the coffee drinking family Preston, Suzanne and I had encountered on our way to the hot springs ten years before.

The hills of this watershed are laced with roads. Each square mile averages six miles of road and twenty-seven miles of skid trails. All are private. None are paved. Many are impassable except by four-wheel drive vehicles. Or by foot.

These numerous tracks which thread, ungridlike, up and down, over and around, correspond to lines of ancestry macraméed through the population. Posterity, not thinned out by population explosion, is apparent, but so tangled I'll never get it straight. When Dorothy Halliday or John Biaggi or Junior Stornetta begins, for the umpteenth time, to clarify for me whose great-grandmother and whose cousin by a second marriage — "No, that one was just a stepfather after so-and-so was killed in the wagon accident" — I realize I'll never manage to untie all the bloodline knots.

The Moungovan clan, however, didn't leave any of their clan behind. Lots of word and deed, but no kin, even though there were such a lot of them. As the family worked the new ranch, the number of Moungovans increased. A 1902 list of students at the Garcia School shows a Moungovan in nearly every grade, 1 through 6, and two in grade 7.

One week in July 1893, the editor of the local paper, the *Point Arena Record*, who routinely groused about subscribers who didn't pay — "If people would do their duty we could make the *Record* equal to any newspaper published north of San Francisco" — was happy to mention Michael Moungovan had "left us enough silver to make him clear on our subscription book to 1894." Then in October of '95: "Michael Moungovan pleaded guilty in Justice Symonds' court Tuesday to the charge preferred against him by Mrs. E. Cox, and was dismissed on paying the cost of the court. What were these charges? I was curious to know, but the *Record* had nothing more to say on the matter, neither that week nor any that followed. What could this conscientious breadwinner have done to offend Mrs. Cox? Something not too awful since he got off so easily. Ukiah gave me no information — wrong court system.

I keep looking for answers, but I wonder why. What difference does it make? Does anyone really want to know? Is it possible my research is less in the service of the telling than the telling is a pretext for the snooping. *Egged on by a mulish curiosity…*

Maybe that's why I'm so smitten with Thomas Moungovan. He was even more curious than I am. His dogged questioning perpetually exercised both his knack for calculation and his keen eye for detail. He was high-spirited and enterprising, too. As a child he was paid to patrol the river with a long pole. Wherever he found a log jam, it was his job to break it up. At nineteen he was offered a job by a neighbor who had been hired by James McNamee of Fish Rock to run a bark camp on the Garcia. The neighbor told Tom he would be "an especially good Jayhawker." Tom had no idea what a Jayhawker was, but he wasn't about to admit it. He'd seen the huge wagons full of bark driving to the Point Arena wharf — that was the sum total of what he knew about tan barking, but with a four-square confidence in his ability to learn, he took the job.

First the tan barking crew had to make a new road. This was the spring of 1906. The big quake had destroyed last summer's road, covering it with several hundred thousand cubic yards of dirt in a landslide which had also dammed the Garcia North Fork. With six mules, a road scrapper, and some dynamite, the crew constructed a usable road in two days.

Now forty men were going to peel trees. Each with a pole ax, they worked in pairs, the most experienced acting as head peeler. Telling Tom, "I want you to jayhawk all this big basin until you get lower down," the boss set him to work with "Bubbly Bill." Bubbly Bill pointed out a tree for Tom to start on, but young Tom needed to watch for a while to figure out what he was supposed to do. He took out his file and commenced filing a spot on his ax while he furtively eyed his partner. Bubbly walked a short distance to another tree, took a careful swing and whacked the bark a few inches above the ground. After making a few such cuts, he pried up a large piece of bark and, using the three-foot-long ax handle, notched one foot from its the end, measured up four feet and cut a ring through the bark all the way around the trunk. Next he gave the bark a sharp lengthwise blow with his ax, pried at it a little, tapped it lightly. Presto! The whole piece fell to the ground, at which point he reached up four feet higher and started over. After cut number two, he moved on to another tree.

By now Tom understood the process and was ready to begin jayhawking tanbark. "My first cut was perfect and I felt that I was a full-fledged bark peeler. Unfortunately, my second cut was far too high, which made the ring six inches too long and Bubbly boiled over. I began to realize why Boss had said that I would make a good jayhawker. It was because there were times when I could stand on the higher or upper side of the hill and take off a third ring and the tree could be left standing for further production of bark."[3]

Trees could be peeled and left standing, in which case, unless hit by fire, they lived to produce new bark. But the ones that were felled to get the third peeling, naturally, did not. Tom Moungovan was 6′4′′ tall.

He loved the woods and woods work. For most of his life he worked, in various capacities, for the L.E. White Lumber Company, owner of the Garcia Mill properties from 1892. By 1912, with its primary venture in full swing at Greenwood, the company was fed up with its operations on the Garcia. Water volume had gotten too low to hoist the ties easily. Ties now had to be separated by twenty-five foot intervals in order to get them on the rollers. Then a strike among some of the tie makers led the company to decide against opening any new timber land on the Garcia. Since ties were made only on cutover land, and there was to be no new cutover land, the pursuit of tie making came to a slow halt.

Of more consequence than these on-the-spot problems, however, was the pickiness of the customer. The railroads — as soon as they determined the smaller the wood's grain, the longer a tie would last — began to specify, "no tie with less than eleven grains to the inch." The L.E. White Company resolved to close down the flume and just in time, too. The flume was no sooner dismantled than creosote put an end to the redwood-tie business altogether.

The last day of the flume was a sad one for twenty-five-year-old Thomas Moungovan. With solemnity and ceremony, he took the last tie from the flume and placed it on the rollers at Rollerville. At the top, he personally put it onto the railroad car headed for the wharf. Afterwards, he gave the men the rest of the day off, then rode his horse back up the river to the North Fork flume, diverted the water to its proper channel, then went back downstream to remove the foundation from the elevated flume. The structure slumped; the boards split. On downriver he continued, stopping to ask property owners if they wanted the company to take away their portion of the flume. Most were happy to get the good lumber and chose to do it themselves. Two years later L.E. White Company sold all of its holding on the coast.

❦

I'm on my way to my daughter's house to pick up some steelhead steaks her boyfriend saved for us. Paul is a Bed Rock employee; he drives one of Bill Hay's gorgeous, sparkling maroon trucks. He and my daughter live beside the river in a mobile home Billy owns. During fishing season, on any day he doesn't have to go to work, Paul dons his waders, grabs his gear and a six-pack and jumps in the river.

Eureka Hill Road winds and unwinds beneath the wheels of my car. Where the road passes over the river I always stop. My eyes — previously fixed on the inert, lackluster, black-dotted-yellow — savor the sight of the living ribbon of water passing below. I've heard in the old logging days, railroad ties made on Eureka Hill were brought by wagon to this bridge where they were cast into the water to float the rest of the way to the flume at Buckridge.

Even when it is so shallow its ribs stick out, the Garcia River is alive — a living, breathing, moving ribbon connecting everything it passes through in both time and space. It is a natural delineation, more authentic than any political jurisdiction.

❦

In the days of the Garcia Mill, children walking the wagon road beside the river on their way to school came upon a man lying beside a moss-covered log. Nearby a black mule stood. It was early in the morning, so early that it was still rather dark and the children couldn't be sure what they saw was really a man, so one of them plucked up his courage and went closer. It was a man all right. "Are you okay," the boy asked, shaking him. He was stone cold and the youngsters hightailed it away from there. Before going to school, they rushed to the mill store to tell the storekeeper. Pretty soon the tale of the mysterious dead body was causing a stir in the mill town. No one knew who he was, nor did they ever find out.

The body had been removed by the time the children headed home that cloudy evening. Under the big bay trees where the log lay, the ground was as dark as dark could be. Passing the spot, the littlest girl, always a tad behind everyone else, thought she heard a groan which made her start to cry and run, setting the whole lot into a panic.

Through the following years, every new child entering the mill school had to hear about the ghost on Dead Man's Flat. "If you cross the flat before sunrise," they said, "you'll see the mule standing in the same position by the moss-covered log. As you watch, it will slowly vanish without a sound." The children always banded close together when they got to the flat and walked as fast as they could until they could see the water in the mill dam — the ghost was afraid of water. When the sun stayed up late in the day, the children sometimes forgot to worry, but directly the season dimmed early, they would start to run. One very, very dark evening, the children scared themselves into a veritable stampede, and one girl fell down. She lay on the ground shrieking piteously, but the other kids, far ahead now were afraid to go back for her. At this moment of moral dilemma, the foreman of one of the tie camps came riding by on his horse, and asked the child what was going on. The girl said, "I tripped, and the ghost was trying to grab me."

The foreman was full of questions and the children were delighted to oblige him with the answers. The man became more and more apprehensive and the last thing he asked them was, "Do you think a ghost would bother a man on horseback?" He rode on "trying to look every way at once."

The very next evening, coming home from school, the children had a fine surprise. A brand new trail had been made at the foot of the hill. It was a more direct trail, shortening the twice daily walk by a good five-hundred feet. What's more, not one inch of it was under shade.

I read "The Tale of Dead Man's Flat" in a little stapled-together booklet called *Lore of the Coast* published by the Mendocino County Historical Society. As no author is given, I wonder who wrote it? I wonder where, exactly, is Dead Man's Flat? I try to visualize the river above the mill site. The landscape seems wrong for the story; but, of course, the place has changed radically. The mill was on the north bank of the river, directly across from Buckridge Bar —then Mill Flat — where the Bed Rock plant operates today. The mill town beside it had a school, a store, a hotel, a billiard hall, as well as housing for ten or twelve families. A bridge — originally built for teams before they were rejected in favor of a flume — spanned the river. All of this is gone, and the shape of the river bed has altered. With the big timber removed from its banks, the river's selvages must be equally altered.

When the written word fails me, I look for truth in landscape. Physical signs of things I have previously only read about give me a little time-travel frisson. I have located the precise site of the old Garcia Mill. I have identified the scars left by the lifting works at Rollerville. I have found a slice of the railroad bed that took the logs from Rollerville to the wharf where, scanning the cove for some evidence of the chutes, I recognized, in a large rock, the rusty ring bolt young Tom Moungovan swam out to in the dark.

Thus far one landmark to elude me is the old Moungovan Ranch. It is frequently mentioned, so I am always on guard for clues to its precise location. "...Our favorite camping place was just above the Moungovan place. Just this side of Rollin' Brook,"[4] I read that and I thought, Bingo! Rolling Brook. I know right where that is. Yet "just above" and "just this side" don't put a fine enough point on the location for me to determine exactly where Moungovan Ranch was, not even which side of the river it was on.

I have been thinking I need one of my little time travel strolls. I hoped "Ghost of Dead Man's Flat" would point me in the right direction. The story begins with a reference to the Moungovan Ranch. "On the right bank of the Garcia River, going downstream from the Moungovan Ranch to the Garcia School, was a wagon road most of the way. About half way between the upper and lower end of the dam, which was over a country mile in length, was a low flat. It was covered with a dense growth of pepperwood tree, some moss-covered logs and a tiny brook..." Now surely this tells me where the Moungovans lived, and yet it doesn't. About half way between the upper and lower end of the dam, which was over a country mile in length, was a low flat. What was over a country mile in length? Not the dam. The dam was only as wide as the river. Maybe the extent of water backed up behind the dam...but, surely that's too far.

As I ponder the problem, the telephone rings. It's Dorothy Halliday. Her memoir is ready for the printer, and she is calling me because the press is asking if she wants an ISBN number, a Library of Congress number, a Bar code acquisition number, an Advance Book filing, a CIP Data block, a copyright, a Standard Address Number, a Wilson Cumulative Index, or a Baker & Taylor Profile Questionnaire. After I tell her she needs none of it, I ask if she knows where Dead Man's Flat is?"

She's never heard of Dead Man's Flat and seems to think I'm losing my wits. Can she trust me in the matter of the ISBN number?

"Actually," I explain, "I'm trying to locate the site of the old Moungovan Ranch."

Now she's more surprised than ever. "The Moungovan Ranch? Why, that's right next to Don Stuart's place. On the river there, north of Eureka Hill Road. You know. That big place Bill Hay bought a few years ago. Your daughter lives there."

REFERENCE NOTES

1. Lyman Palmer, *History of Mendocino County*, page 268.
2. Bruce Levene et al., *Mendocino County Remembered: An Oral History*, page 189.
3. T. Moungovan, Bruce Levene et al., *Mendocino County Remembered.*
4. Bruce Levene et al., *Mendocino County Remembered*